Beyond 100 Percent:
Rebuilding Life After It Breaks

For anyone who needs a hand, a map, or hope after being reminded how fast life can change.

Dedicated to my grandmother, the ultimate survivor. The strongest, softest, and wisest person I have ever known, you rebuilt your life after the unthinkable, time and time again. You are still my greatest teacher, my inspiration, and my clearest example. I hope to spend the rest of my life trying to honor what you showed me. I love you so much.

AUTHOR'S NOTE

This book is a work of creative nonfiction. While inspired by real events from the author's life, some names, identifying details, locations, and circumstances have been changed to protect the privacy of individuals. Certain scenes have been reimagined, condensed, or combined to convey emotional meaning rather than exact chronology. Conversations are reconstructed from memory and may not represent verbatim accounts.

DISCLAIMER

The information in this book reflects the author's personal experiences and perspectives. It is not intended as medical, psychological, or professional advice and should not be used as a substitute for consultation with qualified healthcare providers.

Readers are responsible for their own decisions and actions. If you are experiencing a medical emergency, mental health crisis, or emotional distress, please seek assistance from appropriate professionals or emergency services.

CONTENTS

PART I

THE BODY

1

—

THE MOMENT EVERYTHING CHANGED

"The whole world is a very narrow bridge,
and the essence is not to fear."

LIFE can change course in a heartbeat. Or in my case, when a blood vessel in your brain decides to fail.

About thirty-six hours before I collapsed, I returned from an international trip. Exhausted, I crashed into bed at 10 PM, knowing I had to wake up early the next morning to catch a flight from my home in Sacramento to Portland, Oregon, for work. The next morning, I woke up feeling confused. I drove all the way to the airport before I realized I had forgotten my ID. As a frequent traveler, that had never happened to me before.

Life can change course in a heartbeat. Or in my case, when a blood vessel in your brain decides to fail.

I went home with plans to work remotely the next morning. By that night, my head hurt and I felt oddly disconnected from myself. I assumed it was all related to jetlag and planned to go to bed early that night. The next day was important, full of meetings about how we would integrate AI into multiple departments. I needed to be at my best.

But when morning came, I couldn't focus. I tried eating a light breakfast with coffee, but that didn't help. I tried to meditate, but the headache and strange "jetlag" feeling wouldn't subside.

My first meeting began at 7:30 AM on a Teams video call, though I was the only one with my camera on. Lawyers and technical teams from India and various locations in the U.S. discussed a vendor we were evaluating. I tried to contribute as I usually would, but I found it hard to speak. I paused for a long time and said, "ahh...ahh..." between many of my words. I made an excuse about my internet connection, muting and unmuting myself to create the illusion of technical issues. I don't think anyone noticed.

When the call was over, I found it impossible to move my cursor to the "end meeting" button. I had to place my left hand over my right one, using both hands to move the mouse, and eventually managed to end the meeting.

Something was wrong. *Very wrong.*

The sensation was like being drugged, but not in a pleasant way. When I tried to get up to walk toward the door of my small home office, my legs collapsed beneath me. I fell backward, my head just beyond the doorway, my legs still inside the room.

I tried to call for help, but instead of the words I meant to say, only an "AHHHHH" sound came out.

My daughter's voice floated down the hallway, responding with, "Yes, Abba?"

She usually had her headset on listening to music, frequently missing the instructions we gave her, as teenagers tend to do. Fortunately, she heard me.

Only, what I was saying made no sense at all.

I called out again, still unable to form any words.

"Yes, Abba?" she replied once more.

Clear thoughts formed in my brain: *Something is very wrong. I can't move. I need help.*

But there was a chasm between thought and speech that seemed to be obstructed. I tried once more, and produced an even longer, louder, just as unintelligible, "AHHHHHHH!!!"

I couldn't raise my head to see, but I could hear her step into the hallway and then rush to our bedroom while calling my wife, who was just about to take a shower. Wearing only a towel, she came into my field of vision and asked, "What's wrong?" When I couldn't answer, she called 911.

My wife stayed with me, her hand on my chest, as I lay on my back trying to make sense of what was happening. My vision narrowed, like a theater curtain closing on a final act. *Is this it?* I thought.

My vision narrowed, like a theater curtain closing on a final act. *Is this it?* I thought.

Just yesterday, I had been the person everyone depended on. The problem-solver. The rock. The one who made things happen through sheer force of will. I had just returned from visiting friends and family in Germany and Israel. My calendar was full. My mind was sharp. My body was reliable. And now, I was on the floor. That version of myself, built over forty-nine years, had vanished in seconds.

My wife had been speaking to the 911 dispatcher, saying, "Please, come quick! He can't move. He can't speak! Please, hurry up!" Then, with her hand on my heart, she recited the Jewish prayer "Shema Israel," and I found myself mentally chanting along with her.

Still unable to lift or turn my head as she leaned over to speak to me, her beautiful cleavage caught my attention. I don't know if it was a primal instinct or simply a way to grasp onto life, but a somewhat random thought came to me: *is it okay to be aroused now?* The familiar sight in this unfamiliar situation triggered the realization that this might actually be the moment I die.

Surprisingly, I wasn't afraid. I actually felt calm, comfortable, and somewhat familiar. I was just sorry to leave. I felt like a kid who's being told it's time to go home when the park is still open and there are rides he hasn't gone to yet. Not in a regretful way, exactly, but with a profound sorrow that I'd never see my daughter grow up, never hug my mother or kiss my wife again. As my consciousness teetered on the edge of life and death, I only wished for more time.

Earlier that year, I had taken an EMT course and had even volunteered on two ambulance rides. I thought back to those scenarios and mentally ran through the possibilities. There was no pain in my left arm, so probably not a heart attack. I could smile (at least, I thought I could), so it must not be a stroke. It continued to feel like I had been drugged. Had something been in my morning yogurt?

Eight minutes after my wife had made the call, both the fastest and longest eight minutes of my life, three first responders walked in. I noticed they all three had mustaches. The scent of their uniforms mixed with the familiar smells of my home office and the coffee I had spilled onto the carpet when I fell. Those everyday details suddenly seemed precious, as if they belonged to a life I was leaving behind.

Two of the paramedics stepped over me, into my office, while asking their standard evaluation questions. I was able to answer a few of them, slowly. I knew the answers, but speaking required monumental effort. They asked if I could walk and tried supporting my effort, but we all quickly realized that it was not going to work. Again, I knew exactly what walking entailed, and it also wasn't pain that stopped me. The best I can explain is that it was a profound inability, coupled with bone-deep exhaustion and a strange detachment from my own body.

I was simultaneously a boxer who'd just been knocked out and the trainer in the corner, watching with resigned understanding as the referee waved the match over. "No point trying to stand him up," this clinical observer within me thought. "Get him out of here, he's done for this round."

I was simultaneously a boxer who'd just been knocked out and the trainer in the corner...

The absurdity of the situation amused me. How bizarre it was to be so mentally present yet physically absent. I remember smiling at the paramedics, then their exchanged looks confirmed what we all understood, and they lifted me onto the stretcher.

It took a second for my eyes to adjust to the sunlight as we passed through the doorway. I was struck by the vivid beauty of our little suburban paradise. The different shades of green in the trees, the feathery clouds in the sky, I took a mental photograph of these images, hoping to hold onto their beauty as long as I could.

An ambulance and a huge fire engine came into view, with at least eight firefighters standing nearby. Not all had mustaches, I noticed, and there was one female firefighter. Every trivial detail was cataloged in my mind, as if my brain were trying to anchor itself to normalcy while my life was upended.

When they loaded me into the ambulance, a sudden quiet enveloped me. The distinctive smell of sanitization and alcohol overtook the fresh air of my neighborhood and the calming scent of my home even before the door had closed. Then the siren wailed above us, somehow syncing with my racing heartbeat.

The sensation of drifting away from myself continued. My vision narrowed even further, until I could only see the details of whatever was directly in front of me. A paramedic attempted to insert an IV into my left arm and missed. He moved to my right arm and missed again, this time without noticing. I wanted to tell him that I had EMT training and plenty of experience with difficult IVs in my army days, but speaking was still too difficult. I figured they would notice and fix it at the hospital.

The paramedic talked the entire way to the hospital, which was nice in its own way. But my mind was elsewhere. *What's happening? What's the damage? Is it getting worse? Will it stop?*

Fear shivered through my body. I reminded myself that I'd soon be at the hospital, and that I'd been in emergency rooms before. I looked at the calm face of the paramedic, who took rides like that all day, every day, and thought, "I'm an easy case. It's all going to be okay." I just had to trust the process. At the same time, part of me still wondered if these would be my final minutes alive. I tried pushing the fear away as I had learned to do over time, but it kept surging forward. From then on, it never fully disappeared, remaining a constant, unwelcome companion.

Four minutes later, the racing ambulance had arrived at the hospital. The sunlight blinded me momentarily as the doors burst open, replaced a mere heartbeat later by the harsh fluorescent lights of the emergency room. My world now consisted of the ceiling, bright lights, the inside of various scanning machines, and strange faces leaning over me. Doctors came and went, calling out orders that nurses and staff followed. I tried to track what was happening but lost all orientation of time and place. It felt like a long international flight, white noise, artificial light, being surrounded by people yet utterly alone, floating high above the vast nothingness of an ocean, entirely at the mercy of others.

Then, something unexpected happened.

I cried.

My whole *body* cried.

All defenses down, I surrendered completely. A dam had broken open for the first time in decades, with floodwaters rushing out that I couldn't have stopped even if I'd wanted to. And it felt good.

I wasn't overtly sad or happy, I was simply giving in. This flood of emotions was the complete opposite of the calm "drifting" or observing that I'd experienced all morning long. It was total immersion. I was fully, overwhelmingly present. At that moment, I felt more alive than I had ever felt in my entire life. A voice inside of me confirmed that I was going to make it, and I believed it. I felt it in my bones.

I was still scared. But I was also still *here*.

As the doctors worked around me, my wife's hand found mine, and I allowed my eyes to close. In the narrowing spotlight of my consciousness, I held onto that one certainty: *I was still here.* The curtain had nearly fallen, but not completely. Not yet. And maybe, just maybe, it would rise again on a different stage, for a different act.

I just had to survive the darkness.

Choosing My Words

Fluorescent lights and unfamiliar faces broke through the darkness.

I surrendered to the expertise of these strangers, focusing my remaining mental energy on remembering as much as possible while giving my brain a rest. Somewhere between the scans, I don't exactly remember when, doctors had said my symptoms indicated a stroke. The scans were to confirm that diagnosis, suggest what type, identify the exact size and location, and provide more details. Periodically, the heads of doctors and medical staff would hover over me, telling me these things in a calm, almost nonchalant way. Sometimes they explained what was happening and why, sometimes in great detail. But I was not able to keep up.

In my engineer's mind, I worried that overthinking might worsen my condition, so I tried to clear my head. I watched the ceiling tiles, counting them to stay focused. My limbs remained as distant and unresponsive as if they belonged to someone else.

My left arm became a hub of medical access. Beyond the failed attempt in the ambulance, it hosted a PICC line, IV line, intravenous blood pressure monitor, and another access point.

A PICC line is a tube placed in your arm to inject medication directly to your heart when needed, and the procedure to place it lasted twenty agonizing minutes. First, a man and a woman arrived to perform the procedure. He was Filipino, roughly my height (meaning short), in his forties, displaying the confident movements of someone who had placed hundreds of these lines before. She was also short, keeping both of them out of my line of sight for much of the procedure, and it was clearly her first time. She seemed overwhelmed from the moment they entered the room.

"Watch how I approach the patient," he said from the doorway. "You always want to stand here, introduce yourself, explain what you're doing before you do it."

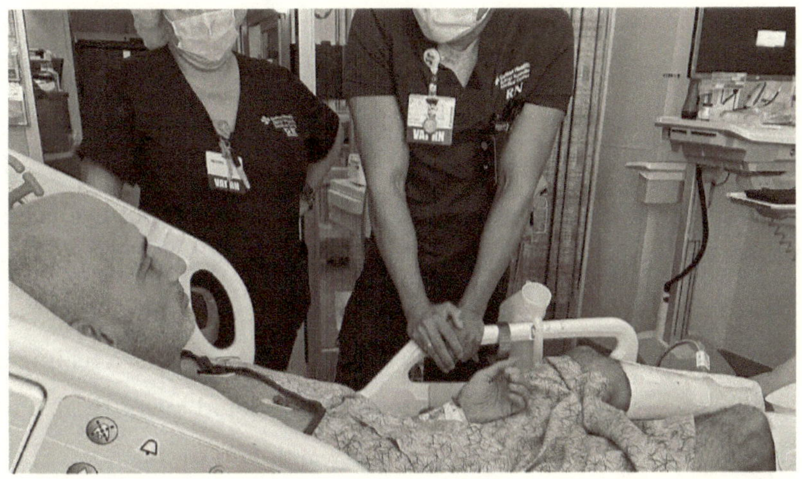

This continued throughout the procedure, as he patiently explained the reasoning behind every action in exhaustive detail, where to place the equipment, how to open each sterile package, how to put on gloves. Everything he did came with a detailed explanation followed by a demonstration and then her attempt to follow along. She was trying but visibly struggling with the information overload.

"It's okay," he reassured her. "It will take a few more procedures before you'll be ready to do one alone."

Inside, I was screaming. It felt like being stuck in terrible traffic when you're already late for the most important meeting of your life. *Shouldn't they be rushing? I'm literally dying here!* Every few seconds, I looked back at the clock hanging directly in my field of vision. Its hands were barely moving, as if time itself were playing some cruel joke. If we had been in traffic, I would have been the person punching the steering wheel and screaming, except it was all happening in my head.

I wanted to yell at them to "hurry up already!" and "train on someone else!" But talking remained difficult. And what could I say that would actually help? Would they move any faster if I spoke up? Or would I just make things worse?

Beneath my frustration ran a deeper current of fear. I had no viable choice except to surrender complete control and trust these strangers with my life, something I'd spent forty-nine years avoiding whenever possible. It felt like I aged two years during those twenty minutes.

My brain seemed to work perfectly, but I couldn't express myself. Finding words and constructing sentences required tremendous physical effort, like lifting heavy weights. This forced me to speak very slowly, giving me time to choose better words to communicate more clearly. It didn't always work.

For example, I learned I was lying on something resembling a fishing net that could connect to a ceiling lift. When needed, they would lower an arm from the ceiling, connect all corners of the net, and use a remote to lift me up. Like a fish in a net, I wiggled in the air, squished and dangling as they transferred me from my bed to the scanner bed before lowering me down. The second time I was transferred this way made me laugh. I tried sharing the joke in my head, but all I could say was, "Fish." They didn't get it. I thought, *If my brother were here, he would have understood.*

When my friend Niv arrived, the staff encouraged him to speak Hebrew with me, saying stroke patients often retain their mother tongue when speech is impaired. With my wife, her close friend, nurses, technicians, doctors, and other staff watching, Niv was the only one in the room who understood my language. I nodded to confirm I understood him, but when it came to answering, it was just as difficult to speak Hebrew as English. I responded with a single word, "ken" ("yes" in Hebrew), and said nothing else.

Everyone was afraid I'd lost my Hebrew, but I had a different concern. Switching between languages is challenging even without a stroke. Everyone there spoke English, the staff, my wife, and even Niv. If I gave the impression that my Hebrew was better than my English, all communication would shift to Hebrew. And speaking Hebrew was equally hard as English. Since I couldn't explain all this, I had chosen the shortest, easiest way to keep communication in English only.

Plus, I didn't know if thinking was good for me now. When injured, you should rest the affected area and definitely not push it, but was that the same for brain bleeding? Would using my brain make things worse? If speaking was difficult, it must involve the affected area of my brain. Should I also try to think less?

I couldn't ask anyone these questions because speaking was too challenging, and I worried the effort itself might cause more brain bleeding.

Facing My New Reality

A few hours or days later, it was all the same to me, I was transferred to the ICU. It was a short bed ride away, guided by the volunteer who had transferred me before. I never heard him speak, but I remembered his calming face. He gave the impression of having done this for years. He knew exactly where we were going. He projected an understanding of my situation without the pity everyone else showed, or at least pretended to show.

I tried to pay attention to every detail as he used his badge to open doors that closed behind us. I hate not knowing where I am; at least when it was all over, I could backtrack and know where I was. For the most part, I could only watch the ceiling as bright, cold fluorescent lights flashed by.

Two doors closed behind us, then silence fell. A sharp turn, a short quiet walk down a corridor that looked like all others, one more set of big doors, and then we arrived at a noisy new section of the hospital. The sign above the double doors announced we had reached the ICU.

It looked exactly as I'd imagined, a wide corridor with large rooms on both sides, equipment everywhere including in the hallway. The wing was L-shaped, with a busy nurses station at its corner. We stopped there for two nurses to check the bracelet on my wrist and direct me to my room. Back offices, whose purpose remained mysterious, were tucked behind the station. My room was at the end of the corridor.

Inside my room, I first noticed the entire wall could open for easy access for large beds or equipment. The volunteer and now three ICU staff rolled my bed near the middle of the room, each taking their position around the bed. The volunteer counted backward, 3, 2, 1, and they all knew exactly what to do, transferring me to the new bed in seconds.

From my bed, I could see all the way to the end of the corridor's entrance if my curtain was open. I could also see part of the bustling nurses station, where, I quickly learned, something was always happening. So, I watched the volunteer walk all the way back through the two wide doors as the nurses connected me to nearly every machine in the room. They talked with each other using medical terminology I vaguely understood, while also introducing themselves and asking questions. All I remember was how quickly everything happened, how automated it all seemed, and how I had zero control over what was happening. *Trust the system*, I kept reminding myself. *This will all be over soon.*

The room was large and without windows. In one corner, there was a door to what I assumed was a toilet or bathroom, though I never found out. A curtain on a rail could surround my bed when needed. Machines filled the room, some turned off and the rest connected to me. On one side of the bed, there was one large, soft chair and one metal chair. There were numerous outlets on the wall, in all different colors, and a white clock hanging over the doorway. The hospital scent had grown stronger as soon as we entered the ICU's corridor, but there were also hints of people's perfume, *perhaps from visitors?*, soap, and a strong smell of eggs from breakfast trays. When we entered the room, all of those smells vanished instantly, replaced only by the antiseptic smell of a freshly cleaned hospital room.

My wife arrived just as the nurses had finished connecting me to the equipment. She looked tired and worried, as if her entire world was crashing down around her. I don't think she'd slept in what seemed like years. My heart broke, seeing her that way. My instinct was to protect her, but I knew I couldn't. Not yet. Niv stood beside her, trying to maintain a positive mood, though his face also showed fatigue and concern. The head nurse explained the treatment plan and orders to us all, providing my first full briefing. Unfortunately, I was overwhelmed and couldn't follow everything she said. I managed to ask her to give me the essentials only and explain details later.

Minutes later, another nurse came in and explained again that doctors believed I'd had a stroke caused by a blood vessel leak. To observe the bleeding and help it heal, she said they were keeping my salt levels high. That didn't sound sophisticated. *Is that all you can do?* But I stopped myself, figuring she had probably simplified things for me, or I didn't fully understand her explanation. *Trust the system. Stroke is common; they know exactly what they're doing.*

My wife discussed practicalities with Niv, my work, her work, insurance, communicating with my family in Israel, our daughter...I could tell it was overwhelming for her, too. These were responsibilities I typically handled in our marriage, now falling entirely on her while she was also worrying about me. Niv reassured her, repeating what the nurse had said: I was stable now, the bleeding was contained, and it was just a matter of time for my body to heal. He suggested she go home to rest and take care of our daughter, who had just experienced what might be a life-changing trauma, seeing her seemingly invincible father helpless on the floor, then calling for help that saved his life. She took his advice, and they both left.

This left me alone for the first time, finally able to rest without anyone else around. I didn't have to be a subject, a patient, a husband, or a friend. I preserved this feeling with most of the nurses' check-ins. I felt no judgment or expectations from them. They would just walk into the room, fix things, and walk out. But I was never truly alone for long.

Life in the ICU was hectic. Nurses visited every two hours, shifts changed multiple times daily, meals arrived three times a day, and in between, I was taken for imaging or visited by specialists, social workers, patient advocates, managers, and visitors. The corridor outside always seemed to be in a state of urgency, making my room a safe, peaceful haven as long as the curtains were closed.

But peaceful havens without sleep can easily become unending nightmares. My sleep schedule depended entirely on the pace of nursing shift changes, periodic tests, and the beeping machines that surrounded me. One night, a particularly loud machine kept beeping, waking me every few minutes. Normally, nurses rush in when alarms sound. But not this time. It was the middle of the night, I could only tell based on the time I kept in my head as nurses came every two hours to shift the pillows under me and turn me slightly to my other side.

That day, my wife and I had discussed administrative matters about work and insurance, and the possibility of transferring to a Bay Area hospital, leaving us both exhausted. I had finally fallen asleep when the loud, long beep jolted me awake like someone screaming in my ear. Expecting the nurse to come check on me, I drifted back to sleep. A few minutes passed, and just as I found my sleep again, BEEEEEP! *What was that? Which machine? Where is the nurse?*

My back was sweaty and starting to itch, but I was too tired to call for help, caught in that gray zone between sleep and wakefulness. Then, BEEEEEP! *What? Where am I? Hospital. Should I call the nurse? She'll be here any moment. She's probably busy with more urgent patients.*

My back felt wet with sweat. My hospital gown stuck to my skin and started itching. *Is this made of polyester?* I was hot. I was cold. I was deeply uncomfortable, unable to turn, unable to scratch my itching back or remove the fabric that had stuck to me. It nearly broke me, to the point where I wished I could tear off all my wires and walk out, or at least scream, "Make it stop!" It was worse than a nightmare. At least you can wake from those; this was one I couldn't escape.

I knew I had to change my attitude, but I wasn't awake enough to do that. BEEEEEEP! *What? Oh yes, hospital, nurse taking care of urgent patients, she'll come soon.*

I felt my legs sweating under the compression pumps, but I tried not to think about it and focused on getting back to sleep...BEEEEEEP! *Damn it! What machine is beeping? Is everything okay? Where is the nurse? Was she just here a moment ago, or was that yesterday?*

BEEEEEEP! *Enough!* I finally pushed the call button. She poked her head in for just a second to ask if it could wait five minutes, they had just started their shift change. It was morning, though without a watch or window, I had no other way to tell.

That shift was the last time I saw that particular nurse. I remember her as kind and empathetic; she seemed to genuinely care and try her hardest. I couldn't be angry with her, even after such a night. All the ICU nurses, especially the day nurses, acted with the confidence of experienced professionals. They spoke as if they'd been doing this for years, and I felt like they were on my side, rooting for my recovery. Of course, they had to follow medical procedures and schedules, but beyond that, they listened to me and worked with me on solutions.

When I finally told the morning shift nurse about my sleepless night and why, she immediately knew which machine was beeping and fixed it. Apparently, it wasn't even connected to anything. She placed another cotton sheet on my bed, changed my gown, removed the compression machine from my legs for a few hours, darkened the room lights, and ensured I wouldn't be disturbed by visitors for the next four hours. She even saved my breakfast for when I woke up. I slept like a champion, then woke up hungry and longing for coffee.

That long, painful night reminded me of my time as a young, sleep-deprived soldier, fading in and out of dreamless sleep without knowing which side of the thin line between awake and asleep I was actually on, no brainpower for anything beyond basic functioning, completely drained of feelings and emotions. The closest emotion I could access in that state was anger, but without any of the willpower it requires.

As I floated timelessly in the gray zone between wakefulness and fragmented sleep, a strange realization formed. The body that had carried me through life, through military service, travels, fatherhood, career achievements, now felt like foreign territory. My right arm lay beside me, visible and feeling pressure when touched, yet it refused my most desperate commands for it to move. An impassable canyon had grown between intention and action.

> The body that had carried me through life, through military service, travels, fatherhood, career achievements, now felt like foreign territory.

Beeping machines counted out the seconds of my new reality. I was fighting to heal a vessel in my brain, while facing the collapse of everything that used to define me, independence, capability, control. My entire world had been upended in an instant. The tears that had broken through decades of restraint were an acknowledgment, a surrender. The necessary first step toward whatever came next.

These first days had made it clear: whatever path lay ahead would demand a strength I'd never needed before. I would need to rebuild my body, yes, but also my entire way of being in the world.

And the first step was to understand what it meant to occupy a body that no longer recognized me as its commander.

$\diamond \quad \diamond \quad \diamond \quad \diamond \quad \diamond \quad \diamond \quad \diamond \quad \diamond \quad \diamond \quad \diamond \quad \diamond \quad \diamond \quad \diamond \quad \diamond \quad \diamond \quad \diamond \quad \diamond$

REFLECTION SPACE

"Every ending is a doorway in disguise."

We build our lives for stability and predictability, striving for control and to avoid the unexpected. We buy insurance in case our home catches fire or someone breaks in. We wear sunscreen, take our vitamins, and teach our kids to look both ways before crossing the street. We build careers or businesses that will last. We do all this while knowing that shit happens. You can't dodge it forever. It's the oldest fact of life, we're just trying our best to postpone the inevitable. Someday, it will happen to us.

And then, one day, it does.

Maybe you wake up in a hospital bed, or you're sitting in a doctor's office when you hear the diagnosis. Maybe it's a phone call in the middle of the night, or an email from your boss. One moment that says, "Life will never be the same."

That moment comes for all of us, in one way or another.

What I learned, and what I want to offer you now, is this: You must accept that it happened. That it happened to *you*. Surrender to it.

This is the first step in a long journey, but it's the most important one you'll ever take. Allow this understanding to sink in before moving forward in any direction.

PRINCIPLE #1: SURRENDER

Surrendering doesn't mean giving up, in fact, it's the opposite of quitting. It's the first real act of courage. Surrender means letting go of the fight against reality, against what is. Stop trying to force your will, your wishes, on things that are out of your control. Only then can you redirect your energy toward healing.

So, take a breath. Let the truth settle: This happened. You are here now. You don't have to know what comes next. You just have to stop fighting what has already arrived.

That's where healing begins.

2

WHAT'S NO LONGER MINE

A time to keep, and a time to cast away.

–King Solomon, Ecclesiastes

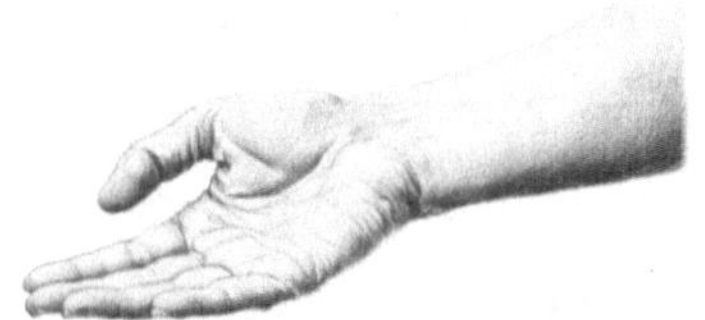

AT some point during the first or second day in the ICU, a team of doctors visited. They tried explaining everything to me, my wife, and Niv so we'd all understand. I wish I'd recorded that conversation, because it was difficult to follow. They seemed to be in a rush, though they answered all our questions.

I did grasp two essential points: First, I had suffered a hemorrhagic stroke that they believed was caused by a bleeding vein, and second, the first three months would be critical for my recovery.

All of my questions focused on that second point. It's not that I didn't care about the cause, I did, but it had already happened. I was fortunate that they had managed to stop the bleeding, and they said they wouldn't know more about the cause until after my next MRI, which couldn't happen until months after the bleeding subsided. In the meantime, my focus was on recovery.

Unfortunately, at that point, I had very little say in what my body did or did not do. For example, the bathroom posed a significant challenge.

Let me rephrase that: number one got an upgrade, but *number two* became a challenge. For urination, I didn't even have to get off the bed, just tilt to one side, aim into the designated container (called a urinal, but it was a urine bottle), and enjoy the relief it created. This was clearly one of the best advantages of being a man.

The salt and liquids from my IV made me need to pee frequently. The first few times, I needed help; I couldn't move anything on my right side, so a nurse or my wife would hold the urinal for me. I felt no embarrassment from this. Actually, I felt proud of myself and happy about what I saw as an upgrade over walking to the bathroom every hour or two. In fact, I carried on this tradition as long as I could, even when I got home many weeks later. To be honest, I still wish I could go that way at home, especially in the middle of the night or in the early morning when I'm barely awake.

Number two was a different story. Without going into details, I simply didn't go for the first few days. At home, I usually go once or even twice a day, though it is highly correlated with my emotional state. When nervous or stressed, I tend toward constipation. I figured that would be the case now. But after a few days without going, I needed to prepare. I didn't want to do it lying on the bed with a bedpan. I'd done that once long ago, in another lifetime, and it was a humiliating experience that I had no desire to repeat if I had any other option.

A negotiation began between me, the nurses, and Niv (as much as he disliked participating). We evaluated our options and decided on a commode chair, also known as a portable toilet. This gave me some sense of normality, as well as the comfort of sitting upright. With the curtains closed, I'd have privacy while still being able to call for help with the emergency button if needed.

Now, I needed to eat.

Even though it had been several days, I didn't feel the urge to go. I wanted to make it quick, but I was terrified of "pushing" too hard. I'd had hemorrhoids before, and my logic suggested that pushing might revive the bleed in my brain as it had with my hemorrhoids. On the other hand, I wanted this to be a one-time ordeal while also avoiding diarrhea. So, I decided to take a little stool softener (Miralax) with my largest meal. It worked perfectly.

I felt incredibly proud and satisfied, as a successful bowel movement tends to feel, especially after such buildup. However, I couldn't wipe or clean myself. I reluctantly called the nurse. As soon as she saw my face, she said, "Don't be embarrassed. I do this all the time. It's part of my job, and it's very important to keep you clean."

"I'm not embarrassed," I lied.

The whole situation reminded me of a joke my father used to tell, which I shared with Niv and the nurse: *All the body's openings compete for who is more important. They argue and make their claims, all while insulting the butthole. The butthole says nothing. It just goes on strike until they all beg it to return.*

We laughed, but I felt the message loud and clear. Even the most basic bodily functions, which I'd taken for granted my entire life, now required planning, assistance, and sometimes negotiation. I had lost the autonomy over even the most private aspects of existence.

The Difficulty of Letting Go

Time dissolved into a meaningless blur. In between these events, I simply lay there, staring at my lifeless right hand with a mixture of desperation and rage. My fingers mocked me with their presence. I could feel them when touched, could visualize every movement in my mind, but they remained stubbornly still, as if they belonged to someone else entirely. It was like being trapped beneath an invisible lead blanket, able to feel but powerless to move.

I knew this feeling. Almost twenty years ago, I'd been in an accident that left casts on both my legs and arms. But the dread of being restrained against your will is instinctive, a primal fear of claustrophobia that almost anyone can relate to. Panic flashes through your mind when you realize you can't move, like being trapped in a collapsed cave with nowhere to go. I knew nothing would help except time, but that knowledge offered no comfort while being completely at the mercy of circumstances beyond my control, watching precious minutes tick away.

The medical staff moved around me with practiced efficiency, offering well-meaning suggestions. "Let's adjust your pillows," they'd say. "Should we raise the head of your bed?" But their help only underscored my helplessness, each failed attempt at comfort fed into the growing storm of frustration.

The movements I could make became increasingly aggressive, each shift more forceful than the last. I tried every position I could manage, but nothing helped. The frustration built until something inside me finally snapped. A primal sound erupted from deep in my chest, "ARRRR!", and my body seized in what doctors would later describe as a spasm. Every muscle clenched, my legs and arms stretched uncontrollably taut.

Then it happened again, this time more intense and with my legs shaking. All the pent-up tension had exploded within me. I wanted to scream at the top of my lungs, to trash the room, to smash every beeping machine and slam the door as I ran away from this nightmare. But I couldn't even do that much, I was trapped in a body that wouldn't obey my commands.

My wife later told me it was the first time she had seen real fear in my eyes. She was right. I was terrified. In that moment, the reality of such complete lack of control over my own body, my life, and everything that came with it finally sank in with a crushing weight.

But then, my grandmother's words came back to me. I could hear her saying, "The mind must stay strong," and I drew in a deep, shuddering breath. I held the air in for a few seconds, exhaled loudly with a sigh, then did it again.

Something shifted inside me. I needed to give in without giving up. I had to accept what was happening. Accept that my body and brain were different now. I pushed aside the added thought: *And it will probably never be the same.*

That was tomorrow's battle. For now, it was enough to acknowledge that this wasn't a nightmare I would wake from. This was my new reality.

First Signs of Optimism

The medical response to my spasms was swift. A nurse called the doctor, who ordered an immediate twenty-four-hour EEG monitor to ensure these were "just" spasms and not seizures. Little did I know, I was about to become a walking (well, lying) art installation.

The EEG technician arrived soon after with what looked like a fishing tackle box full of wires. "Good news!" she announced cheerfully, surveying my bald head. "We're saving at least twenty minutes because I don't have to shave you!" We shared a laugh, the most genuine one I'd had in what felt like forever, and she got to work.

The process that followed was like a very strange, very smelly makeover. Each wire was carefully glued to my head with a cold, strong-smelling epoxy that made my eyes water. "Don't worry," the technician joked, "this is the latest summer fashion in Europe." By the time she finished, I had what looked like a technicolor ponytail of wires cascading from my head. Niv couldn't resist taking pictures. "For future blackmail," he said with a wink.

That night, as I lay in bed still decorated with my electronic crown of wires, I thought about my grandmother again. She had always said that survival wasn't just about enduring, but about finding hope in the smallest victories. I contemplated what that might look like in my situation, as spasms continues to roll through my body.

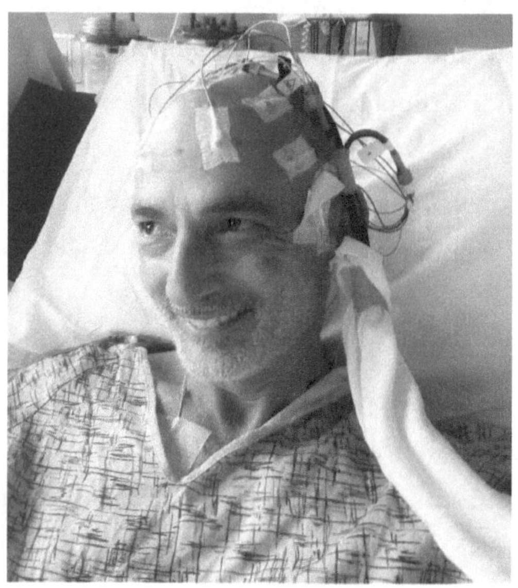

Then, something remarkable happened. A spasm had taken control yet again, but this time *my right side moved* as well. The movement was not under my control, and not in any way I could replicate, but it had *moved.*

My body had moved!

The realization hit me like a bolt of lightning: the connections in my brain weren't completely severed. My brain could still send signals to those muscles, even if I couldn't yet control the signals themselves.

That tiny spark of movement became the small victory I had needed. A promise of possibilities to come. It was like discovering a light switch in a dark room, even if you can't reach it yet, just knowing it's there changes everything.

The next morning, the doctor shared the EEG results with the kind of anticlimactic delivery only medical professionals can master. "Well, you're not having seizures," he said, scrolling through notes on the computer. "You're just extremely tired. Try sleeping more." I couldn't help but laugh at the simplicity of the prescription. "Sleep more." He made it sound so easy.

What had started with frustration and fear, then peaked with rage, had ended with an unexpected gift of hope. My journey to recovery was just beginning, but now I had proof that my grandmother was right. As long as the mind stays strong, the body can find its way back.

As if the universe wanted to reinforce this lesson, more signs began to appear. One morning, I felt an unmistakable tickle in my nose signaling an incoming sneeze. I took a few short breaths, experienced that familiar pause, and then it happened: an explosive sneeze enlisted my entire body as a willing participant. To my amazement, my right arm and leg joined the performance! It wasn't controlled or graceful, but again, it was movement. Real, undeniable movement. My brain had issued an order, and my right side responded.

The encore came midday, right after lunch. I was completely exhausted. Half-conscious and fighting sleep, I surrendered to a massive yawn that turned into a full-body stretch. From the crown of my head to the tips of my toes, once again, *every* muscle joined in. It was like discovering a hidden door in a familiar room. The pathways were there, waiting to be rediscovered, and my brain knew the way. I just needed to find the right keys to unlock these natural movements again.

These movements were like whispers from my nervous system, telling me not to give up. My grandmother would have called these "God's little hints," small miracles that show up exactly when you need them most, reminding you that healing follows its own mysterious timeline.

One of these moments transformed my understanding entirely. During a routine examination, when the nurse ran her thumb along the curve of my foot, my toes moved. Not a spasm, more of a reflex, and a direct response to outside stimulation. The words came almost as instinctively: "Holy shit, I moved my toes!" But while the excitement in my voice made my wife and the nurse smile, what I really wanted to explain was that this was a moment of enlightenment.

As someone who had spent years working with computers, everything had suddenly clicked into place. My brain's CPU, the thinking part, was intact. The lack of movement wasn't a processor problem, it was an I/O problem. An input/output failure. The spasms, the sneezes, the stretches, and now this toe movement were like different ports lighting up on a motherboard, showing that the basic circuitry was still there. The central computer was running fine, and the connections themselves hadn't been destroyed. The communication lines had been disconnected, waiting to be rewired.

My grandmother's words about the mind staying strong took on new meaning. She had always said healing follows its own path; now I understood that this path would be about reconnecting, rewiring, and relearning. The hardware was intact; I just needed to rebuild the network.

That night, as the nurses came to check my vitals for the thousandth time, I found myself responding differently. Where frustration had been my constant companion, I now felt something like curiosity. *What would my body do next? What hidden connections might reveal themselves tomorrow?* The rage hadn't disappeared completely, it would return many times during my recovery, but the bulk of it had transformed into something more useful. It had become determination.

"You seem different tonight," the night nurse observed as she adjusted my IV.

"I think I am," I replied. "I'm starting to figure out the rules of this new game."

She smiled, clearly used to patients having all sorts of revelations in the middle of the night. "What game is that?"

I thought for a moment, feeling more patient with my slow pattern of speech. "It's like putting together a jigsaw puzzle when someone has mixed pieces from different boxes together. You don't try to finish the whole picture at once. You find one corner, one edge that fits, and build from there."

"Sounds like a good strategy," she said, checking something off on her clipboard. "Small steps add up, right?"

I smiled. "Yes, though I'm hoping this puzzle has fewer pieces than it looks like from here."

She laughed softly. "Just don't try to finish it tonight. Celebrate every piece that you find, not just the finished picture."

It's like putting together a jigsaw puzzle when someone has mixed pieces from different boxes together. You don't try to finish the whole picture at once.

As I drifted toward sleep, that thought settled in me like a seed. Small victories accumulated. The progress wasn't dramatic, but it was sustainable. And sustainability, I was beginning to understand, is everything.

My mind cycled through the day's revelations, joined by something else my grandmother used to say: "Even in the darkest night, your eyes eventually adjust. You begin to see shapes, outlines. Not everything at once, but enough to find your way."

And sustainability, I was beginning to understand, is everything.

I gazed at my toes, which had just performed their tiny miracle, and felt a surge of something I hadn't experienced since this whole ordeal began: possibility. Not optimism, exactly, I was still too practical for that, but a sense that there was a path forward. For the first time, I could look at my circumstances as a complex problem to be solved with patience, strategy, ingenuity, and the remarkable resilience of the human brain. I was beginning to understand how well it can forge new pathways, adapt to damage, and find alternative routes to accomplish what once seemed impossible.

My eyes were adjusting to this new darkness.

I couldn't see the whole path yet, but I could take the next step. For tonight, that was enough.

Learning to Focus on Myself

A chaotic but predictable routine developed in the ICU. There were hospital staff coming and going, medical tests at my bedside or elsewhere, visitors arriving and leaving, bathroom visits, machines beeping, wires and lines protruding from my body, conversations outside my door...But despite all of the commotion surrounding me, for the first time in years, I had to focus solely on myself. I had to fight the instinct to care for my daughter, my wife, my parents, my siblings, they all depended on me, each in different ways, and I loved them deeply. In any other circumstance, I would have done anything for them. But now, after brushing extremely close to death and now pinned to a bed, the best thing I could do for them was to think about myself.

This wasn't easy. Helping others gives me purpose and a sense that I am doing important work that makes a difference. It's part of my identity. I'm the older brother and the "successful" one with financial stability, so it fell to me to help my immediate family, especially my mother. A year ago, we sadly had to place my father in a home for people with dementia. I had visited him while in Israel just before the stroke. It was hard seeing my once-vibrant, alpha-type father now tied to his chair. He had always been full of boundless energy, always joking and acting silly with his many friends. Now he was barely making sense, head bent down, staring into the distance. When our eyes met, his turned red and filled with tears. For a moment, it felt like I was looking directly into his soul, where he could say that he loved me. It lasted less than a second, and then he resumed shouting at something invisible in the distance.

There was no single "event" that caused his condition, just a rapid deterioration of memory and cognition until my mother couldn't provide the around-the-clock help he needed. They lived in a small apartment in a northern town, where my grandmother used to live before she passed away. It was on the ground-floor apartment of an old three-story building, with back access for my grandmother's electric cart. (My brother and cousin used to "borrow" it for joyrides until they crashed it completely.) A small garden surrounds three sides of the building, which my grandmother tended carefully, later instructing us grandchildren how to care for it. It had given her great joy, and now it gives my mother the same pleasure.

Those memories and thoughts were all I had in the ICU. I couldn't plan tomorrow or next week, couldn't distract myself with mundane entertainment. I wasn't in the mental or emotional space to focus outward. I was still trying to process what the hell had just happened. It wasn't the first time I had dodged death, but this time it had been closer than ever before. And it felt like it wasn't over yet.

I knew the toll this was taking on my wife, who was always there, right by my side. I could only imagine how my mom was holding up back in Israel. Or my sister, Vered, who lived close to her. They probably felt as helpless and anxious as I was. Our roles had shifted. I was no longer the caretaker, but the one needing care. This reversal felt foreign and uncomfortable, yet somehow necessary. For now, self-preservation wasn't selfish, it was simply the only way forward.

I placed my functioning left hand over my unresponsive right one. The warmth of one hand against the coolness of the other created a strange sensation, as if I were simultaneously the healer and the one being healed. Once again, my grandmother's wisdom echoed in my mind: "Even in the darkest night, your eyes eventually adjust."

For now, self-preservation wasn't selfish, it was simply the only way forward.

She was right. The darkness hadn't lifted, but my vision was adapting. I didn't yet have a strategy for this recovery, but I could feel one forming. Each tiny victory revealed what might *become* possible, one connection at a time.

For tonight, I closed my eyes and surrendered to the darkness, letting go of the man I had been, not yet knowing who I would become, but certain, at least, that there was a path forward.

REFLECTION SPACE

"Even in the darkest night, your eyes eventually adjust."

–My grandmother

What would happen if you stopped rejecting or apologizing for needing support? What if you said, "Can you help me?" That single shift, from struggling to maintain control to embracing humility and gratitude, might be the most healing move you make.

For many of us, the hardest part is not just needing help, it's accepting it. And even harder: asking for it.

I had spent decades being the one people turned to. I fixed problems, held things together, kept people afloat. Then suddenly, I couldn't even wipe myself. It's one thing when they move you around like a puppet during medical procedures. It's another when they are involved in your most intimate daily care tasks. It's even more difficult when it's not a "professional" caregiver like a nurse helping you, but someone close to you, like a family member or a friend. The difficulty was mostly in what it symbolized: the collapse of my independence, the end of being "the strong one."

Here's what I learned, and what I want you to remember:

ASKING FOR HELP:

When something like this happens, it's your turn to take care of YOU. Everyone who sticks around in that moment wants to help in any way they can. Let them.

The people who truly love you don't love you because you're helpful. They love you because you're you. If someone only sticks around when you're useful, that's not love. That's convenience. And it's not worth building your identity around.

Learn when to ask for help. Know how to accept help. Give yourself permission to be vulnerable. That's wisdom, not weakness. It's courage in a different form.

3

RULES FOR RESILIENT ROOTS

I GREW up near my grandmother, both physically and emotionally closer to her than any of my cousins. She always knew what to say, and you could tell her anything. She was my inspiration, and remains so even now, the toughest, most resilient, smartest person I've ever known. Her life story reads like something from a history book. For me, it was simply the background of the woman who shaped my understanding of strength.

My grandmother had survived the Holocaust while taking care of her younger sister in the Nazi camps. After liberation, the terrible truth emerged: they had lost everyone else. Their parents, brothers, cousins, aunts, uncles, all gone, taken like sheep to the slaughter. Just the two of them remained from what had once been a large, loving family.

They made their way to Israel, a newly formed country still fighting daily for its existence. While my grandfather joined the forces protecting their new borders, my grandmother built their home from nothing, often sleeping with one eye open as danger lurked nearby. And just when it seemed they might find peace, unimaginable tragedy struck again. Her eldest daughter, my aunt whom I never met, was killed in a horrifying car accident right before her eyes. For months, she barely spoke. The doctors weren't sure she would recover. I've seen photographs of my grandmother from that time, and her eyes were always hollow, her body present but her spirit seemingly gone. Somehow, even from those depths, she found her way back to life.

My grandmother knew more about time and resilience than anyone. She knew that rebuilding a life isn't a quick process but a patient one, measured in small improvements and sometimes no improvement at all. Eventually, gradually, remarkably, even the failures add up to something strong and enduring.

Decades before my collapse, when I was about thirty years old, I was diagnosed with cancer that was spreading fast in my body and required aggressive chemotherapy. It sucked every ounce of life out of me. I lost all my hair. I wasn't able to hold food down and had to keep a bucket near me at all times. It felt like I hit rock bottom. Then one day, my grandmother came to my room. We sat near my window, looking outside at an oak tree that provided shade to a bench we used to sit on together. "Nir," she said in her accented voice, "we grow from the bottom. Like the oak tree." She pointed down to the base of the tree and then slowly raised her finger upward along its trunk. "It was once just a small sprout in the dirt."

Up until now, I thought she meant that we grow from our lowest points, that hitting rock bottom was the start of something new. That is still true. But now, I understood another meaning to her words. The oak doesn't become mighty overnight. It takes years of slow, patient growth. It weathers storms, endures droughts, and stands firm through countless seasons. Sometimes it grows so slowly that no one notices the change from one day to the next. Other times, it is set back after losing a branch to a storm. But still, it is growing.

> The oak doesn't become mighty overnight. It takes years of slow, patient growth. It weathers storms, endures droughts, and stands firm through countless seasons.

Like the oak tree's invisible root system spreading underground, my recovery was happening in ways I couldn't always measure or see. I could imagine myself as that oak tree, sending roots deeper even when no visible growth appeared above the surface. Some days, I might only gain a millimeter of movement, barely perceptible to anyone watching. Other days might bring no visible progress at all. But beneath the surface, unseen by medical scans or physical assessments, my brain was forming new connections, one tiny neural pathway at a time.

Every time I struggled to move my right finger even a fraction of an inch, I could hear her voice: "From the bottom, Nir. Like the oak tree." I understood that those improvements were sprouts pushing through dirt, beginning the growth that would eventually, with patience and time, reach toward the sky.

The Marathon Mindset Rule

The doctors had said the first three months would be most important for my recovery, and that over the following six months, for up to eighteen months after, I might even return close to my former self. This was like waving a red flag in front of a bull, my competitive spirit was instantly triggered. There was something I could *do* about my condition.

I had spent seven years in the Israeli Defense Forces, commanding an elite company whose sole mission was to navigate to precise destinations and scout for strategic targets. Like those military missions, I now had coordinates to navigate toward. The doctor had marked an X on my recovery map and had even given me a timeline for reaching it. I decided I would find a way to reach that goal faster than anyone before me. I would break every recovery record they'd ever seen.

Suddenly, I was filled with determination, will, motivation, and a sense of mission that I could regain control over my life. I wouldn't be at the mercy of others much longer. It wasn't up to trusting the process; it was up to me.

I also knew I had to temper my enthusiasm and give it time. Three months was a long time, six months even longer, and eighteen months could seem like forever. I'd need to be smart about this. The only thing that could derail me was giving up too early or pushing too hard too soon. Giving up seemed unlikely, but this wasn't just a sprint of a few days or a few weeks, it was a two-year marathon. I'd need to control my impulse to sprint.

THE MARATHON MINDSET RULE

This became my first rule of recovery: the Marathon Mindset. As the days turned into weeks, this Marathon Mindset became my foundation. There would be more principles to guide me, more lessons to learn, but this commitment to patient, persistent growth, like the oak tree, would carry me through my darkest moments. After all, my grandmother had survived unimaginable things, yet somehow rebuilt her life, time and time again. If she could endure all that, surely I could face this challenge with the same quiet determination.

I made a promise to myself and to her that I would return to this rule every time I thought about pushing too hard or wishing for more progress. Keeping a Marathon Mindset requires determination, persistence, and acceptance. This was where I would find the patience for the long journey ahead.

My grandmother's wisdom had prepared me for this marathon long before either of us knew I would need it. Her legacy taught me that the longest journeys are completed not with dramatic bursts of speed, but with steady, determined steps forward, mile after mile, day after day.

Her legacy taught me that the longest journeys are completed not with dramatic bursts of speed, but with steady, determined steps forward, mile after mile, day after day.

The 1 Percent Rule

Pushing too hard is my natural instinct. Maybe it's from my seven years in the army, or perhaps it's from growing up as an Israeli man to an alpha-male Tunisian father, maybe it's just who I am or a combination of all these, but when I set my mind on a goal, I give it everything I have. When I thought about my recovery as a marathon, I remembered Krembo from the cult comedy *Operation Grandma* offering his ridiculous advice: "*To run a marathon, you start as fast as you can and constantly speed up.*" We always laughed at this absurd strategy, but secretly, that's exactly how I approached challenges my entire life, full throttle, damn the consequences.

But this recovery marathon demanded something different. My neurologist had made it clear: "The brain doesn't heal on your schedule. Push too hard, and you might injure yourself and set yourself back." I secretly added to that wisdom: "Move too slowly, and you'll miss critical windows for neural rebuilding."

This space between patience and urgency was unfamiliar territory for me, and I needed to thread the needle perfectly. That's when I remembered a story from a coaching book about the British cycling team. For decades, they were mediocre, until a new coach implemented what he called "the aggregation of marginal gains." He sought just 1 percent improvement in *everything*. Not just pedaling, but sleep quality, nutrition, even the pillows cyclists used. Within five years, they dominated world cycling.

THE 1 PERCENT RULE

Just 1 percent. It sounds insignificant, almost insultingly small when you're struggling to rebuild your entire life. But here's the magic: that 1 percent compounds. One percent better each day means you're twice as good in seventy days. Four times better in 140 days. The math is on your side.

This became a daily whisper to myself: *Just get 1 percent better today.* Some days that 1 percent came from physical therapy, other days from cognitive exercises, and sometimes, on the hardest days, it came simply from resting properly or maintaining a positive mental state. Everything counts when you're rebuilding yourself piece by piece.

On frustrating days when I could barely see progress, I'd ask myself, "Did I improve by just 1 percent today?" Almost always, the answer was yes. That tiny win would lift my spirits enough to try again the following day.

The beauty of the 1 Percent Rule is its flexibility. It makes room for inevitable setbacks, necessary rest days, and frustrating plateaus. It acknowledges that recovery isn't a straight line, it's a winding path that occasionally back-tracks.

The 1 Percent Rule was quickly becoming a philosophy for life itself. Small improvements, accumulated faithfully, would create transformations that I couldn't yet imagine. On this long road back to myself, the pace of healing might be slower than I'd like, but its power was unstoppable.

The Rest Rule

Sleep continued to elude me in the ICU. I was disturbed every few hours by someone checking on me, the beeping machines, or the vivid dreams that sometimes jolted me awake whenever I fell into a deep sleep. In my dreams, I could move my whole body, and a part of me, my aware self, realized I was moving my fingers by command from my brain. I tried desperately to stay in that moment of control, sometimes managing to maintain that feeling for a brief second, sensing movement in my actual body. But it almost always ended as I lost the thread of that dream and I awoke to numb, unresponsive fingers.

Each morning, I remembered these dreams, or at least the feeling of moving my right side. Then it would return to stillness in waking life. Perhaps it was only a dream, I can't be certain, but I had an unmistakable feeling that it had been real.

The first such dream came on my third night in the hospital. In it, I could move my fingers, gripping something. The next morning, I clearly remembered the feeling. I looked at my hand and focused on my fingers, then tried sending that same command from my brain, but nothing happened. Then, I placed my left hand next to it and tried moving both hands' fingers simultaneously, remembering the connection I had made in my sleep. I kept trying, moving both the fingers from both hands individually or together, with greater intention and force. My left hand's fingers moved fully, the skin visibly stretching as I pointed it up and closed it. But on the right...*something moved!* A very slight, almost undetectable movement in my right finger, but I knew it was there.

Now I had something to work with! I felt elated and proud of my progress, bragging about my extraordinary achievement to everyone. "Look, I can slightly move one finger. You have to pay attention to see it, but it moves!"

My intuition, later validated by the neurologist, was that the pathways in my brain were damaged, but new ones would form if they received the signal to do so. So I made these calls whenever I could. First, I tried to move both sides simultaneously, tapping my fingers on both sides. Eventually, I didn't need the left hand; I knew when I was sending the command. All day long, that's all I did. I tried harder, closing my fist or spreading my fingers. I couldn't straighten, point, or open it fully, but I repeated what I could do. *Close, release, close, release.*

Each small success fueled my determination. After a few days in the ICU, I had regained movement in four of my fingers, each at a different level, correlated to when I had first noticed motion. The most advanced was my index finger, closely followed by my middle finger, which by now I could close with about 25 percent of my normal grip strength and slightly open, though not completely. Next came my thumb at about 15 percent grip power, but with better range opening it. The ring and pinky fingers were "followers," meaning I could barely move them without moving my other fingers, and when I moved my other fingers, they also moved. I could independently flex my ring finger, just a little.

However, just a few minutes of trying to close and open my fist, barely moving it at all, left me sweating and breathing heavily. Honestly, trying to move one finger took more effort and exhausted me more quickly than my most intense pre-stroke workouts. That meant I also needed to rest, letting my body and (mostly) brain recover.

I knew rest was crucial for recovery from physical training, but I had always been terrible about doing so. Even when my body signaled it needed recovery, my brain would insist that was exactly when change happens and that I should keep going. But recovery is different. The doctors told me this, and while I questioned how much doctors knew about recovery, when the therapists told me the same exact thing, I paid attention.

Muscles rebuild after exercise, and the brain rewires itself during rest.

My brain needed two things to heal: the bleed had to shrink, like a bruise fading over time if left undisturbed, and new neural connections had to form. My neurologist confirmed that most of that process happened during sleep. Muscles rebuild after exercise, and the brain rewires itself during rest.

The Humor Rule

Every shift change followed the same routine. They would ask the same questions, "Do you know where you are?" "Do you know why you're here?" "Do you know the year and month?" "Can you tell me your name?" Then they'd ask me to smile, lift my arm, close my eyes, and keep them up. Finally, they'd feel my legs and arms and ask if sensation was equal on both sides.

This happened several times daily. I understood they were just doing their job, but after a while, it started to irritate me. They sometimes wouldn't even wait for me to finish answering before moving to the next question. The more unseen I felt, the more rage built up inside. Can't you see I'm OK? Are you just following a protocol? Am I just a number to you?

I remember the exact moment this thought came. With anger and frustration bubbling up, I told myself to stop. I closed my eyes, took a deep breath, and let it all out.

My grandmother once told me not to be so serious; life is serious enough. She had a dark sense of humor that I suspect I inherited, and she used to say things like "Life is a fatal disease." When asked

My grandmother once told me not to be so serious; life is serious enough.

how she was doing, she would answer, "Getting old is not for kids." Everything depends on how you look at it, and "bad" things are the easiest to laugh about. They do it in cartoons all the time, like someone slipping on a banana peel or, my all-time favorite, the coyote from *Wile E. Coyote and the Road Runner* falling into his own traps.

THE HUMOR RULE

That morning, I promised to stop taking everything so seriously. I could joke about the situation as easily as I could get irritated by it. Laughter was something I missed. Every time it happened, I felt physically better. So the next time a nurse began the questions, before she even finished the first one, I answered all of them at once: "I'm in the ICU, it's July, I had a stroke..." and finally, putting on a big smile and raising my left arm in victory: "... and yes, it feels the same on both sides!"

You should have seen the looks on their faces. They didn't know whether to continue with their questions or break protocol. Oh, the little things that could bring me joy.

That evening, as the hospital quieted, I looked down at my index finger, commanding it to bend. It responded with a slight, trembling curl, barely visible, but undeniably mine. In that small movement, I saw a framework for healing begin to take shape. My body was becoming a territory I could reclaim through patient, strategic effort.

My body was becoming a territory I could reclaim through patient, strategic effort.

This approach, a Marathon Mindset, 1 percent improvement, a rule of rest, and a humorous perspective, began to form the first pillar of my recovery efforts. Healing the body required more than physical exercises or movement patterns. I needed to have a comprehensive philosophy for rebuilding neural pathways, restoring strength, and reclaiming control over my physical self. And unlike my previous approaches to fitness challenges, pushing for maximum effort and quick results would not be effective. This pillar demanded patience, consistency, and listening deeply to my body's signals. Every finger movement, every attempted step, every small victory would build upon this foundation. Without it, nothing else in my recovery would be possible. As my grandmother might have said, it was like the roots of the oak tree, invisible yet essential, spreading beneath the surface long before any growth could be visible above ground.

I drifted toward sleep with my grandmother's wisdom echoing in my mind. For the first time since the stroke, uncertainty no longer felt like terror. The questions about tomorrow now carried a hint of anticipation. What new movement might emerge? What challenges might I overcome? A new day brought a new opportunity for my roots to grow. This was a pillar I could build from, 1 percent at a time, with just enough rest and humor to make the long journey bearable.

REFLECTION SPACE

"The mightiest oak was once an acorn that held its ground."

When everything feels like it's falling apart, it's easy to want fast answers and big progress. But recovery doesn't work like that. There are no shortcuts. It can be slow, quiet, unpredictable, and even messy. Most of it happens underground, like the roots of an oak tree. The strongest growth happens out of sight.

While this chapter summarized the foundation of the recovery framework that I came to follow, it's important to know that these realizations came to me slowly, and only in retrospect did I realize that the framework had been there all along. If I wanted to sum it all up in three words that I reminded myself of all the time, it would simply be, "Give yourself a break!"

Now that the framework does exist, however, I want to turn it to you. Let's look at these rules, these roots, and ask how they might show up in your life.

1. **THE MARATHON MINDSET:** If you are reading this book, it means a Band-Aid solution won't work for you and your situation. This is going to be a marathon. The main ingredient in successful recovery, whether from illness, trauma, burnout, or deep emotional loss, is time, not just willpower.

   Are you expecting yourself to "bounce back" too fast? What would change if you treated this like a two-year journey instead of a two-week comeback? (Everything, right?!)

2. **THE 1 PERCENT RULE:** There is no magic "recover pill" that heals the body or the soul. The magic happens over time with consistency and small, incremental steps. One day it's getting out of bed, another day it's making that phone call, or doing one exercise, or even a good night's sleep. Anything that moves you an inch forward.

   What is the one thing you can do today to be 1 percent better than yesterday? (And, can you let that be enough?)

3. **THE REST RULE:** We are terrible at this one (I know I am). We want to be doing something productive, and we think pushing and working are the ways to be more productive. But most of the real work happens when we're sleeping, sitting still, or just being. Your brain, muscles, bones, and even soul need downtime to process, to rebuild themselves, to heal. I like to think that making time to rest, is working smarter.

   Do you listen to your body when it tells you it's tired? Can you include rest time in your days without feeling guilty about it?

4. **THE HUMOR RULE:** This one's simple: laugh. Laugh at the absurdity, the pain, the awkwardness of it all. Not because your situation is funny, but because it reminds you that you're still you underneath all this chaos. I know that my grandmother would agree that this is the perfect time for self-humor and even dark humor. It doesn't mean you're not taking it seriously. It means you're human.

   Ask yourself: what is something about your current situation that would be hilarious in a movie? (Yes, even this.)

Recovery is happening in ways we can't always see. Some days you'll grow a millimeter, some days you'll lose ground, and some days nothing visible will happen at all. But beneath the surface, if you follow these rules, your roots are spreading deeper.

You don't have to do it all today. Think about it, let it sink in, maybe tomorrow you'll give it a try.

____

____

____

____

4

FIRST STEPS FORWARD

Every step teaches the foot where it wants to go.

THE first meal I recall having was a tray of hospital food placed before me as I sat up in bed. The nurse offered to help, but I insisted on doing everything myself with whatever ability I had. This was a workout in itself, but a couple of days later, two therapists came in after breakfast and asked if I wanted to try getting out of bed. You should have seen my smile! Without hesitation, I responded that I absolutely, definitely, 100 percent wanted to get out of bed. I also asked if they would teach me to do it myself. They laughed until they realized I was serious. Then they told me it probably wouldn't happen while I was in the ICU, but that they'd see how I was doing. For now, getting out of bed with assistance was excitement enough.

I wanted to sit in the patient chair near the bed. It had a tray holder, so I thought eating my meals there would help me feel slightly more normal and less like a patient. The nurse overheard me and joked that my eagerness to leave the bed hurt her feelings, as though I didn't want to be with them. We all laughed, and she made plans to rearrange the room and some equipment I was connected to in order to make that happen.

The next day, I eagerly awaited the PT team, ready to move from bed to chair. This time, two different therapists arrived, an older man in his fifties and a younger woman. Both appeared physically fit and, like the other medical staff I had worked with, projected confidence and professionalism. They knew I wanted to move to the chair and stay there even after they left, and my lunch tray waited outside the room. I couldn't see it, but I could smell it.

The first step was to turn to the side of the bed, leaving my legs dangling over the edge. It felt strange. Then we used a device called a Sara Stedy to transfer me from bed to chair. They guided me to hold my left arm in a certain way, made adjustments, and placed my right hand alongside it. Finally, they asked me to stand with their support.

And I stood up.

The movement was short and quick, only requiring me to straighten my legs and lock my knees. I am not a tall man, so my legs did not reach the floor while I was sitting on the bed and hardly reached the Sara Stedy, which meant they were almost straight right away. But when my knees locked, my back straightened, and I raised my head up, everyone was at eye level for the first time since entering the hospital. I remarked aloud that I finally didn't have to look up to everyone.

Then they rotated the seat pads behind me so that I lowered back a bit and rested my knees against them. I was still closer to standing than sitting and took a moment to appreciate the position. I felt strong, or at least less weak. I felt free, or at least less dependent. I felt optimistic, and even a little proud. They rolled the Sara Stedy so that the chair was right behind me. They helped me stand again, removed the pads, and assisted me in lowering into the chair. I got stuck momentarily when I couldn't release my right hand's grip on the handle, but the nurse helped me lower myself until I sank into the chair's cushion. *Success!* I raised my eyes again to look at everyone in the room. It felt...strange. I used my left arm to place my right one on the armrests and realized I was breathing hard and sweating, both from physical effort and the adrenaline rush of fear, excitement, and change. I needed water.

Before they left, the PT team instructed me on how to return to bed and made me promise never to attempt it alone, only with a nurse's assistance. I promised, though I wasn't brave or foolish enough to try.

Finally, the nurse placed my lunch tray in front of me and removed the covers from the plates. I tried using my right hand, but I could only move my index finger and connect it to my thumb with minimal strength. That wasn't helpful for eating, so I had to use my left hand.

All the while, I kept reminding myself that I only needed 1 percent improvement each day. A slow and steady pace would help me finish this marathon.

Regaining Perspective

When the physical therapists came for my next session, the older one shocked me by casually saying, "Let's get you up and walking today." A jolt of excitement and terror shot through me. With some help, I put on socks and sat on the edge of the bed. I felt both excited and terrified but trusted them completely. It was easier to trust the physical and occupational therapists than it was to trust the doctors, especially the specialists. They have spent many years sharpening their expertise in a narrow domain, all within a competitive environment where they need to build a name for themselves. The more experienced they are, they more determined they are about their recommendations. Specialists seem so confident in their knowledge that I have often suspected they'd never admit ignorance.

While doctors know to fix you up, save your life, prescribe you the right medicine, or operate on you and stitch you back up, they spend such little time with you. On the other hand, therapists have experience in the recovery process. They know what works and how long it takes, not just from reading it in a book, but from direct experience with people. All in all, I appreciate modern healthcare, but I wish it were more transparent.

With the guidance of the therapists who'd helped me move to my chair, I grasped the walker with my left hand and prepared to stand. Then the therapist helped position my right hand on it, and suddenly, I was vertical again.

The first sensation was almost like vertigo, a disorienting shift in perspective after days of horizontal living. Then came awareness of my body's weight, the pressure on my feet, and the slight wobble in my stance. But the most striking difference, like I'd noticed the day before, was being at eye level with others again. No longer looking up at their faces from down below, I stood among them as an equal.

"We'll go slowly," he assured me. "We'll be right here."

The nurse and the therapist guided me to shift my weight between my left and right legs. I even tried moving my right leg forward with some success. My hip was moving more than the leg itself, but this still gave me reason for optimism. The slightest movements encouraged me, confirming that the right side was reluctant yet not entirely absent.

"Look up, forward. Try taking another step," the therapist encouraged.

Just like they had been from the beginning, both my wife and Niv were present for these first steps forward.

Niv had dropped everything to come to the hospital as soon as he heard about my stroke. We'd met in 2015 at an Israeli poker night in Portland, Oregon. He's tall and handsome, with long hair and tremendous energy. His presence is memorable, you either like him or you don't, but you don't forget him. I liked him right away.

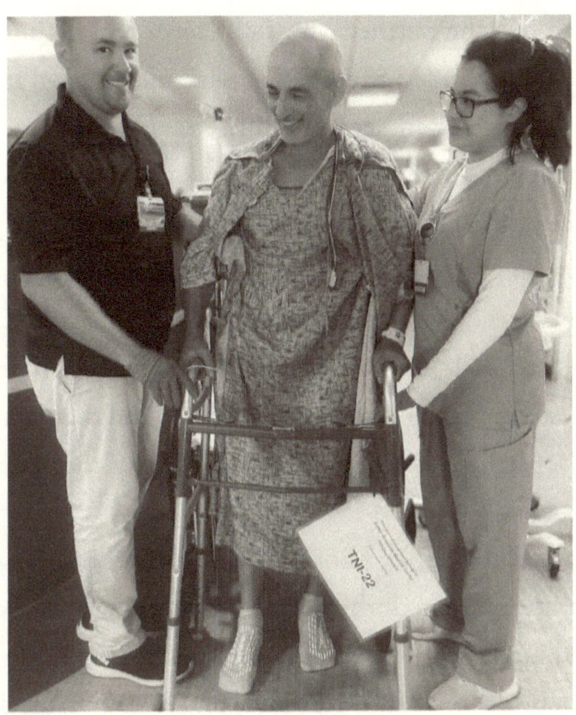

We stood out from the other players, both clearly there for fun and laughter. For us, poker was just an excuse to gather with other men our age, even though most of the other guys were engineers who took everything much more seriously. He and I drank beers and whiskey as we played, occasionally slipping outside to smoke what was about to be legalized in Oregon. That's where we bonded, trying to stay dry and warm under the cold Oregon skies, smoking weed and laughing about nonsense. We could share jokes that only someone familiar with Israeli cult movies and comedy sketches would understand or we could have deep, philosophical conversations about life's meaning.

Our friendship grew even closer when we went on to work together, first as colleagues from different departments and later in a direct reporting relationship. He excels professionally not just because of his mental intelligence but because of his emotional intelligence, charisma, and endless drive. When his wife heard what happened to me, she notified him right away, and he immediately flew to California to be with me. He'd tried joking with me as usual in the ER, but his nervous, frightened expression betrayed him.

As far as the hospital knew, Niv was my brother, and he certainly seemed like it. Perhaps his most significant contribution for me was to remind me about laughter, silliness, and small talk. Whenever a nurse or another professional entered my room, especially a woman, he'd make us all laugh. They often stayed after completing their task just to talk with us, mostly with him. This made the staff feel noticed and appreciated, creating a small bond that continued each time they returned, especially when Niv was present. My care seemed to improve from this as well.

I was equally grateful that Niv was there for my wife. She had sent our daughter to the neighbors, thrown on clothes, and chased the ambulance to the ER the morning they had taken me. The whole event had been extremely traumatizing.

My wife has always been the sensitive one between us. If I couldn't cry or connect to my emotions, she had a direct line to hers. She also possessed emotional intelligence and maintained a vibrant social life, managing both our social calendars and informing me about birthdays and special occasions. Whatever was "expected" of me came through her first, including who we would meet and what to wear.

A few months before my stroke, she had started a new job as a senior executive at a non-profit organization addressing rising antisemitism, an issue dear to her heart. It was demanding work, and with me traveling for several weeks, everything had fallen to her. Now this. To make matters worse, all our insurance came through my work, so she suddenly needed to handle that as well as all the administrative tasks involved when a husband is hospitalized. She liked and respected Niv more than any of my other friends, and his support helped us both tremendously.

Now, I stood there in my enormous green hospital gown, my backside exposed, a topic that generated much conversation, supported by them both.

I hesitated, unsure whether my right leg would support me enough to hold my balance. Then, summoning my courage, I shuffled my left foot forward ever so slightly. *Success!* Next, I focused all my mental energy on one simple command to my right leg: *Move forward.*

I stood there in my enormous green hospital gown, my backside exposed, a topic that generated much conversation, supported by them both.

Nothing happened.

I tried again, concentrating even harder and visualizing the movement.

Again, nothing.

Refusing to give up, I discovered I could compensate by slightly swinging my pelvis, using the momentum to throw my right leg forward in a circular motion. It wasn't elegant, but it worked. *I'm walking!* I shouted in my head. My right foot moved ahead of my left, and I took another step.

We only ventured to the nurses station in front of my room and back. After five to ten minutes spent taking no more than ten total steps, the effort had completely depleted my energy. I returned to the armchair sweating, thirsty, hungry, and exhausted. A staff member arrived with my lunch tray right on time.

I ate lunch that day feeling a profound sense of accomplishment. *I had walked today!* Even if it wasn't truly walking as I once knew it, and even if I couldn't move my right leg properly, I felt happy and optimistic. And I suddenly longed to see the sun. I knew it was mid-July, and according to everyone who visited, it was one of the hottest weeks on record. I wanted to feel that warmth on my face, though I didn't mention this desire to anyone. I just kept eating, listening to my wife and Niv discuss the weather and their plans for later that day.

With the three-month recovery counter ticking in the back of my mind, I had asked the therapist for homework, exercises I could do in bed or while sitting to regain leg function. There weren't many, and most required sitting, so for the next few days, I spent as much time in the chair as possible, practicing all of the arm and leg movements that I could.

The physical achievement of those few steps, however modest, had represented a reclamation of my vertical self. My standing identity. Problems that had seemed overwhelming from a prone position now felt more manageable. The world that had loomed over me now met me at eye level.

It's remarkable how much of our human experience is tied to this vertical posture, how much of my own experience was tied to it. We stand to speak, to be counted, to be seen. How often had I wished to be two inches taller? At school, I had gotten into fights whenever someone made a comment about my height. Now, in those first wobbly moments on my feet, I was beginning to discover what is truly important.

Reconnecting Body and Mind

The physical therapists also showed me in-bed exercises that focused on my shoulder, the part of my right arm closest to my body (proximal). They explained that typically, stroke patients regain movement first in joints closer to the body, proximal before distal. That pattern held true for my leg but not my arm, where movement started in my fingers (distal) and worked upward toward the wrist, elbow, and shoulder.

With fingers able to grip handles, I practiced moving my wrist like I was operating a motorcycle throttle. My wife's face was priceless when I joked about wanting a new bike (or was I joking?). By the seventh day, I could bend my elbow just enough to notice, perhaps 2 percent of my normal movement.

Once I could use my shoulders to move my arm upward, I practiced the "seatbelt on, seatbelt off" movement the therapists taught me. At least, I thought I was doing it right. While I later learned I was doing it incorrectly and had injured myself in my enthusiasm, I was thrilled to be using my entire arm. It opened up so many possibilities, from moving in bed to reaching for objects, eating, and basic personal hygiene. It represented major progress, signaling an upper body that would soon return to my control.

I was also making daily breakthroughs with my mind's connection to my body, discovering important clues about how recovery works. Each new movement was preceded by a visualization, whether in dreams or while awake. I began by mentally commanding the part to move. It was frustrating and exhausting, but eventually, I'd see signs of life, a tendon stretching or a faint movement. At first, I thought this was just coincidence. Then I was suspicious, then I accepted that "it's all in my head" referred to the very real neural connection between body and mind. Every tiny victory, every small movement became a celebration, a promise that this connection remained intact, simply waiting to be reawakened.

My family members became a constant reminder of the connections that can hold even when all seems lost.

I love my younger sister and brother dearly, and I had just seen them during my visit to Israel. It had been the first time in many years that Roy and I were both in Israel simultaneously. We spent time with our sister, our mother, and extended family before I returned to California the day before my stroke.

When he heard the news, he was in Tel Aviv, riding one of those electric scooter rentals you unlock with an app. In Tel Aviv, as in most cities with e-scooters, there are no designated lanes, so riders navigate between sidewalks and roads based on conditions. They're also quite fast. The news of my condition distracted him, and he got into a serious accident that nearly cost him his leg. Needless to say, he couldn't come to California to visit anytime soon.

Did I mention we share an exceptionally dark sense of humor?

Now, imagine our first video call, both of us in hospital beds, wearing hospital clothes, me with half of my brain "cooked" and he with a severely damaged leg. We looked at each other for a long moment, and as I struggled to say something funny, he beat me to it, making me laugh so hard that it almost hurt. My brother laughed because I was laughing, creating a feedback loop of unstoppable mirth.

He and I share a special language of total nonsense. We can hold a conversation about absolutely nothing for hours, changing accents, slipping in and out of mostly made-up characters, one sentence leading to another as we complete each other's thoughts. Together, we can build stories with no point whatsoever until one of us breaks into the kind of laughter where you have tears running down your face, you're choking, can't talk, can't even say a word, can't even breathe.

Jokes kept forming in my mind, but I couldn't find the words, put them into sentences, or deliver them with proper timing. *What's the most important part of a joke? Timing!* I had nothing but delay now, and somehow that itself became the joke.

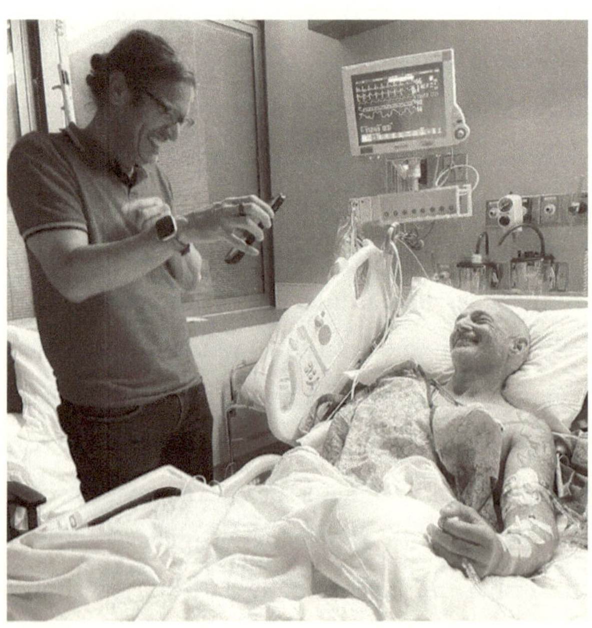

We used to say to each other, "It's funny in my head," alluding to the "movie" running through our minds that we couldn't articulate because it was moving too fast or because we were choking with laughter. Now the joke had a new dimension: it was funny in my head, but my medical condition prevented me from getting it out. The absurdity of it all only made me laugh harder.

It was cathartic. I had missed him terribly and wished we were together in Israel, at his rented apartment in Tel Aviv or staying at my sister's place, just the three of us laughing like we used to. Just a week ago, we had all sat around a campfire with my sister and her children, celebrating one of my cousins' birthdays. My brother and I had started one of our nonsense conversations, making everyone laugh until my mom choked and cried while others rolled their eyes in mock exasperation. This memory brought more tears to my eyes, not only from laughter. I felt waves of gratitude for the simple joy of connection that I'd taken for granted before.

The thought of "what if this had been it?" came to my mind. The timing of my stroke, just two days after seeing my family in Israel, created a narrative arc that seemed almost deliberate, as if I had been granted one final reunion with everyone I loved before nearly dying. There was a poetic quality to it all that made me contemplate whether there might be meaningful patterns in what otherwise appears to be random chance.

While I felt comfortable being vulnerable with my brother, I wasn't fully comfortable with myself feeling this way. This felt especially prominent when I realized there were people around during our video call, my wife, Niv, and nurses coming in and out of the room. I was already struggling with the new reality of not being able to speak my mind fluently, of everyone growing quiet when I tried to talk, sometimes attempting to help by completing my sentences. I wasn't ready for this kind of attention.

I tried not to dwell on it, but the awareness was constant. Eventually, whenever

I wanted to say something, I weighed the importance of my thought against the effort and time it would take to express it. I had never been particularly talkative, but now that every word required deliberate choice, less became more.

Another connection formed during that call with my brother, which I had felt but not fully articulated before. While we found humor in our parallel misfortunes, there was something deeply symbolic about experiencing similar limitations at the same time, despite being thousands of miles apart. It felt like more than coincidence, as though our lives were fundamentally intertwined in ways that transcended physical distance. I saw it as a metaphor: what happens to one of us happens to both. My brother couldn't walk; I couldn't control half my body, and we were both in recovery. Our connection was unbreakable, even across the Atlantic and without words.

My mother was also back in Israel, but I was more hesitant to speak with her. I didn't want to worry her more than necessary. She already had my father to worry about, and now my brother was hospitalized as well. Plus, in the early days after my stroke, I was afraid that my own stress or worry for her could trigger another bleeding episode. I couldn't bear to see her worried and probably crying. Not calling her felt like a deliberate choice to be selfish, putting my health before the people I loved most.

Instead of a real-time conversation, where I'd have to respond to her questions and potentially reveal the full extent of my condition, I decided to record a video message so she could see and hear that I was at least somewhat okay.

It took five attempts to get it right. I used voice-to-text to write a script so I wouldn't repeat myself or forget key points, with a list of seven or eight topics I wanted to cover. Eventually, I managed to record a message without too many pauses, without saying "Ohhhh" before every sentence, without crying, and covering most of my points just once. I sent her that version.

I preferred to be alone while recording these messages, each of which left me choked up or crying. Imagining her inevitable question, "How are you doing?" led to deeply reflective thoughts. After objectively describing my circumstances, that I was in a hospital bed, struggling to move and talk, I wanted to give her a glimpse into my inner world. I wanted to tell her how grateful I was to be alive. My feelings of love and appreciation for her, for her unconditional love throughout my life, had mixed with empathy for what she must be going through as a mother. As a parent myself, I finally understood how a child's suffering becomes a parent's agony. Now I needed help rather than providing it. I had to accept care rather than giving it. This reversal challenged my fundamental sense of self. Who was I if not the capable one, the provider, the rock that others relied on?

After I pressed "send," something clicked. The message that should have taken two minutes had consumed nearly an hour of concentrated mental labor that left me physically exhausted. And the struggle had revealed a critical dimension of my recovery that had been lurking beneath the surface all along. While my physical limitations were immediately visible to everyone, the way my right side dragged, my clumsy attempts to use my hand, the cognitive challenges that remained largely invisible to them were more frightening to me. Finding words, organizing thoughts, maintaining focus, remembering what I'd just said, these mental processes had once been my superpower. Now, they required exhausting effort.

I had been approaching my recovery primarily as a physical challenge, but this experience forced me to confront a harder truth: my mind needed its own dedicated rehabilitation approach.

This realization became the seed of what I would later call my Mind Pillar, the second essential component of my recovery framework. While my Body Pillar focused on movement and strength, this emerging Mind Pillar would encompass the equally crucial work of rebuilding cognitive pathways.

I didn't fully understand it yet, but both pillars would require the same patience, the same incremental progress, the same strategic rest, the same capacity to laugh at myself when I inevitably messed up, all while following its own timeline, with its own tools, milestones, and breakthroughs. What worked for rebuilding a muscle wouldn't necessarily work for reconstructing a thought process.

At the end of the day, I felt both overwhelmed and strangely comforted. Overwhelmed by this new dimension of recovery I was only beginning to understand, but comforted in the knowledge that identifying the challenge was the first step toward addressing it.

I had named it now. I could feel its shape. And what you can name, you can tackle. One percent at a time.

I had named it now.
I could feel its shape.
And what you can
name, you can tackle.
One percent at a time.

REFLECTION SPACE

"A journey of a thousand miles begins with a single step."
–Lao Tzu

There's something about standing up after being stuck in bed that hits deeper than just "getting vertical." It's emotional. Existential, even. You're no longer looking up at the world, you're at eye level with it again.

This was when I first started to feel like myself again. But it wasn't really about the steps, it was about connection. With my body. With the people who stayed. With the version of myself that I was slowly becoming.

And those first steps, literal or not, can be terrifying. Your identity wobbles as much as your body does. So I want to offer you this space to reflect, not just on standing again, but on what it means to reclaim movement in your own life, physical or otherwise.

Ask yourself:

What "first step" have you taken? Maybe it was small. Maybe no one noticed. But you did. Count it. Celebrate it.

What's your relationship with your body right now? Not how it looks. Do you know your body? Do you listen to it? Do you trust it?

Who helps you feel stronger? I was lucky to have Niv and my wife by my side. Who brings you ease, or laughter, or just shows up? Who can you lean on, even a little?

Who reminds you who you really are? I was grateful to have my brother Roy to call. Who do you have an unbreakable connection with?

Maybe you're here because something knocked you down, an illness, an accident, a breakup, a breakdown, grief...Whatever it was, it's okay to still be rebuilding. To feel awkward. To move funny. To not have it all together yet.

Remember: your body is not you, but it is your partner. Whatever you're recovering from, physical or not, your body is part of that journey. You are both in this together. Let it be.

Start wherever you are. One percent at a time. That's enough. You're already on your way.

PART II

THE MIND

5

—

NEW SURROUNDINGS, NEW CHALLENGES

Letting yourself fall apart isn't weakness. It's the only way the pieces can find their way back together.

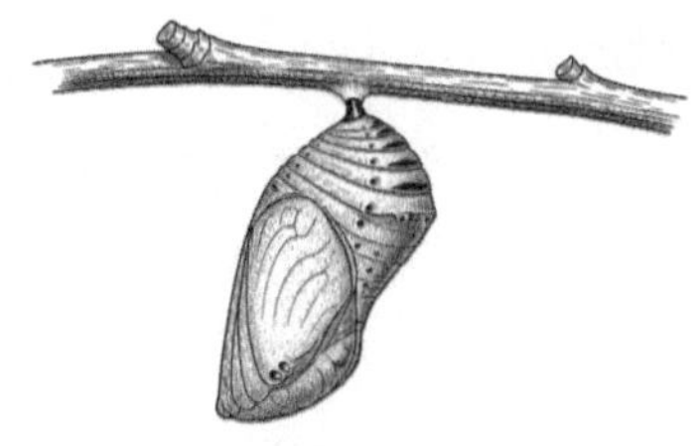

I'D cried more since the stroke than in the previous thirty years combined. Even when I had tried to cry intentionally in the past, it never happened. The closest I had come in recent times was after October 7th, 2023. Watching the horrifying news from Israel, listening to survivors, feeling their sorrow and pain while being unable to do anything about it had broken me apart. Something big was happening, and still is, as of this writing, that I couldn't fully grasp. Life would never be the same. And still, the tears would not flow.

> I'd cried more since the stroke than in the previous thirty years combined.

In childhood, tears came easily. This quality was not appreciated in a young boy, and certainly not in a man. I'd spent years training myself to suppress my emotions. But as soon as I arrived at the ER, amid the chaos of exams, people, and machines, I wasn't worried about any of that. When I saw my wife, the dam broke. All of my emotions came rushing forward, and I didn't try to hold them back.

I felt helpless, scared, profoundly alone, and afraid everything would soon end as the metaphorical curtain closed completely. I didn't need comfort or reassurance for these feelings, I just needed to cry. To feel the sadness and pain, which, surprisingly, felt good to do. For the first time in years, my emotions had overpowered my ability to control them, spilling out with a level of catharsis I hadn't experienced since childhood.

For years, I had approached life as merely a challenge to overcome without allowing it to touch me deeply. Now, I wanted to feel again.

Since then, I had tried to keep that door to emotions open. For years, I had approached life as merely a challenge to overcome without allowing it to touch me deeply. Now, I wanted to feel again. This didn't contradict my determination to overcome the obstacle of this setback; it added a dimension to my recovery.

THE FEEL EVERYTHING PRINCIPLE

Just as I had made a rule to make room for happiness and laughter, I should also make room for sadness and crying whenever it appeared. If feelings are a spectrum of frequencies, like light, I wanted to remove my filters to see the entire spectrum. Feelings aren't good or bad, they're just feelings. Chemical reactions in my body serving a purpose, just as dark colors make the brighter ones appear more vibrant by contrast.

I'd heard that, as men age and testosterone decreases, they often grow more emotional and cry more frequently. I knew such a man. He had once been the epitome of masculinity, a strong former soldier who worked with horses and cattle (still does), but who also published a book of poetry. I'd seen him cry over both happy and sad events. I aspired to that balance, minus the cattle work and lowered testosterone. I came to think of him as a "Sensitive Samurai." This was a journey into a new way of being, while rediscovering parts of myself that had long been neglected. And somehow, strangely, I felt grateful for the opportunity, even as I grieved what I had lost.

These thoughts and realizations accompanied me as I prepared to move to the rehabilitation unit. Seven days in the ICU had yielded remarkable progress. I had stood again. I had taken steps. I had begun the journey back to myself. Now, it was time to move forward, both literally and figuratively. Despite my strategy of moderation and rest, the clock was ticking. The doctor's words kept echoing in my head: "The first three months...the first three months..." And as they say, "It's easier to restrain a wild horse than push a dead mule." I was the wild horse in this scenario, full of determination, perhaps too eager to make rapid progress, and I hoped to find a rehab facility who could restrain me.

My natural instinct was to accelerate my recovery with more repetitions and more difficult exercises. I was looking forward to working with therapists who could both keep up with me and pull me back when needed. To give me the platform to run fast, but also to say, "That's enough for today" or "Let's not risk injury by attempting that yet."

We found a rehabilitation center that seemed to provide everything I was looking for, and it happened to be attached to the hospital I was in. We had to pull some strings to arrange for transfer from the ICU to an intermediate unit for a night or two until a room became available. Then, with mixed emotions and gratitude for the staff who had guided me through those initial days, I prepared to leave the ICU. I said goodbye to my favorite nurse as she disconnected me from the monitors, then promised to return walking independently, carrying a box of those Belgian chocolates we had talked so much about.

Eight days after I'd arrived, the two big doors at the end of the corridor opened for me once again. Though I was still lying on my back, this time my head and torso were elevated, and I felt less shocked, more observant. I was able to look around at more than just the ceiling tiles, even making eye contact and exchanging smiles with hospital staff and random visitors. The more of these small moments of contact with people I had, the bigger my smile grew. The road ahead would be long and filled with challenges I couldn't yet imagine. But having stood at eye level with the world, I knew that each small victory would carry me forward. One step, one day, one percent at a time.

New Rule: Don't Get Injured

My transitional bed was in the internal unit, and it immediately struck me how much quieter it was than the ICU. Nothing seemed urgent here. I remained connected to my PICC line "just in case," but everything else had been removed. The room offered more space for visitors, a door to the bathroom with a shower, and the most important thing: a window to the outside world. The sunlight streamed into the room as I was wheeled to meet it, no longer isolated in a bubble devoid of time and space. Simply being able to tell if it was day or night gave me a sense of contact with the outside world.

When the new nurse arrived to perform their usual checks, he also mentioned "showering," so casually that I asked him to repeat. He confirmed what I thought I'd heard: he could help me shower if I wanted to. *Oh*, how I wanted to!

It was one of the best showers of my life.

Layers of stickiness peeled off my skin, the hospital grime washing away as warm water ran over my body, dripping from my head to my face and shoulders.

It was a sensory symphony, the muffled sound when water covered my ears, the fresh smell of water and soap combining to an almost hypnotic effect. It felt like a spa treatment, right there in a commode chair in a hospital shower. I couldn't care less that the nurse was there, adjusting the water temperature and helping soap areas I couldn't reach. Privacy was a luxury left at home.

Lost in this utopic world, I grabbed the rail, pushed myself an inch above the commode chair, and bent just slightly forward to clean my underside. Then I reached for the soaped cloth, and slipped.

In that heart-stopping moment between slip and fall, time slowed. My mind sprinted ahead with terribly clarity: The nurse reaching to catch me, my body crashing against the hard tile and wet floor. The crash, the sharp pain. The doctors shaking their heads, the X-rays, the new injuries, the additional days or weeks of recovery. The absurd stupidity of it all. All my progress erased because of one careless moment.

My heart kept racing as I fell back onto the secure commode instead of tumbling to the floor.

This moment crystallized what would become my fifth recovery principle: the "Don't Get Injured" Rule.

Back in Portland, Niv and I both had dirt bikes. Our motto was to have fun but make sure we'd wake up in our own beds tomorrow. Meaning, don't get injured. Here, the "Don't Get Injured" Rule became non-negotiable. One bad fall wouldn't just ruin a weekend; it could erase weeks or months of painstaking progress. The fastest way to go backward is to try pushing forward too hard.

> The fastest way to go backward is to try pushing forward too hard.

THE DON'T GET INJURED RULE

Every action, every decision had to pass this test: Is this worth the risk of undoing everything I've worked for? Usually, the answer was no.

I couldn't bear the thought of explaining to my doctors, my wife, my daughter, or myself how I'd sabotaged my recovery through some avoidable, foolish risk.

Back in my room, skin clean but ego slightly bruised, I reminded myself that I wasn't fully recovered. I needed to keep reminding myself of this, especially on good days, when the progress made me feel invincible.

A New Level of Freedom

After the shower, I learned that leaving the ICU also meant I could wear my own clothes. The nurse tossed my polyester-blend hospital gown into a basket in the corner, then helped me into my own cotton garments with familiar scents and textures. I had underestimated the importance of underwear before spending this week without it. Showered, and now clad in a simple pair of shorts and a T-shirt, I felt human again.

The improvement was evident when Niv arrived later that day and an idea came to mind. Through the partially open door, I had spotted a wheelchair in the corridor. I wondered if he could push me around in it, even if we were limited to the hallway, for a taste of freedom and a change of scenery. I asked the nurse for this, and he agreed.

The nurse had just enough time to help Niv transfer me to the wheelchair before he was called back out to the nursing station. We were almost ready to roll, except that my right leg kept sliding off the footrest. Impatient and resourceful, I had Niv use one of my shirts to wrap my leg and secure it to the footrest. A test drive up and down the corridor by my room proved that our prototype solution had worked.

I'd never enjoyed asking for help or needing assistance. Honestly, I had never understood how some people could readily ask others to invest time and effort on their behalf. I viewed them as selfish, self-centered, and even weak. Asking for help had been my last resort, and even then, I carefully considered whom to ask. Throughout my life, this dominant, competitive mentality had earned me nicknames like "Lone Cowboy," "Napoleon," and "the Captain."

Looking down at my leg, strapped to the footrest with a shirt, I had to laugh. The Lone Cowboy needed a makeshift harness just to keep his leg from sliding off. Napoleon couldn't conquer a simple shower without nearly falling. Some captain I was, commanding a vessel that refused to respond to half my orders.

Yet as Niv pushed me through that fluorescent-lit corridor, I realized something important: the operating system had crashed, the hardware had failed spectacularly, but the reboot was complete and somehow the core programming remained intact. My 1 Percent Rule was working. Each small victory, finger movement, standing up, making a joke that landed, asking for help, was a line of restored code. Maybe not the same as the original, but it was at least functional and, in some ways, upgrades had been installed.

the operating system had crashed, the hardware had failed spectacularly, but the reboot was complete and somehow the core programming remained intact.

Mere days ago, I'd arrived on a stretcher, wondering if I would leave alive. Now I was sitting up, moving forward, making plans.

I tightened my improvised leg strap and pointed ahead. "Let's do an exploration mission of this place," I told Niv in Hebrew, my sense of humor returning along with my determination. "I need to identify all strategic positions before the full operation begins."

REFLECTION SPACE

"In every new beginning, some other beginning's end is concealed."
–Talmud

There's a moment in recovery, or grief, or change, when you move away from survival mode and the pull toward doing more kicks in. That urge to speed things up, to prove you're okay, to make everything "normal" again. I know it well.

After leaving the ICU, I felt like I was finally coming back to life. I could wear my own clothes, roll down a hallway, even laugh at myself again. But with that freedom came a new challenge: not pushing so hard that I'd break everything I'd just started to rebuild.

It's a strange dance, stretching yourself but not snapping. Holding your balance. Acknowledging that you are not okay, physically or emotionally.

So, I invite you to reflect:

Where are you trying to rush something that needs more time? Can you ease up a bit? Not to quit, but to soften your grip?

Where are you holding yourself to old standards that don't fit your current reality? Can you let go, just a little?

What does "freedom" look like to you now? Are you chasing it in a way that supports your healing or risks it?

And maybe most important:

Can you sit with the discomfort of "I am not fine" without trying to fix it all at once? Try it.

Then, notice what emotions come up. Anger, sadness, fear, or even joy…Again, not to fix or analyze those emotions, but just to notice them.

That's been one of the hardest lessons for me to learn. Some things need space. Time. Rest. Attention without urgency.

Progress isn't just forward motion. It's also knowing when to pause. When to hold back. When to laugh at yourself and say, "Not today, cowboy." How to rebuild wisely, even if it's not quickly.

And that, too, is healing.

6

——

DON'T FORGET TO EXHALE

When you breathe properly, you heal properly.

THE route through the hospital and out to the rehab facility was confusing. Even the volunteer transporting me, a short man with wide shoulders and a small mustache, admitted that if he hadn't brought another patient there that day, we might have gotten lost.

We went up one elevator, down a different elevator, over a bridge used for parking extra beds, through corridors lined with large imaging equipment, and passed patient rooms with monitors outside their doors. I tried to identify the cafeteria, or at least a sign showing where it was, but I saw nothing. Finally, we arrived in a room of similar size to the one I'd been in, with the same beige and brown color scheme. It was furnished with comfortable-looking chairs, a sink with a large mirror above it, a cabinet with shelves and drawers, and, to my delight, *no* medical equipment whatsoever.

A whiteboard displayed my name, the names of staff members on the current shift, my room privileges, and most importantly, my shower days. There was also a bright red paper next to the whiteboard that the nurse explained was a waiver. If something happened while I was doing something I didn't have "approved privileges" for, like getting out of bed without assistance or going to the toilet alone, they wouldn't be responsible.

Taking Stock

My schedule included one hour each of physical therapy, occupational therapy, and speech therapy daily. It wasn't as intensive as I'd hoped for, I wanted to maximize every minute of those critical first three months, but it was still early to judge.

My first session was an assessment with Rob, one of the few male physical therapists. Beyond evaluation, he gave me tips, corrections, and exercises I could do independently in bed or in my wheelchair. This resonated perfectly with my emerging recovery strategy. I could supplement the formal therapy with my own effort, applying my 1 percent improvement approach throughout the day.

As part of this initial assessment, we discussed goals for my stay, which would likely be one to two weeks.

"What would you like to be able to do when you're released home?" he asked. "Walk? Shower?" he suggested, offering the typical benchmarks most patients aimed for.

I answered instinctively, from somewhere deeper than rational thought: "Independence."

I elaborated that I didn't want to rely on anyone, not even my wife, for anything. If that meant home adjustments or using equipment, so be it. I had never liked being helped or feeling weak or vulnerable except in rare circumstances and with very few people. This was a core part of my identity now threatened by my condition. So, I asked him to document it: "My goal is to be able to live without help at home, without relying on my wife being there, and that includes driving!"

The mention of driving seemed to surprise him. It was ambitious given my current state, but I needed it to be a target on the map, something concrete to work toward.

He smiled and wrote something down without commenting, probably having heard countless unrealistic goals from patients who didn't yet comprehend the long road ahead. But I wasn't approaching this like other patients. I had my framework forming, with my incremental steps, my marathon runner's perspective. And now, I felt a level of purpose that I hadn't experienced since before the stroke. I was ready to reclaim myself.

My first meeting with the rehabilitation doctor illustrated how drastically my circumstances had changed from the ER to the ICU to now: after Dr. Matthews sat near me and introduced herself, we had an *actual* conversation. She took her time and conveyed interest in me as a person, not just a case. In contrast to the dehumanizing routine exams that had been required in the ICU, we talked for a while before she finally said, "Before I leave, let me examine you."

Dr. Matthews asked to see any movement I could manage with my right side. I was extremely proud to demonstrate my newest progress. The previous night, I discovered I could lift my leg ever so slightly from the hip joint, about 50 percent of the times that I tried. Unfortunately, I tried too hard to succeed on the first attempt. While I had hoped to show her what a big boy I was, instead I threw my abdominal muscles into a sharp cramp. I stretched out on the bed arching my back, trying to release my muscles while describing to the worried faces around me what was happening. At the same time, the word "cramp" evaded me, leaving me scrambling to find other terms between the "ouch" and "eyyy" sounds that more readily escaped my mouth.

The doctor placed her hands firmly on my belly and started massaging my abs. After the pain subsided, she reminded me, gently but firmly, to take it easy and not overdo it. I bowed my head in shame and said, "Yes, ma'am," and we proceeded with the exam.

After she left, I noticed a terrible expression on Niv's face. He hadn't known what was happening. One moment I was talking normally, the next I was twitching in pain, and the worry weighed heavily on him. At that moment, my promise to the doctor to take it easy turned into a promise to myself. I would never again put him or anyone else through such unnecessary worry.

The next doctor I met was a neurologist named Dr. Daniel. He didn't look like a typical doctor. He was my age, wearing a nice button-up shirt similar to one I had at home, without the typical stethoscope and coat that's supposed to come with the job. He looked more like a colleague than the stream of people representing the medical system I was surrendering to. Perhaps that's why I opened up to him so much, so soon.

Dr. Daniel sat with his back to the window, facing me as I enjoyed my new wheelchair. I don't remember how the conversation started, but it progressed with me talking and him listening. Despite my speech continuing to be a struggle, pausing often, sometimes losing words mid-sentence, my thoughts flowed freely for the first time since the stroke. It was as if the dam holding back my pre-stroke life had suddenly broken, letting everything rush out at once.

I was extraordinarily candid about my mental state and stressors leading up to the stroke: my father being placed in a dementia care facility; my visit just before the stroke where I realized he barely recognized anyone, couldn't make eye contact, and was restrained to prevent falls; my chaotic work situation, having just been fired along with my team, then rehired under three different managers without a clear job description; the several startups courting me to join as CEO; my constant worry about my aging mother living far away in Israel; my sister struggling nearby her, and my brother whom I desperately wanted to help; all of them being too distant to support as I wished to do; tensions in my marriage; my beloved daughter, born with a neurological condition and having endured numerous surgeries, and my worry about her starting high school the following year...

The words continued to pour out as the doctor listened with great patience and full engagement. I talked about the absence of local friends or community. About the situation in Israel since October 7th, 2023, which had forever altered the lives of all Israelis, and my heartbreaking meetings with families of hostages and killed children during my recent visit. I told him I had felt betrayed by the liberals I once identified with, who now seemed to wish me harm. I said I did not feel safe anywhere in the world. I explained my nightly ritual of marijuana, lately accompanied by beer, my daily gym visits to release built-up anger.

I don't know how long I was talking. Maybe ten minutes, maybe half an hour. My thoughts raced at normal speed, but articulating them remained challenging, like trying to push water through a half-blocked pipe. He listened patiently, leaning forward, his hands clasped, nodding and maintaining an attentive expression. As I spoke about these personal stressors without interruption, I realized just how much I was carrying. My brain might have been injured, but my awareness of each of these factors remained intact, perhaps even heightened by my new perspective.

By the time I finished, I felt like a one-ton weight had been lifted off my shoulders. I had needed to vent, to express everything without judgment or personal attachment, without anyone trying to fix anything.

By the time I finished, I felt like a one-ton weight had been lifted off my shoulders. I had needed to vent, to express everything without judgment or personal attachment, without anyone trying to fix anything. He said what I expected him to say. That it was a lot, that I had much on my plate, that even the most relaxed person would feel stressed, and that I should focus on recovery and take it easy. When he left, the space he created for me to see my whole self, not just my broken body but my overwhelmed mind, remained.

Better Out Than In

The last doctor I met became my favorite. He asked to be called Dr. M, promising that I wouldn't be able to pronounce his full 16-letter name, not even by the time I was released. He was right.

Unlike every other medical professional I'd encountered, Dr. M seemed to deliberately avoid talking about my condition. He visited daily, and each day followed the same pattern: we made small talk about everything and nothing, then just before leaving, as if it were an afterthought, I would ask something related to my situation. In a world where I had been reduced to a collection of symptoms and measurements, his approach restored my identity as a person with interests beyond my medical condition.

During his first visit, as he was leaving, he advised me to use the bathroom whenever I felt the need, even if I was in the middle of therapy. "The last thing you want is constipation. So drink plenty of water, and when you need to go, go! Don't be a hero," he said. Those simple instructions hid wisdom that I would carry throughout my recovery: there's no virtue in unnecessary suffering, and sometimes the most basic needs take priority over everything else.

One of our early conversations centered on coffee, a daily ritual that had anchored my mornings before the stroke. I mentioned that Andrew, a father of one of my daughter's best friends who lived nearby, had brought fresh Starbucks coffee to me daily while I was in the ICU. Black, medium roast, no sugar or cream, just as I liked it. Andrew came every single day, stayed no more than ten minutes, and then left. The familiar taste of that coffee had been my first reconnection with normal life, a reminder that some pleasures remained unchanged, even when everything else was upended.

Those ten minutes had meant more to me than Andrew could have imagined. They made me feel seen, cared for, and connected, even in my weakest moments. When you're in the hospital, visitors create a sense of belonging, the comfort that someone is thinking about you, and the reassurance that you're not alone. Each visit, however short or simple, quietly says, "You matter."

This discussion, centered primarily around coffee, led to a lengthy conversation about hospital coffee. After describing the excellent coffeemaker he had in his office and acknowledging there were no good alternatives without driving, he offered a simple idea that struck me as revolutionary: why not get my own machine? He assured me that coffee wouldn't negatively affect my condition, and noted that it wasn't about the drink itself. Making my own coffee, exactly as I liked it, represented a small but significant victory over helplessness. It was a way to take back a small piece of control, creating a tiny island of normalcy in the clinical desert of rehabilitation.

During another lengthy visit, I mentioned being unable to nap because people constantly entered and woke me. He suggested placing a "Do Not Disturb or Wake Up" sign on the door during naps, with "By Doctor's Orders" added to it. Once again, the simplicity of this solution was genius, a straightforward way to balance my Rest Rule with the requirements of the facility. Dr. M's human approach, treating me as a person rather than a patient, modeled recovery as a holistic return to fullness as a human being rather than a series of medical benchmarks to achieve. This, paired with my initial conversation with Dr. Daniel, where I had finally vented all my accumulated stress, revealed a pattern I'd been missing. Both experiences underscored the vital importance of not just what we take in, but what we consciously release.

In my EMT training, I had learned that breathing is as much about inhaling oxygen as it is about exhaling carbon dioxide, a waste product that becomes toxic if it remains in our bloodstream too long. I saw this pattern everywhere. Our bodies don't just absorb food; they must get rid of waste. When we move, some muscles tighten and others relax. The body builds strength not during exercise but during recovery afterward. Our entire existence depends on this fundamental rhythm of receiving in and releasing out.

> Our entire existence depends on this fundamental rhythm of receiving in and releasing out.

Our emotional lives also require regular release. That's what had happened in the ER when tears came so unexpectedly. Feelings are simply visitors passing through. Joy, sadness, anger, fear, all need to be felt, acknowledged, and then released. My body knew that all those feelings I'd been holding for decades finally had somewhere to go, and that's when the dam broke. When I vented to Dr. Daniel, I felt lighter not because he solved my problems, but because he simply listened while I released what was inside of me.

This pattern even holds within our relationships. We often hear about surrounding ourselves with people who energize and support us. But it's just as important to release the ones that drain us. Letting go of people who deplete your energy isn't cruel or selfish, it's necessary maintenance. Sometimes, being alone is important as well. Just as our lungs must exhale to make room for fresh air, our lives require the space that comes from solitude or ended relationships.

> Letting go of people who deplete your energy isn't cruel or selfish, it's necessary maintenance.

Time itself functions similarly. I had always been future-focused, planning, preparing, projecting, but rarely fully present. But reflection on the past and preparation for the future are only valuable when balanced with full presence within the current moment.

Within the context of Dr M's admonishment to "go" when needed, this concept of release made me think of Shrek's famous line: "Better out than in, I always say!" (Something I often repeat at home, making my wife roll her eyes with a sigh.) I had been mentally constipated for years, full of ideas, feelings, and stress that had nowhere to go. My stroke, terrible as it was, had forced a release, clearing space for something new to emerge. Better out than in, indeed.

> I had been mentally constipated for years, full of ideas, feelings, and stress that had nowhere to go.

REFLECTION SPACE

"Sometimes, the most important thing you can do is nothing."

Healing is the balance between adding something more and letting something go. For so long, I'd been holding everything in, tension, stress, pressure, control. My identity had been tied to pushing through, managing everything on my own. But here's what I learned: sometimes, the most powerful move is to exhale. To let it out.

What are you holding that you don't need to carry anymore?

Anger about what happened to you? A grudge? Fear about what comes next? Grief for what you've lost? Sadness? Resentment toward people who "didn't understand" or those who didn't show up? These feelings don't go anywhere until you let them out.

Do you have someone who can simply listen, not fix or advise? Could you be that person for someone who needs that, even for a little while?

Where in your body or life are you clenching? Are you trying too hard to keep it together? What thoughts, feelings, or conversations have you been avoiding? What would it feel like to finally let them out? Maybe all at once, or maybe just start with one and then see.

What relationships or situations are draining you? Who leaves you feeling depleted? What commitments are you keeping out of guilt rather than choice? Maybe it's time to let them go.

How can you reclaim tiny bits of control? What small piece of your old routine or identity can you bring back into your life right now? For me, it was a coffee maker and a "do not disturb" sign. Small things, but they made me feel human again.

Remember: your body knows how to breathe. *"Better out than in."*

Inhale the good stuff, but don't hold it in. Exhale the waste, toxic thoughts, draining relationships, impossible expectations.

Just breathe.

Let yourself feel without solving. Rest without guilt. Let go of something that's no longer serving you.

Even a tiny release can make space for something new.

86

Beyond 100 Percent: Rebuilding Life After It Breaks

7

—

BEYOND THE PHYSICAL

The wounds no one can see often take the longest to heal.

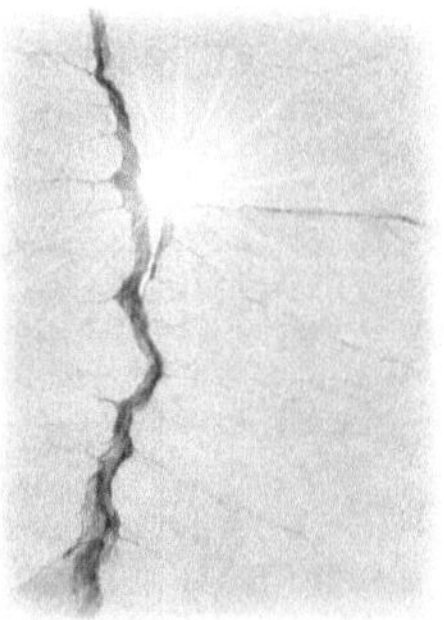

Mʏ first speech therapist met me in my room exactly on time for our planned appointment. Something about her seemed familiar, though I couldn't place who she reminded me of. We walked together, or rather, I rolled myself as she walked beside me, to her small office at the end of the corridor. She commented on how hot it was outside even though it wasn't yet 9 AM. I offered her chocolate and told her about the fancy coffee machine that was supposed to arrive any day. Then I parked my wheelchair near her desk, locked it, and waited as she pulled a few binders from her shelf and organized them.

"I'll be evaluating your condition today to determine the best treatment approach," she explained. "Where do you feel your cognitive changes are most noticeable?"

While my right arm and leg advertised my condition to the world, the most profound damage remained invisible. Even I felt like I was discovering my cognitive challenges incrementally over time.

No one who watched me struggle to walk could see the mental fog that sometimes descended without warning or the frustration I felt when common words vanished from my vocabulary mid-sentence.

At first, I thought it was a "wiring" issue, that my brain functioned the same but needed to find the right paths to speech. But I was coming to terms with the reality that my brain was not okay. I told her about my word-finding difficulties and about recording a video message to my mother five times and still not being satisfied with the result. I confessed that I'd barked at my wife to "stop completing my sentences," and how I'd regretted it before I'd even finished speaking. I described how I couldn't multitask anymore, either, and that I was experiencing "glitches," moments where I completely forgot things, made unusual mistakes, or lost my train of thought.

She listened attentively, typing notes into her computer. Then she said, "I'm going to run a standard assessment. Just answer the best you can."

The test was embarrassingly simple, like naming ordinary objects and identifying basic patterns. I grew increasingly frustrated. *What am I, a six-year-old?* The entire session felt like a complete waste of my time.

Before my stroke, my cognitive abilities had defined me. As a child, national tests identified me with a high IQ, in the 95th percentile. In my eighth-grade yearbook, my picture was captioned, "The computer of the class, the bright student, where you'll easily find the answer to every question..." Throughout my professional life, I prided myself on continuous learning and intellectual challenges and surrounded myself with people who were smarter than me.

My work relied heavily on both emotional and intellectual intelligence. As a manager, I influenced peers, led teams, and worked with partners and customers in a rapidly evolving field that required constant adaptation and learning. I relied on communication skills, analytical thinking, and quick problem-solving. My brain was my superpower.

Now I faced a terrifying question: *What if I never returned to my former mental capacity? Who was I if not the quick-thinking, articulate problem-solver I'd always been?* I could imagine adapting to physical limitations, but losing my mental edge threatened the core of who I believed myself to be.

> *Who was I if not the quick-thinking, articulate problem-solver I'd always been?*

In the next day's session, we finished the evaluation tests and discussed my goals, but I left feeling just as frustrated. That night, looking at my upcoming schedule with yet another hour of speech therapy, I sighed deeply, dreading another round of first-grade questions.

Then a sobering thought hit me: *Oh my God, if these are the questions they ask stroke patients, then...*

Suddenly, my dread was overpowered by a wave of gratitude. I was lucky, incredibly lucky, to find those questions to be insultingly basic. There are people whose strokes leave them unable to answer at all. That could have been me.

I realized I needed to apply the same approach to cognitive recovery that had been working for my physical rehabilitation. I needed to give myself grace, take incremental steps, and celebrate small victories.

One particularly memorable speech therapy session occurred when the therapist asked if I could recite the alphabet. I smiled, thinking this was becoming yet another waste of time. When I reached Z, she said, "Great, but you forgot a letter."

"I did?" I asked incredulously.

"Yes," she confirmed, "let's do it again and count."

I repeated the exercise, and she was right, one letter was missing. She placed a keyboard before me and asked me to type the letters from A to Z. I did, and *still* one letter was missing. I examined the keyboard row by row, trying to identify the missing letter. It was Y. From then on, we joked that "Nir forgets Y."

These little "glitches" or "oopsies," as I called them, continually reminded me that I hadn't fully recovered. I'd find myself in the middle of a sentence, suddenly blanking on a common word or losing direction frequently, which pre-stroke rarely happened. Once, I went looking for my toothbrush while holding it in my hand the entire time. Humor became a crucial coping mechanism in these moments. If I couldn't fix these glitches immediately, I could at least find the comedy in them.

In another one of my speech therapy sessions, the therapist suggested telling a simple story I knew by heart. "A Tale of Five Balloons" came to mind, a children's book in Hebrew that my mother had read to me countless times and that I had later read to my own daughter when she was small.

In the story, when a balloon hits a rose and pops, the other children comfort the sad child by saying, "Don't cry; that is the end of every balloon." My daughter had loved that section, her tiny hands clapping in perfect rhythm with mine as we recited the lines together. Telling it properly involved making hand gestures and clapping at specific moments.

I closed my eyes as I recounted the story, and I found myself transported back in time. I was no longer in a sterile therapy room but lying beside my young daughter on her toddler bed in our old house. The memory was startlingly vivid: The warm, clean scent of shampoo in her damp hair after her evening bath combined with fabric softener we used on her blankets. The collection of stuffed animals clustered in her room. The way she always insisted I stay beside her until she fell asleep, one small hand holding onto my shirt as if to make sure I wouldn't leave too soon.

Without warning, tears filled my eyes and spilled down my cheeks. I couldn't continue the story. My voice simply stopped working, replaced by a tightness in my throat that wouldn't let words through. The therapist waited patiently, and I believe she offered a tissue. I barely noticed her presence. All I could think about was my daughter.

My little girl had grown into a beautiful teenager, and she had been the one to find me collapsed on the floor, unable to move or call out with more than sounds. Her invincible, all-knowing father, the one who could fix anything, had been lying helpless, taken in an ambulance, and left in a hospital where she herself had been so many times before. *How had it affected her? Had it shattered some fundamental sense of safety in her world?*

She had gone to stay with my brother-in-law in upstate New York while I recovered. She sent me text messages and occasional short videos of art projects, dogs, and her new cooking experiments. But our phone conversations remained brief and somewhat superficial. The emotional landscape between us was too raw, too complicated to navigate while I was still struggling to find my way back to myself.

When I finally composed myself enough to speak, I apologized to the therapist for the emotional outburst.

"Don't apologize," she said quietly. "This is part of recovery too, perhaps the most important part."

She was right. I needed to feel those feelings. To let them surface without hiding or "overcoming" them. I didn't need to "be strong." I just needed to *be.* Cognitive rehabilitation was about reconnecting with who I was, as a father, as a husband, as the

> "This is part of recovery too, perhaps the most important part."

person I had been before the stroke and the person I was becoming after it.

As I continued to build my recovery framework, I realized that this Mind Pillar demanded as much attention as the Body Pillar, though in different ways. Physical progress was visible and measurable, I could see my arm lifting higher or count more steps walked. But cognitive improvement worked almost in reverse. It revealed itself when things went wrong. To track progress, I needed to assess how frequently I forgot words mid-sentence, got lost in familiar places, or found myself holding my toothbrush while still looking for it. The less these things happened, the better I was doing.

Technology became my ally. I researched cognitive rehabilitation apps and subscribed to the paid versions of several top-rated ones. While word puzzles came highly recommended, my dyslexia (which affects both English and Hebrew equally) ruled them out. Instead, I found games that challenged memory, attention, and processing speed.

I committed to complete at least one session daily with each app, though I typically did more. I have no shame admitting that the toilet became my cognitive training center. Instead of mindlessly scrolling through social media during those private moments, I exercised my brain. My wife sometimes wondered why I was spending so long in the bathroom. "Brain training!" I'd call out, which usually ended the questioning.

Unfortunately, unlike counting steps, there was no app or tool to measure the frequency or severity of these mental hiccups. I had to rely on my own internal sense of how I was doing: *Was I having fewer "Y" moments this week? Could I follow conversations more easily? Did I find myself saying "what was I talking about?" less often?*

This internal barometer became my primary measurement tool, and despite its lack of scientific precision, it served me well. After all, the whole point of cognitive recovery was to restore my ability to think clearly and trust my own mind. What better test than to accurately assess my own progress?

Beyond the Physical

Our community Rabbi visited me every Friday afternoon. I was never a religious man; I found it hard to believe or connect with the stories and related even less to the do-and-don't-do chores. Still, I respected the tradition and saw it as an important aspect of growing up, my identity, and the notion of belonging. I wanted that for my daughter, but I rarely visited the synagogue. We would go together, despite her resistance, for maybe an hour on the holiday. I don't know how the Rabbi found out about my condition, and I did not ask.

The first visit was right after I moved to the ICU. Niv and my wife were in the room discussing something about insurance and work. Unable to follow the conversation, I was zoning out when the nurse said that we had a visitor who identified as our Rabbi and asked if it was okay for her to let him in. Niv and I looked at each other with cynicism as my wife replied.

I recognized him from his walk. He walked like a Rabbi. He looked like a Rabbi. Wearing black pants and jacket over a crisp white shirt, a long curly beard, and big glasses with smiling eyes behind them, he could not be mistaken for anything else.

He always carried two bags. One was a paper bag with two candles, a challah bread, and few candies. The other was a Tefillin bag. Tefillin are two leather boxes that Jewish men are supposed to put on their arm and head when they pray every day. The last time I did that was for my Bar Mitzvah when I turned thirteen.

He asked how I was doing. I answered with just a few words and my wife elaborated. He said that he and the whole community were praying for my recovery. That tomorrow and every time they read the Parsha, they would say a special prayer for me. He said that if there was anything we needed they were here for us. Then he asked if I wanted to put on Tefillin.

I showed him my left arm, where you are supposed to wrap the arm piece. It was occupied by too many tubes and had no space for Tefillin wraps. My right arm was…well, it wasn't cooperating. To both of our surprise, the Rabbi looked at Niv and said that he could put it on for both of us. Niv was also non-practicing and, as he confirmed, had also not used Tefillin since he was thirteen. But he offered his left arm and asked for a Kippa (head cover) without hesitation.

Niv held onto my bed with his right arm as the Rabbi wrapped the Tefillin on his left and then placed the head piece on his head. Then he repeated the prayer's words as the Rabbi said them one at a time. When he finished, the room was quiet. My wife had tears streaming down her face.

Without a hint of cynicism or sarcasm, I had genuinely hoped to feel something physically change. I was open to anything that might help my recovery. But I didn't feel anything. I also wanted to tell the Rabbi that when I was lying of the floor, seeing my curtain close as I was waiting for the ambulance to come, I was chanting the Shema. But words were still a struggle, so I let it be for now.

The next time he came, I was in the rehab unit, and there was no announcement from a nurse. Just a knock on the half open door on Friday afternoon and a familiar smile. Once again, he carried two bags and asked if I wanted to put on Tefillin now that my arm was free of tubes. "If you want, you can be next," he said to Niv.

The notes of humor in the room faded as I wrapped the Tefillin on my arm and over my head, placing the leather box in between my eyes. The Rabbi held a written prayer in front of me that I read aloud. When I finished, he quietly said, "Now might be a good time for your own personal prayer." Without thinking twice, I closed my eyes. In that brief moment of silence, I felt an unexpected sense of comfort, a gentle connection. Quietly, I said, "Thank you," as tears blurred my vision.

I smiled at Niv, who had an intense look on his face, and nodded my head.

He nodded back.

The Rabbi asked if he could sit with us for a little longer, and I said yes. I don't know why, but I wanted to tell him about the Shema. I described to him what had happened that morning, how I had felt the curtain closing with nowhere to turn for help, the realization that those were my final moments, and how I found myself chanting the Shema.

As I spoke, a memory came rushing back, clear, powerful, untouched by time. Not from the stroke, not even the past few years, but from a lifetime ago. I paused, then shared it quietly, as if I myself were hearing it for the first time. Like the Shema, it was a story I'd never told anyone before then.

"Twenty-five years ago," I began softly, "after my army service, I was backpacking in South America with no return date in mind. Just me, my girlfriend at the time, and a small group of friends from high school. After traveling through Ecuador and visiting the Galapagos Islands, we made our way to Peru. There, we headed for Machu Picchu, then joined a two-week expedition into the Amazon.

"There were seven of us, three girls and four boys. On our way back to 'civilization,' riding in a small minivan on a muddy dirt road, the sound of a loud gunshot sliced through the night. At the same time, three armed men wearing ski masks appeared in front of our vehicle. They put a gun to the driver's head and forced the vehicle to an isolated spot in the jungle."

I swallowed hard, choosing my words carefully.

"It was violent and terrifying. They forced us out of the vehicle, beating us and shouting constantly. With my broken Spanish, I couldn't understand much, just enough to know it was bad. In the chaos, they separated me from my girlfriend. When I tried to resist, one of them punched me, shoved me to the ground, pressed his boot against my back, and pushed the back of my head down into the mud with the barrel of his rifle. I understood him shouting in Spanish, 'I'm going to kill you.'"

For a moment, I went silent, reliving this memory that I'd pushed away all those years. The memory was so vivid I could still feel the cold metal edge of his AK-47 pressing against my skull.

"I stopped breathing. At that moment, with my face pressed into the mud, I felt total helplessness, complete surrender. I knew it was the end. I was only waiting to hear the gunshot, while knowing I wouldn't actually hear it when it came. And in that hopeless moment, instinctively, I started whispering the Shema."

Niv and the Rabbi listened silently, their eyes wide, faces soft and full of compassion. When I finished, there was a quietness in the room that felt sacred. I took a deep breath and sighed, releasing the tension I had carried in that memory for so long. I hadn't shared everything that had happened that night, but it felt like I'd said enough for now.

The Rabbi placed his hand on my shoulder and said quietly, "You have strong instincts. Perhaps your soul has always known where to turn when there's nowhere else to go."

Niv, still silent, nodded again, conveying in a look what words never could.

There, on that peaceful Friday afternoon, the third pillar of my recovery began to take shape, the spiritual healing that had to accompany the healing of my body and mind. It wasn't about Judaism or religion, even though it touched on the same profound questions and deep instincts that often lead people toward faith. Rather, my journey was one of surrender, connection, and trusting something greater than myself, even if I couldn't fully grasp it right now.

Three pillars. Three fronts in this battle. My military training kicked in; you can't effectively fight on multiple fronts without having a clear strategy for each.

As I drifted toward sleep, my mind categorized tomorrow's challenges like mission objectives: stand for two minutes (Body), remember the therapists' names without prompting (Mind), find one moment of genuine peace amid the chaos (Spirit).

Rehab would be humbling. I had to relearn the basics of being human. Things I'd mastered as a toddler would now require my full concentration and determination. The thought should have been depressing, but instead, I found myself almost looking forward to it.

After all, how many people get the chance to learn how to walk twice in one lifetime?

◆ ◆ ◆ ◆ ◆ ◆ ◆ ◆ ◆ ◆ ◆ ◆ ◆ ◆ ◆

REFLECTION SPACE

The deepest healing happens in places no one else can see.

Not all wounds leave visible scars. The ones you can't see often take the longest to heal.

This chapter surprised even me. I thought I was writing about what was not visible, about forgetting the letter Y, recognizing that my brain is in not okay, or breaking down while telling a children's story about balloons, but it became much more. Things I hadn't faced in decades, feelings I thought I'd outgrown, and fears I hadn't fully admitted emerged. Just like the memory I'd buried so deep I'd almost convinced myself it didn't matter anymore.

Crisis has a way of cracking us open, sometimes revealing the hairline fractures that have been there all along, waiting.

So, I want you to think about this:

What invisible wounds are you carrying? What's lurking beneath the surface that this current crisis might be bringing up?

Maybe it's old grief you never fully processed. Maybe it's trauma from years ago that you thought you'd "gotten over." Maybe it's the story you never told. Maybe it's the stuff you've buried so well that even you have forgotten it, or the fear you shrugged off. Can you sit with it for a moment? Let it breathe? Is there anyone you trust with it? If your answer is no, are you sure?

How has your identity been shaken? What part of your identity feels under attack right now? Your role in a relationship? Your looks, or your strength? The one who has it all together? The provider?

For me, losing my mental sharpness threatened who I thought I was at my core. It's terrifying when the thing that defines you suddenly feels uncertain.

What's your version of the Shema? Where do you go when there is nowhere else to go? What's that thing you whisper when nothing else works, when you know this might be it for you, the curtain is closing?

Maybe it's a prayer, a breath, a song, a line from a book, someone's face, hug, or voice. Whatever it is, hold onto it. You don't need to explain it. It's yours, and you are fortunate to know this about yourself.

Remember, sometimes the most important work happens in places nobody can see. The cognitive exercises nobody notices. The emotional breakthroughs that happen in private. The old wounds that finally come to light.

Your crisis might be revealing hidden damage that's been there all along. That's an opportunity to heal things you didn't even know needed healing. Seize it.

8

RELEARNING THE BASICS

The most humbling lesson of recovery is discovering how many miracles we take for granted every day.

URING the evening shift change, a new nurse I'd never seen before came to my room and introduced himself in that efficient yet friendly demeanor that good nurses master. After taking my vitals, blood pressure, temperature, and all the numbers that defined my medical existence, he studied something on his mobile terminal with a slight frown.

"We don't have a current weight for you," he said, pressing buttons on the outside of my hospital bed. "The last measurement is from over a week ago, when you were still in ICU."

I had no idea that my bed could weigh me. That external panel, with its mysterious display and additional options, belonged to their world, not mine.

The nurse looked at the display, then at me. "You're down about ten pounds from your pre-admission weight."

Ten pounds. In just two weeks. Before the stroke, I had desperately tried to *gain* five pounds. As a naturally skinny guy with a fast metabolism, every ounce of muscle mattered, both for vanity and, as I now understood, for recovery. But now? I was literally disappearing.

The nurse saw my concern and added, "Let me get a more accurate measurement after I finish my rounds. We'll reset the bed without you on it first."

The more precise measurement was even worse: eleven pounds gone. Eleven pounds of hard-earned muscle that I needed to help rebuild neural pathways and physically recover.

"I spent months trying to gain weight before this happened," I explained. "Three meals a day, snacks, protein shakes, everything."

He considered this, tapping his pen against the terminal. "We could arrange double portions for all your meals. Or maybe just double protein, if you prefer?"

"Double protein sounds good," I said, grateful for the suggestion.

"I'll ask the dietician to come see you tomorrow morning. She can set up a personalized meal plan."

The dietician arrived the next morning, a short woman with curly hair and a thick accent that I recognized immediately as Catalonian. I casually mentioned what I knew of Barcelona, and what should have been a brief nutrition consultation was derailed by an additional ten minutes of animated conversation about football and, specifically, Messi. I basked in the familiar subject, momentarily transported out of the sterile hospital environment and into the vibrant world of sports that I loved.

"So," she finally said, pulling a clipboard from her bag, "about your meals for tomorrow."

I must have looked confused because she laughed and asked, "What? You think we just bring whatever we want?"

"Is there...a menu?" I asked.

To my absolute shock, she pulled out a printed menu. An actual menu, with options, as if this were some bizarre medical-themed restaurant. I stared at it with the wonder of a child discovering a toy store.

"I can choose?" I asked, still incredulous.

"Of course! You get two snacks daily too."

My head nearly exploded at this revelation. *Hospital food with options* and *snacks?*

The initial excitement of choice wore off after about a week when I realized the menu was a simple rotation of the same limited options. Routine is essential for healing, but too much autopilot dulls the mind, another delicate balancing act I needed to master.

The body doesn't distinguish between rehabilitation exercises and marathon training, both demand energy, nutrition, and care. As movement returned and therapy intensified, my body was working harder, and I needed more fuel. This became a crucial insight about the body's role in healing: You need physical resources to rebuild what has been lost.

I took this job seriously. I ate everything that they placed before me (except those sickeningly sweet desserts), consumed every prescribed snack, and occasionally woke in the middle of the night to eat again. The nurses joked that I was eating for two, me and my recovery.

When I eventually regained those eleven points (and added five more), I developed what my wife affectionately called my "Buddha belly." And I couldn't have cared less. In the hierarchy of recovery concerns, vanity had fallen several notches. Each pound represented more of myself that I'd rebuilt. You can't heal the mind or spirit if the body is starving.

> Each pound represented more of myself that I'd rebuilt. You can't heal the mind or spirit if the body is starving.

Rethinking Simple Movements

Eating itself presented its own complex challenge. Once I got about 50 percent of my grip and wrist movements back, I could use my right hand to eat. At first, we added a rubber cone to the handles to improve my grip where the other 50 percent was lacking, but the main challenge was the process of movement. It was like driving an excavator, you know, the tractor with the arm on the back for digging, but with the need for much more finesse.

For example, I had to teach my brain how to eat the leaves of a salad. It sounds simple at first, but with the plate of green leaves in front of me, fork in hand, nothing happened. I simply stared at the situation, expecting the next steps to just happen automatically, like they had the countless times before. But my brain couldn't execute the sequence.

I tried and failed to follow my instincts. Somehow, I hadn't tilted the fork horizontally first to stab and grab.

Inspired by the excavator analogy in my mind, I broke down one movement at a time, one step after another. For the curious, it went something like this: First, grab the fork with your fist (the stronger grip at the time), then position it slightly below eye level, with 2/3 of it above the plate. Tilt it to approximately 80 degrees, then use your elbow to drive it to slowly but forcefully stab a few leaves. Rotate it back horizontally, guide it to your mouth. Take the bite. Pull it out. Repeat.

Brushing my teeth was an equally elaborate process, even though I used an electric toothbrush. The hospital staff had suggested brushing even more frequently than twice a day and using mouthwash too. They said it was to avoid bacteria that might cause further complications. They didn't have to tell me twice; I didn't have room for more complications.

At first, I simply used my left hand to brush. But as soon as I could hold the electric Sonicare that my wife brought from home, it became my favorite occupational therapy exercise. I planned to increase complexity from just holding it and moving my head, to trying different holding positions, to different hand motions, all the way to complex position changes and finger movement acrobatics.

Having almost five decades of tooth-brushing experience helped, but I discovered through trial and error, mostly error, that it wasn't just movement, strength, and coordination that had been affected by the stroke. For complex tasks involving several steps, I also had trouble remembering and sequencing those steps.

The simplest example was when, a few days after learning to brush my teeth acceptably with my right hand, I decided to complicate things by switching hands. *Why not?* My strategy was to push myself a little further each time, and the left hand was fully functional. It should have no trouble with the task.

I reached for the toothpaste with my right hand. At that angle, it wasn't easy but felt manageable. Holding it to open the lid created another dilemma for grip and hand positioning.

Following my "let's make things more complex" strategy, I transferred it to my left hand to unscrew the cap with my right, but then found myself simply staring at it, unable to process the next step.

Conceptually, I knew what to do. But to actually do it, I had to break it down just as much as the salad fork: *Hold the lid, turn it in the right direction, pull it up. Next, switch the toothpaste lid with the toothbrush. Squeeze the toothpaste while moving the brush slightly.*

Put the brush down, grab the lid, close the toothpaste, place it on its head, grab the toothbrush, continue brushing, all while keeping a casual expression like you know what you're doing. Like this never happened. Like you're not freaking out. Like you're okay.

But as I began to brush with my left hand, I realized I was still holding the toothpaste in my right, and I wasn't sure what to do with it. Any knowledge I had of potential options refused to connect to the part of my brain that could give the orders and orchestrate muscle coordination. Another mental manual formed for this process too: *I need to put the toothbrush down, and before that I need to close its lid. To do that, I need to hold the lid with my other hand, but the other hand is holding the toothbrush, so I need to put it down…I am not okay.*

Like a more detailed IKEA assembly manual in my mind, I gradually relearned what had once been automatic.

Building a Recovery Blueprint

One piece after another, I began to form a recovery blueprint, guiding my path back to the movements that had once been familiar. The simplest acts involved not just muscle, not just strength, not just sensation, but a tremendous amount of coordination and sequencing.

My mind craved structure, something concrete that would help me navigate this unfamiliar territory. Drawing on my analytical background, I began to break the recovery process into distinct steps, just as I had broken down each individual task. This became my personal recovery blueprint.

Step 1: Practice Visualization

"The mind must lead the body," my grandmother used to say. Only now did I truly understand her wisdom: My first breakthrough had been the realization that recovery began not in the muscles but in the mind. Whether during my dreams or through conscious effort while awake, the crucial first step was to mentally command a part to move. Sometimes I'd visualize tiny sparks forming new connections in my brain, imagining the healing energy flowing to damaged pathways.

What surprised me was how exhausting this mental exercise proved to be. As strange as it sounds, just sending brain commands was more tiring than any actual movement would have been when I was healthy. After fifteen minutes of focused visualization, I'd be drenched in sweat, as if I'd run for miles.

Step 2: Look for Signs of Life

Eventually, mental calls would produce actual results, though they were barely visible at first. My arm began by flexing; my leg, by extending, but these movements started as simply as tendons stretching without actual motion.

The first time I saw my right index finger move slightly in response to my command, the movement was so minimal that Niv had to lean close to confirm he could see it too. But that tiny flicker represented proof that the connection wasn't completely severed. I celebrated these microscopic victories as though I'd summited Everest. Each was evidence that my brain was forming new pathways, working around the damaged areas to regain its abilities. Recovery was possible.

Step 3: Build Strength

After basic movement returned, my focus shifted toward increasing my range of motion and strengthening the muscles. This was the simplest step conceptually, but it required relentless consistency.

Whenever an exercise became easy, I'd add resistance, carefully, making sure I wasn't overdoing it. I discovered that diversification was crucial. Finding new ways to train the same muscles kept my brain engaged and building new pathways. I also learned to take frequent breaks and alternate between muscle groups to prevent exhaustion. Week by week, I tracked these improvements meticulously, photographing how high I could raise my arm or measuring how many seconds I could hold a position. I could literally see my arm lifting higher, my grip getting stronger. This step created the most visible progress, which helped me to maintain motivation.

Step 4: Practice Tasks

This final step, which I correctly anticipated would be the longest and most complex, involved applying my recovered movements to actual functional tasks. Brushing teeth, eating with utensils, getting dressed, these required sophisticated coordination across multiple muscle groups. My lagging cognitive recovery added to the challenge, as I often struggled to remember and sequence these steps correctly.

THE RECOVERY BLUEPRINT

Step 1: Practice Visualization—The mind must lead the body

Step 2: Look for Signs of Life—Celebrate microscopic victories

Step 3: Build Strength—Relentless consistency, incremental resistance

Step 4: Practice Tasks—Apply movements to functional activities

Nothing was effortless anymore. Each task required planning, attention, and deliberate execution. But there was an unexpected gift in this arduousness: each remastered task brought a sense of wonder at the intricate machinery of the human body and a renewed appreciation for the astonishing capabilities we typically take for granted. The intricate symphony of muscle contractions and neural signals that comprise even the most basic human movements had always happened beneath my conscious awareness. Now, forced to reconstruct these processes deliberately, I gained profound appreciation for their miraculous complexity.

One evening, while struggling to find words during a phone call with my sister, I realized that my cognitive challenges followed remarkably similar patterns to this physical recovery process. The blueprint I'd created for physical healing applied almost perfectly to my mental rehabilitation as well.

Just as I had visualized finger movements before they happened, I found myself mentally rehearsing sentences before speaking them aloud. Memory issues, both retrieving words and retaining new information, required the repetition and gradually increasing complexity of the strengthening phase. And the most sophisticated cognitive functions like problem-solving, multitasking, and planning became the equivalent of task practice, requiring multiple mental skills to work in harmony.

This revelation was strangely comforting. The same principles that were guiding my body's return could guide my mind's recovery too. I didn't need two separate approaches; I needed one integrated framework that honored the profound connection between body and mind. They weren't separate territories, but a single, interconnected system. What healed one would help heal the other.

> They weren't separate territories, but a single, interconnected system. What healed one would help heal the other.

Marking Incremental Progress

At work, we often repeat a famous quote: "If you can't measure it, you can't improve it." So, before I had even left the ICU, I devised a rough system for gauging my recovery that told me my arm was at approximately 45 percent of its full capacity, while my leg lagged behind at perhaps 10 percent. These percentages weren't scientific measurements by any means, but they helped me track proportional progress in a realistic way.

One percent improvement became my daily goal, but some days brought breakthroughs, a new movement, a task accomplished, while other days seemed to yield nothing visible at all. But I reminded myself that neural connections were forming beneath the surface of awareness, and healing continued even when progress wasn't apparent. There would be days when progress stalled or even seemed to reverse. Instead of forcing solutions, I learned the hard way that

I needed to accept those setbacks as part of the process. No need to fall into despair, simply let go for now, rest, shift my focus, and try something different tomorrow. Easier said than done, I hate to admit.

As time went on, I tried tracking my progress in every way I could think of. I took pictures with my phone of the daily therapy schedule, recorded a daily journal (which I called my "Captain's Log"), and used my smart watch to log all my exercises. I had no real intention of ever going back through this data, but I liked knowing it was there if I needed it. The act of tracking gave me a sense of moving forward rather than standing still. Documenting each small step forced me to acknowledge that movement was happening, even when it felt imperceptible.

This tracking also provided much-needed perspective during low moments. During one particularly dark day, about three months into my recovery, it felt like my body was betraying me by not making any progress for what seemed like weeks. I was convinced that I had permanently plateaued. In the midst of this pity party, I happened to start scrolling through old photos and journal entries in my smartphone. What I saw shocked me: just two weeks earlier, I hadn't been able to perform several movements that had now become routine. The evidence of progress was right there, in my own documentation.

> What my emotions told me and what the evidence showed were completely different.

What my emotions told me and what the evidence showed were completely different. From then on, whenever I felt stuck, I made a point of reviewing my records. The data rarely failed to prove my discouragement wrong. The human body doesn't heal in straight lines. It pulses forward, rests, consolidates, then advances again. Accepting this rhythm became as important as pushing for progress. By breaking the overwhelming journey of recovery into distinct, manageable steps, I had transformed an impossible mountain into a series of achievable hills.

I would test and refine this blueprint over time, discovering nuances and exceptions for my specific situation. But the core approach, practicing visualization, looking for signs of movement, building strength, and practicing tasks, provided the structure I needed to navigate the uncertain terrain of recovery.

Perhaps most importantly, it gave me agency in a situation that could easily have left me feeling powerless. I couldn't control what had happened to my brain, but I could control my approach to healing it. That alone made all the difference.

> I couldn't control what had happened to my brain

REFLECTION SPACE

"The mind must lead the body."
–My grandmother

Progress rarely announces itself with a drumroll. Most of the time, it's not even noticeable. This chapter reminded me how many miracles we take for granted every day. When everything breaks, we get a choice: stay frustrated at how hard the basics feel, or honor the miracle of getting to learn them again. I've done both. No judgment either way. Don't feel stupid if you have to think through what used to be automatic. Start where you are.

What are the "basics" you need to relearn?

Sleeping alone? Getting out of bed? Making conversation? Managing money by yourself? Trusting your judgment? Looking in the mirror without shame?

How are you tracking your progress?

If you're not, you should, because feelings lie about progress. Think about what your "Captain's Log" would look like. Write it down, take a picture, record a voice memo, use your phone, or keep an old school journal. Document something, even if it seems pointless. Maybe you'll count the steps you took or the days you didn't cry. Not because you need the proof now, but because one day, when you feel like nothing's changing, you'll look back and realize you're 1 percent better. Those microscopic victories that felt like nothing? They add up. And your brain needs proof that the progress exists, even when it's invisible to you right now.

Don't forget to note where you need to slow down, breathe, and let today's step be enough.

Finally, what's your blueprint?

I had to invent mine one fork-stab at a time. You don't need to reinvent that wheel, so start here:

- *Imagine.* Picture, visualize, see what's possible in your mind.
- *Take a Small Step.* Take even the tiniest action, looking for a sign of life.
- *Strengthen.* Repeat it, gain confidence, build strength.
- *Practice.* Apply it in real life, even if it's clumsy, even if you mess up.

If you're rebuilding after something other than an injury, a breakup, a job loss, depression, grief, the blueprint still applies. Your "practice" might be sending one email, calling one friend, cooking one meal.

Whatever your recovery looks like, the principle holds: break the mountain into hills.

And if today sucked and nothing worked at all? That's okay.

There is *always* tomorrow.

9

—

LEARNING IN MOTION

Freedom takes different forms.

THIS wasn't my first experience with a wheelchair. Two decades earlier, after breaking my left leg, I'd become an expert driver. This time, with only one functioning hand, maneuvering proved more challenging.

For short distances, I used my left leg to push the chair forward while adjusting and turning with my left hand. For longer journeys, I preferred having someone push me. I also needed help getting in and out of it, but once settled, the wheelchair gave me a profound sense of freedom. The bed became a place of rest, as it should be, rather than it being my entire world.

The first time I truly got to explore, Niv pushed me to the nurses station and asked if I could venture outside the rehabilitation unit. "As long as you stay in the hospital, it's fine. Just don't get lost."

Don't get lost? Why would we get lost?

"Push the button," Niv had said, positioning me near the elevator call buttons.

I looked at him, then at the button, and tried hard to straighten my arm to reach it. I was touching it, but the light didn't turn on. I sighed and pushed harder, *success!* The button illuminated, and moments later, the doors opened.

He wheeled me close to the interior buttons, and I reached out, trying to stretch my arm far enough. When I asked him to push me closer, he gave me a disappointed look. "Don't give up," he said. "Make everything part of your training."

He started to deliver one of his motivational speeches, the kind he excelled at, and that I'd sometimes invite him to give at my team meetings when morale needed boosting. I stopped him, finally reaching the button as I assured him that I was fully committed. I would push myself as hard as anyone could expect, and probably harder.

"Okay, no more motivational speeches," he agreed. "Now push one of the buttons from here," he said, rolling the wheelchair away from the panel so I had to reach farther.

We had no particular destination. I just wanted some movement and change. We found the cafeteria, which was supposedly hidden in a remote part of the hospital. Getting there was no problem; finding our way back was another story. At one point, I was certain we were going in circles. We asked for directions, but only the second person we approached knew how to get back to the unit, and only then because he'd just returned from there himself. On future excursions, we turned getting lost and finding our way back into a game.

Throughout the adventure, we spoke in our secret language (Hebrew) so no one could understand us. This opened the door for us to cover everything from joking around to discussing people we knew in common to Niv's upcoming plans. We criticized how disorganized the hospital layout was and complained about the food. We dove into discussions about work and technology and talked at length about what was happening in Israel at the time. We consciously tried to avoid conversations about my situation, what caused the stroke, or my uncertain future.

Later that night, alone in my new room, the reality I hadn't wanted to talk about hit me: *I'd had a stroke.*

This feeling of anxious overwhelm happened a few times throughout my recovery, and sometimes still does. The image of my brain scan with that large dark oval area visualizing my damaged brain would come to mind and I'd wonder if that would become my new permanent state.

My analytical, logical mind told me this reaction was normal. I should have expected such episodes and understood they were part of the process. I reminded myself that it would be delusional not to fear the future, that it's okay to mourn what I'd lost and occasionally feel sorry for myself, at least privately. I told myself it wasn't just acceptable but necessary to experience these feelings rather than remaining detached from reality. Despite all my progress, this was just the beginning of a long journey.

Even though I knew all of that in my mind, the anxiety still took over. I closed my eyes and took a deep breath, inhaling as much as I could and then some more, holding it for a few seconds. I felt my fingers, my head, my whole body tingling, then slowly released the air with a loud sigh. I repeated this two or three times, feeling the calm return. My breathing normalized, my spinning thoughts settled, and the fear mixed with anxiety receded, not gone entirely, but quieter, allowing other thoughts to surface.

After that episode, I knew with certainty that I would recover to some degree. I'd heal enough to do everything I'd done before, perhaps with modifications. But even those could add character. From where I sat, walking with a cane seemed rather distinguished, even sexy. The path forward would be challenging, but I had a clearer sense of purpose, and a new environment that was optimized for my recovery.

Rule of Learning from Experts

The hardest lesson in recovery: being wrong about how right you think you are.

The most significant development in my mobility came during an early occupational therapy session with Meeka, when a man interrupted us to measure me for a leg brace. We had worked extensively on balance. Like most movements that we take for granted, balancing is complex, involving almost all muscles in the body. When I tried getting on my hands and knees to balance on all fours, this seemingly simple and stable position sent me crashing, laughing, face-down on the mat. I tried again, feeling my entire body engage, visibly shaking at points as I focused intensely on creating stability. Absolutely nothing could be taken for granted; everything had changed.

When the man came during our session to measure me for a brace, I asked if I could reschedule so I wouldn't lose the training time. He was willing, but Kat, my physical therapist, had accompanied him and wanted him to stay. As I had feared, most of the session was "lost" to measuring and discussing what type of brace I needed. A few days later, I returned to my room after a session to find a box lying on my bed, like a surprise birthday gift containing the breakthrough I'd been hoping for. That evening, my wife helped me put the brace on, then stood back to survey our work. "We need to get you wider shoes," she said, "but for now, your shiny blue Adidas will have to do."

When Kat arrived the next morning, I was waiting outside my room in my wheelchair, new brace in hand, right shoe off, and a huge smile on my face. As she approached, I waved my brace, explaining that I wanted her to see how I put it on so she could check if I was doing it correctly, to show her the way I tied my shoelaces with it, to ask about the strange new feeling that I wasn't sure was normal...

"No hello, no good morning? And where's my chocolate?" she asked with a smirk.

One of my wife's brilliant ideas was to get me a stash of top Belgian chocolate that I could give to folks. I offered fresh espresso and chocolate to anyone who came to my room, the therapists, the doctors, the nurses, even the cleaning crew. I hadn't forgotten. I held it up with the brace and handed both to her.

"Good morning. Here it is: Belgian chocolate and a brace for her majesty." We both laughed.

As she did every day, she asked if I wanted her to push me to the gym or if I preferred wheeling myself.

I wanted to get there quickly and had too many items to hold, my phone, glasses, the brace, and extra chocolates just in case, but mostly, I had no patience. As she wheeled me down the corridor, she explained that this was a carbon brace. It was light, small, and durable, with just enough flexibility for the motions I needed to protect me when standing and walking. I heard the word "walking" and nothing else.

My wife arrived for a visit just as we arrived in the gym. Then we put on the brace, and Kat asked me to stand. "Don't forget to make sure your chair is locked on both sides," she reminded me, and watched to be sure I placed my feet and used my body weight to maintain balance with both legs like she taught me.

Then she simply said, "Walk."

No walker, no cane.

"Walk toward the end of the room."

A much more serious expression overtook my smile as I concentrated on moving my leg and maintaining balance. Kat walked behind me as I took one small step after another, ready to assist with balance if needed. I reached the room's end feeling relief and pride, only to hear her say, "Now turn and walk back."

Wait, how do I turn?

I had to think about it. I took several small steps in place, turning slightly with each one until I made it all the way around. Then I started walking back. Just before we reached my wheelchair, the destination I had in mind, she said, "Keep walking toward the door."

With a deep breath of determination, I continued walking, now outside of the gym, heading toward the exit door to the parking area. It seemed so far away.

"Look up. Look forward. Don't look at your feet," she kept instructing me from nearby, watching to make sure I stayed safe.

I tried raising my eyes, squinting at the bright light streaming through the two large doors at the corridor's end. I attempted small talk, trying to joke as I always did, but there was too much happening. Walking required my full attention and awareness, especially while listening to her corrections and implementing them.

"Don't swing your hips; use your leg," she said.

"Try to land your heel right in front of you, not too far."

RULE OF LEARNING FROM EXPERTS

Despite having a strong sense of my body, I didn't know what I didn't know. Knowledge is power, enabling real-time awareness and adjustments. Leverage expert knowledge whenever possible.

We were still far from the exit door when I began to tire and we had to turn back. I started making mistakes and nearly fell, so we slowed the pace even more on our return. By the time we reached my wheelchair, I needed my remaining energy reserves to concentrate on a task I had already mastered: sitting down. Once I was finally in the chair, a loud, exhausted sigh escaped my lungs, followed by tired laughter as I released all the tension and focus that had kept me upright for that momentous achievement.

Later, I discovered my wife had walked behind us, recording the entire sequence. A few months later, when I watched the video, I realized the physical reality looked far less dramatic than the emotional experience that I had felt. But it didn't diminish the achievement. *I had walked.* For the very first time. Suddenly, everything seemed possible.

The wheelchair had given me horizontal freedom, the ability to explore, to change my environment, to feel less confined. The brace had given me vertical freedom, the ability to stand, to walk short distances, to reclaim my place in the upright world. I hoped I wouldn't need them forever, but for now, they were liberating rather than limiting. They allowed me to focus on recovery without being completely constrained by my current limitations. Later that day, Meeka pushed me to the gym for my occupational therapy session as I told her about my successful walking session with pride and excitement in my voice. We arrived at one of the large beds in the gym, where she stopped and asked if I needed help getting onto it. But my ego took over. I wanted to show her that I had recently mastered the ability to transfer in and out of my wheelchair.

I narrated the steps aloud, mostly for myself: Park the chair at an angle to the bed, ensuring I wore shoes with tied laces or non-slip socks before moving. Lock both wheels using both hands, including my challenging right hand. Confirm the bed's stability. Remove the footrests, positioning my feet on the ground at the correct angle and distance. Grab the chair's handle with one hand and, if possible, the bed with the other. Bend forward while simultaneously raising my hips so my weight assisted the transfer. Turn. And slowly lower myself. *Done!*

I sat upright on the bed's edge, receiving the compliment I hoped she'd offer.

In occupational therapy, we primarily focused on my upper body, hands, arms, and more delicate functions, increasing in complexity as I progressed. I shared my recent achievements, demonstrating my latest accomplishment of raising my arm straight and nearly performing the "seatbelt on, seatbelt off" movement. She asked me to demonstrate that movement, then placed one hand on my upper back and the other on my right shoulder and asked me to repeat the motion.

Then she positioned a mirror in front of me and requested that I raise both arms and note my shoulder heights. They weren't level. After a few of these attempts, with her hands on my back and shoulder, she explained that I wasn't using the same muscles and joints when lifting my right arm. Since this could create a bad habit and lead to pain later, I should stop raising my arm that way and focus instead on building up the correct technique.

If my expression reflected my internal state, it probably changed dramatically. She had burst my bubble, and for a moment, I felt like a child watching his ice cream fall from its cone or his balloon float away. But I also wanted to hug her. This was *exactly* why I was here in rehabilitation. Despite having a strong sense of my body, I didn't know what I didn't know. This was her profession, and I wanted more of that knowledge.

I expressed my appreciation for this feedback and asked her to continue to educate me. Knowledge is power, enabling real-time awareness and adjustments. I added this as a rule within my recovery strategy and promised myself that I would leverage expert knowledge whenever possible.

❖ ❖ ❖ ❖ ❖ ❖ ❖ ❖ ❖ ❖ ❖ ❖ ❖ ❖ ❖

REFLECTION SPACE

"Every limitation is an invitation to discover a new form of strength."

Freedom comes in stages. Sometimes it rolls. Sometimes it limps. Sometimes it shows up in the form of a brace or a piece of advice you really didn't want to hear. Even so, progress isn't actually about regaining abilities, it's about how we relate to the support that makes those abilities possible.

So, I want to ask you:

Where can you reclaim some freedom (horizontal or vertical)?

What's your version of the wheelchair or the brace right now? What do you need to help you navigate day-to-day (horizontal), and what do you need to help you feel like yourself again (vertical)?

Maybe it's something you have resisted at first. It could be a person, a tool, a medicine, a new routine. Whatever it is, what if you saw it not as a sign of weakness, but as your current form of freedom?

Who are the experts around you?

Are you seeking them out? Do you admit to yourself that you need them? That you don't know everything, and especially that you don't know what you don't know? This is exactly where those experts come in. Nurses, therapists, experienced caregivers, that is what they do, helping people like us for years.

Your crisis might require tools you never thought you'd need. That's not defeat. Survivors adapt. And sometimes, the thing that feels like it's trapping you is actually what sets you free.

____

____

____

____

10

STRENGTH IN RESISTANCE

Life is resistance training. Might as well get good at it.

"Just do it," Kat said, with a wicked smile on her face. That morning, highly motivated and eager to start my next session after walking, I had been met with the familiar faces of Kat and Harrison, the physical therapy intern. They declined my offer of fresh espresso but accepted Belgian chocolates as they announced their excitement.

Today, they planned to elevate my heart rate above 120. "We're going to make you sweat," Kat clarified with an evil laugh. She and I had developed our own, somewhat dark sense of humor. I would often say, "Is that all you can do?" or "That was easy," and she would respond with villainous laughter while tapping her fingers or mimicking Dr. Evil's pinky move from Austin Powers, wondering how she might torture me next.

Harrison connected me to a harness that would attach to a metal rail that ran along the gym ceiling. "You're going to walk on the treadmill," Kat assured me.

"The harness is just in case you fall."

I promised myself I wouldn't fall. The harness was reminiscent of the parachute harness that I had worn thirty years earlier in the IDF. It wasn't uncomfortable, but there were two straps running on both sides of the crotch. If not properly adjusted, when the parachute opened and pulled you upward, those straps were yanked all the way up, producing a high-pitched squeak accompanied by serious eye-rolling pain.

Before I stood and walked to the treadmill, they positioned it beneath the rails and attached the harness. Then they measured my blood pressure. I claimed I was in such great shape that we'd be there all day before my heart rate reached 120, teasing them that my Fitbit watch could track my heart rate just as well in real-time. (Later, we discovered it was actually quite accurate.)

As soon as it was time to set to work, however, I put on my serious face. I stood, climbed slowly onto the treadmill, and began walking. Unlike walking in corridors, where I could adjust my rhythm or stop, the treadmill dictated the pace. It wasn't under my control. I tried not to hold the side rails, focusing on each movement and step.

Kat guided my attention to specific aspects of my movement, as though I was learning to walk again. Since I could only slightly move my hip joint, I had to concentrate on using those muscles to move my leg straight forward rather than swinging my hip and throwing my leg like I'd done the day before. Sometimes, my foot landed on the treadmill's edge with a telltale noise, another detail requiring attention. I looked down at my feet to better aim their placement, wanting them to be aligned with my body. But looking down caused my entire body to tilt sideways, and Kat kept reminding me to look toward the room's far end.

After a few minutes, we stopped to make our first adjustments. I explained the difficulty of looking up while ensuring proper foot placement and suggested we face the large mirror so I could look forward while seeing myself walking.

While Harrison positioned the mirror about ten feet in front of the treadmill, Kat offered additional guidance: shift my weight from one leg to the other, avoid hip rotation, and try to land heel-first.

Now able to watch my whole body in the mirror, I realized I could anticipate when my foot would land too far right and make that noise on the treadmill. Kat's constant feedback helped me adjust, try new approaches, and determine what worked to prevent that misstep. I focused on shifting weight side to side, deliberately exaggerating the movement like a runway model, swinging my hips side to side. This got the best reaction, so I exaggerated further, adding hand gestures and a pout that would make Zoolander proud. "Blue Steel!" I announced, though I was the only one who got the reference. Apparently, my future as a male model was as damaged as my neural pathways.

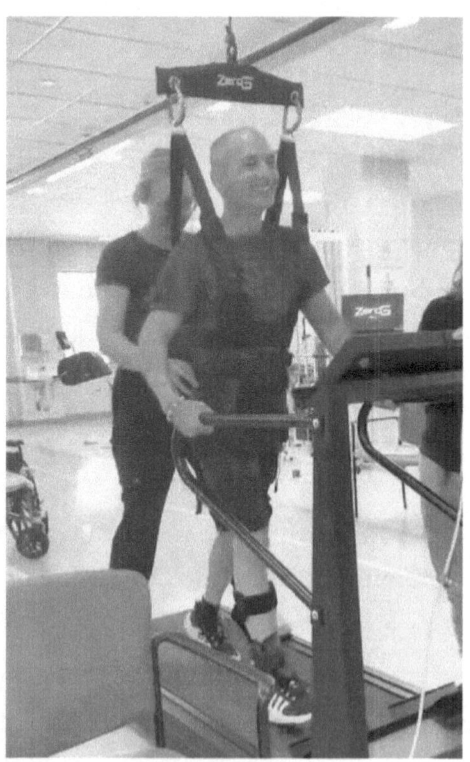

Eventually, I found my rhythm and began making fewer mistakes. And with the noisy treadmill set in the room's center, I noticed I was once again the center of attention. Compliments from nearby trainers boosted my confidence and lifted my spirit. I walked for five-minute intervals, which felt much longer in the moment, then we discussed improvements while they measured my heart rate and blood pressure. The hour passed quickly, and we agreed to continue the next day.

I didn't realize how exhausted I was until I got back to my room. It was still morning, but I asked Kat to help me transfer from the chair to the bed so I could rest. She believed I was ready to do it myself and asked me to demonstrate each step. When I did it all without problems, she walked over to the whiteboard and wrote that I was approved to get in and out of bed without supervision!

I was no longer pinned to a bed. One small step for me, one giant leap for my freedom and independence. This milestone embodied the very essence of my recovery goal, regaining control over my basic movements, reclaiming agency in my most personal space. The day kept getting better, and it wasn't even lunchtime yet.

The next day, I joked that Kat had failed to raise my heart rate or make me sweat. She responded with that evil laugh again, saying, "Wait until you see what I've got waiting for you."

"Give me all you've got," I said, immediately bracing for what that might mean.

As I started to walk on the treadmill, this time without so many movement corrections, she explained the theory behind elevating the heart rate. She said they traditionally worked on individual movements with gradually increasing complexity, but new research showed that when the body operates at high intensity, getting the heart rate above 120, it learns faster. I trusted her, but I imagined my brain bleed as a recently healed fresh wound in my brain's center. I worried that even minor aggravation could trigger rebleeding and set everything back. *Wasn't that why they measured my blood pressure at every session?* The thought of another incident like the one I'd experienced roughly two weeks ago terrified me. It was my first such thought in a while, making everything seem fragile and delicate. Life can change in an instant, and I wasn't ready for any more changes just yet.

I asked whether intense exercise and elevated heart rate might increase blood pressure and if we should consult a doctor, specifically a neurologist, about this. As if she had overheard us, Dr. Matthews entered the gym and walked directly over to us. I asked my question again, and she helped me better understand my situation.

Yes, it was much as I had imagined, a recently healed blood vessel in my brain requiring time for further healing and avoiding high blood pressure. However, I typically had low to normal blood pressure. She agreed there was a chance pressure would increase, though not necessarily from physical activity alone, and we wouldn't push to extremes while continuing to monitor it.

She measured my blood pressure to confirm, which again registered on the low side. "You see," she said, "you have low blood pressure."

My instinctive response was to say, "Yes, even when surrounded by all these beautiful ladies and knowing they're going to torture me."

I caught myself just before completing the sentence. They rolled their eyes and sighed, as people do with old men. After she left, I asked Kat if my comment was inappropriate. She said, "Well, if it had been just us, it would have been fine."

Mental note: avoid inappropriate humor altogether. Yet another skill to relearn in my new reality. I felt comfortable at the gym and wanted to be myself there, so it was easy to say what I thought as I thought it, bad jokes included. But my brain's "filter" was working more slowly than my speech, a reversal of my pre-stroke abilities, where my mind could run multiple social calculations faster than my words came out.

I did sweat that day. They pushed me to breathe hard and maintain that intensity for several minutes at a time. I noticed my right leg beginning to pull upward more effectively and requested an increased incline while maintaining the same pace. That proved to be a mistake, but a useful one for my learning process. By the end, I looked like I'd been caught in a rainstorm, drenched in sweat and feeling approximately as graceful as a walrus on roller skates. But it was progress.

The treadmill sessions became a perfect embodiment of my recovery approach, strategic intensity followed by strategic rest. Learning when to push and when to hold back, holding a balance of exertion and caution, was just as important as building physical strength. This bolstered my emerging understanding that recovery wasn't a simple straight line but a careful dance between challenge and restraint.

> that recovery wasn't a simple straight line but a careful dance between challenge and restraint.

The Variety Rule

The next morning, the look on Kat's face was oddly joyful. She entered my room with a wicked smirk and announced, "We are going to do something new, just for you. Something we have never done here, and it's going to be so much fun." She ended the sentence with her signature laugh, pinky beside her mouth in perfect Dr. Evil fashion.

Two could play this game. "Bring it on," I teased her, with genuine excitement bubbling up. "We both know you don't have what it takes."

Even before the stroke, I loved to keep variety in my training regimen. This passion for novelty extended to every aspect of my life. There was a time when, if you'd asked about my favorite food, I would have answered, "Something I've never tried before." That was my motto throughout my younger years, and that same adventurous spirit would lead to my "Variety Rule" in recovery, constantly seeking new challenges to prevent boredom, plateaus, and routine.

THE VARIETY RULE

If any practice, training routine, or exercise gets too easy, or if I get bored, I need to change it. Similarly, when I'm excelling at something, I tend to like doing it and even get hooked (a nicer way of saying addicted) and too attached. That's exactly when I need to make a change. It can be a small change, as long as it's enough to take me out of my comfort zone and keep challenging me.

Exercising the Variety Rule taught me that growth happens at the edges of discomfort, and Kat was about to demonstrate that lesson in a brand new way. When we reached the gym, she brought out a rubber band, wrapped it around my waist, positioned herself behind me, and explained that before trying a mystery "never-done-before" exercise, we'd start with something simpler. She would pull backward while I walked forward, creating resistance that would elevate my heart rate faster and strengthen my walking.

"You ready?" she asked.

"Born ready," I replied, channeling my pre-stroke bravado.

We proceeded up and down the long corridor, me in front, Kat behind holding what resembled a harness, pulling backward while I pushed forward against the resistance. I tried to focus on my walking technique, but couldn't help noticing the amused looks from staff as we passed nursing stations. The few people fortunate enough to witness our unusual procession didn't bother hiding their smiles.

My heart rate quickly climbed to 120 beats per minute. Hers too, apparently. By the first round-trip, we were both breathing hard and sweating profusely. With each labored breath and bead of sweat, I felt more and more alive. I had graduated from passive patient to active participant in my recovery, challenging my limits rather than merely accepting them.

The next day, Kat maintained mysterious silence from the time we met in my room until we arrived at an unfamiliar station at the gym. She secured me to the contraption with a thick strap with Velcro on one end and what looked like a sack on the other. After she loaded weights into the sack, she stood back and gave me that smile I'd been waiting for.

"Now," she said, "you pull."

We were back in business.

This became my favorite exercise: walking up and down corridors dragging an increasingly heavy sack behind me, focusing on maintaining both pace and proper form. This dual challenge required complete concentration. I kept my eyes fixed about twenty feet ahead on the beige patterned tile floor, avoiding eye contact with the nurses peeking above their computer screens as we passed their stations. While focus kept me in form, their encouraging smiles and occasional cheers meant more than they could know. Each step represented another small victory in my quest for independence, and I was glad to have so many people celebrating the wins with me.

With every interval, I felt improvement, in foot placement, weight management, and consistency of stride length. Usually, we'd reach the corridor's end, measure my heart rate, and if it was elevated or I needed rest, we'd pause briefly before heading back. Through two wide doors, I could just glimpse large windows and a security guard. During one session, when my eyes adjusted to the brightness, I saw beyond them into a large room with a high ceiling. The walls were almost entirely windows, flooding the space with natural sunlight, a stark contrast to the artificial lighting I'd lived under for weeks. A seating area occupied the center, with a long staircase curving along the glass wall to a second floor, and I mentally bookmarked the location of two vending machines for future reference.

Automatic sliding glass doors opened to the parking lot.

That glimpse of sunlight, of space beyond my medical confines, represented the next frontier, the world waiting for me after I mastered these challenges. Like the weighted sack I pulled behind me, my stroke had created drag on my life's momentum. But with each difficult step forward, I proved that resistance didn't have to stop progress. It could actually strengthen it.

"One more round?" Kat asked, noticing my gaze lingering on those windows.

"Make it two," I replied. "And add another weight to the bag."

She laughed, adding the weight as requested. "You're really embracing this resistance training."

"Life is resistance training," I said, surprising myself with the philosophical turn. "Might as well get good at it."

Learning from My Nemesis

"Ready to try the stairs today?"

Those five words sent a chill down my spine. My first attempt on the small set of stairs in the gym had not gone well. Since then, getting to the stairs had become my obsession. I had progressed well when walking on flat surfaces with my brace. Stairs represented a different level of difficulty altogether. It was the ultimate symbol of independence and the most intimidating physical challenge I faced.

"It's me or them," I declared dramatically. "This town isn't big enough for the two of us."

Before long, Kat and I stood at the bottom of the seemingly endless staircase that I had seen during our walking exercises. It curved up along the glass wall, its end barely visible. The light streaming through the wall of windows made it appear almost heavenly, standing sentinel at the border of the outside world.

Looking up from the bottom of the mountain, I had to ground myself in the present moment. Taking a deep breath to focus on the challenge, I reminded myself to start with my right leg first. This went against my instinct, but it was necessary for the proper technique.

I harnessed all my concentration and willpower to kick my right foot up to the six-inch stair, declaring, "One small step for man" as I made contact. My toes hit the next step when I lifted my leg, but I rose to my tiptoes on my left foot to give me enough height to clear the edge. Then I shifted my weight to my right leg, bent slightly forward, similar to standing up from a chair, and pushed myself up to land on the first step. A partial success.

The left leg followed easily. Now I could use this position to build momentum and lift my right leg even higher, hopefully enough to avoid hitting the next step. Each step was its own project, requiring planning, focus, energy, concentration, and willpower. I literally took it one step at a time.

When I saw we were approaching the final step, I celebrated my victory, one step too early. I grabbed the side rail, desperately trying not to fall down the entire staircase, and my therapist stood two steps behind me and pushed me back up to stability. We both took a moment to catch our breath, processing the frightening moment that could have changed my life forever. One second of inattention was all it would take. I vowed never to repeat that mistake, reminding myself of the most important rule of them all: do NOT get injured.

After letting my heartbeat settle, I faced the next challenge: going down. This presented a completely different challenge from ascending. Accurately lowering and placing my right foot mid-step required precision that I didn't yet have. Usually, this movement happens instinctively, in a brief moment as you lower your entire body with the other leg. In reality, there's no margin for error. Miss the step, and you're going down.

It felt like a children's game we used to play at birthday parties, where a pencil is tied to a string around your waist and you dangle it into a bottle between your legs. After trying to dangle my leg to land on the lower stair, I eventually found a technique that worked: I kicked my foot beyond the stair's edge, then pulled it back until my heel hit the edge on its return. Then I placed it firmly on the step and shifted my weight accordingly. It was fast and accurate and (usually) worked.

I proudly explained my process as I took the next step, expecting my left leg to be cooperative enough that I could talk while moving. Only, my right knee locked straight, shifting my center of gravity too far forward.

"Shit, I'm falling!"

Everything seemed to happen in slow motion. I grabbed the rail with both hands as hard as possible while my body rotated and hit the stairs. I ended up partially seated sideways, with only my grip on the side rail preventing me from tumbling down completely.

In spite of the lesson I had just learned on the way up the stairs, I hadn't seen this danger coming. It was the easy step, not the one requiring focus. My mind replayed the moment over and over again. Besides remembering to bend my knee before taking the next step, what else could this "almost" teach me for next time? Perhaps that literally *everything* was different now, even the aspects I least expected?

Kat paused to process it with me. "It must have been surprising and scary," she said.

"Very scary," I agreed. "I don't know how I forgot to bend my knee as I was lowering."

She explained the way knees lock and how my body and brain were relearning walking and stair navigation. She advised keeping a slight bend in my knee to prevent it in the future, then said I needed to help my body relearn through repetition.

We managed to descend the rest of the staircase without further incidents. When we finally reached ground level, Kat noticed the enormous amount of tension I held and began massaging my tight neck and shoulders. "Let's call it a day," she said, and for the first time, I was grateful to end a session early.

Just before leaving the area on our way back to the gym, I stopped to look back at the long staircase. It appeared majestic with the light streaming through the windows behind it, almost challenging me to conquer it. The stairs represented my entire recovery journey. Sometimes progress came step by step. Sometimes I fell or nearly fell. But with each attempt, I learned something new about my changed body and mind. The stairs couldn't defeat me, because I wouldn't allow them to limit the life I was determined to reclaim.

The day before my discharge, I asked to try the stairs one last time. Approaching the now-familiar staircase, I felt a different energy. After weeks of practice, repetition, and small incremental improvements, something had changed in the way my body responded.

I took the first step up with confidence, then the second. We ascended all the way to the landing without incident. This time, I maintained constant awareness of my knee position, ensuring it stayed slightly bent. Step by step, we made our way down. When we reached the bottom, I felt a surge of triumph that far exceeded the modest nature of the achievement.

"You did it," Kat said simply.

"We did it," I corrected her.

It wasn't perfect. My technique still relied heavily on compensatory movements. I still needed the rail for support and my brace for securing my foot. I still moved slowly and deliberately where others moved fluidly and automatically. But I had faced my nemesis and had at least established some terms of coexistence.

This allowed me to approach stairs with respect rather than fear. They were no longer insurmountable, just part of the path. Each time I climbed them, I quietly celebrated a win over something that had once felt impossible.

Every recovery has its own Everest. For me, it was stairs. For someone else, it might be buttoning a shirt, holding a fork, or forming a full sentence. It doesn't matter what the mountain is, the lesson is the same: face it, practice, ask for help, and keep showing up. The obstacle that seems impossible today can become ordinary tomorrow.

Sometimes, the purpose of the obstacle isn't to be conquered at all. It's to change us in the trying.

REFLECTION SPACE

"Growth happens at the edges of discomfort, not at its center."

Often, we move fast not because we're ready, but because we're desperate to be done. But I've learned the hard way that healing has its own speed. If you rush it, it'll remind you who's in charge.

So, let me ask you:

What's your staircase?

What part of your life feels like that huge flight of stairs, overwhelming, impossible, something you might have tried once and it didn't go well? Don't avoid it forever. Don't force it too soon. But don't give up on it, either. One step, literally or not, is all it takes to start. You don't have to conquer it today. (Just between us, I didn't either. Not yet.)

Where do you need to pace yourself?

Maybe you're throwing yourself into recovery so hard you're risking burnout or injury. Maybe you're trying to feel better faster than your heart can keep up. I know that urge to "hurry up and be okay." I know it well. But the strongest move is knowing when to stop, breathe, and wait for your body or your life to catch up.

How are you using resistance?

The stuff that feels hard or slow? That's the workout. Every bit of drag is shaping you. Every frustrating step is building toward something. Maybe it's time to stop seeing "resistance" as a sign of failure and start seeing it as your training partner. (Yes, even people!) The very thing slowing you down might be the thing that's making you stronger.

What "fall" are you still replaying?

Did you mess up, as we all do? Did you say the wrong thing, or miss a step that cost you progress? Learn from it. Don't carry it. Every scar is proof you kept going.

Your Everest might not be stairs. It might be grief. Or rebuilding trust. Or getting back to work. Whatever your mountain is, you don't have to sprint to the top. Just take the next step. With attention. With curiosity. With breath.

Finally, remember the Variety Rule. Don't get too comfortable. If something gets easy or repetitive or if you master it, change it. Flip the order, try something new, do something to avoid going on "autopilot." Growth lives at the edge of discomfort, and you need willpower to stay on that edge.

The path forward curves, dips, and repeats itself. But if you're still walking, you're still winning. You've got this. Even if it doesn't look graceful quite yet.

11

DEEPER REVELATIONS

In darkness, there are always stars to be found,
if only we adjust our eyes to see them.

ENCOUNTERED other patients throughout my stay in rehab, sometimes in the gym, but mostly during meals. Most were in their seventies or eighties, with one exception who appeared to be around my age or younger. Needless to say, when a very young girl was rolled into the dining room by a nurse, she caught my attention.

The girl wore a brace around her chest and back, suggesting a spinal injury of some kind. Other than that, there was no visible indication of scarring or injury. Just a lovely young lady who couldn't have been more than twenty, surrounded by people decades her senior. *If I feel out of place here,* I wondered, *what must she feel?*

It was my first time seeing her, though her voice sounded familiar. I didn't have to strain to eavesdrop because the nurse loudly announced that today was the first time she would be eating in the dining room rather than in her room and confirming that her family wasn't present, she would be eating alone. The next morning, I spotted her in the courtyard after breakfast, just before it got too hot to be outside. This time, she was with someone her age, perhaps a friend or family member. Later, we crossed paths in the gym and exchanged a few words. Her voice continued to sound strangely familiar, though I couldn't place why.

One day, we spoke briefly at the entrance to the dining room. I asked the question that had been so heavy on my mind, what had brought her here? then immediately recognized it as inappropriate. I apologized and suggested she didn't need to answer such a personal question. She simply smiled and shared her story.

I won't share all the details here, but a full-sized grand piano had fallen on her while she was moving into or out of her university dormitory. One moment, she had been a college student enjoying the independence of living in a dorm, and the next, she was lying under a piano, her life forever altered. I didn't feel sorry for her, as so many tend to do when people are in rehab. I didn't view her situation as unfair or judge it as good or bad. Rather, I saw it as an extreme example of the sudden, unexpected changes that can affect not just us but everyone around us.

She remained remarkably calm as she spoke, her smile and bright eyes giving the impression that she was surrounded by a halo. Until just a few days earlier, she explained, she had been in excruciating pain. It had only recently subsided enough for her to leave her room.

Suddenly, I knew why her voice sounded familiar: I'd heard crying and screams of pain day and night, and it had come from her room, from her.

Later that day, I found myself complaining to my wife about what they called meatloaf, possibly the most trivial grievance in the history of rehabilitation. Mid-sentence, I started laughing at myself.

"What's so funny?" my wife asked.

"I just realized I'm complaining about the meatloaf texture while down the hall there's a girl who had a Steinway fall on her," I explained. "I've officially become the pettiest patient in the whole rehab facility."

Sometimes, humor is the quickest path to perspective.

About a week after our conversation, I grew frustrated yet again, this time while working with Meeka on a particularly frustrating fine motor exercise. The task was simple: pick up coins and put them in a pile. But my fingers wouldn't cooperate. I kept dropping the coins or hitting the pile with my wrist. Even worse, I had been successful at this exercise *just yesterday*. I felt my frustration building, to the point where I wanted to swipe everything off the table.

"I'm not making any progress," I said through gritted teeth.

Meeka looked at me with knowing eyes, familiar with the frustration I was feeling. "Actually, you've made remarkable progress. Remember where you started."

I took a deep breath and thought of the girl with the piano. *How would she approach this feeling?* Probably with that same calm smile, that same determination, that same acceptance of the process.

"You're right," I admitted. "Let's try again."

We continued the exercise, and while my performance didn't immediately improve, my attitude did. Viktor Frankl, who survived the Nazi concentration camps and later developed logotherapy, wrote that when we cannot change our situation, we are challenged to change ourselves. The girl with the piano embodied this wisdom. She couldn't change what had happened to her, but she maintained her dignity, her smile, and her engagement with life despite catastrophic circumstances. With her in mind, I adjusted my approach to attempt the task with more patience, more curiosity, and less attachment

> when we cannot change our situation, we are challenged to change ourselves.

to immediate results. Somehow, that shift made the work itself feel more meaningful.

The girl with the piano never knew the impact she had on me. And after that conversation, I never saw or heard from her again. Our paths crossed only briefly in that rehabilitation center, as two strangers navigating life-altering events. But her presence in my journey became a touchstone, reawakening something that had been dormant since long before my stroke. Whenever frustration mounted because I couldn't tie my shoes or my progress seemed too slow, I would remember her calm smile, the light in her eyes despite what she had endured. The enormity of her struggles didn't minimize my own. Rather, it reminded me of the extraordinary capacity for resilience that we all possess.

This encounter stripped away any remaining illusions of control that I'd been holding onto. Nothing remains the same, nothing is permanent, and nothing can fully be predicted or controlled. Her youth made this lesson all the more extreme. I realized I wasn't afraid of death; I was afraid of not truly living. And while we have little control over our health, age, or objective circumstances, our experience of life exists primarily in our minds and, therefore, within our control.

I realized I wasn't afraid of death; I was afraid of not truly living.

Once the immediate pain and shock subsides, our happiness or sadness, satisfaction or anxiety, depression or enthusiasm has little to do with external circumstances and everything to do with how we interpret them. Whether you perceive yourself to be the luckiest or unluckiest person alive is, largely, a choice. I began to see my stroke not just as a catastrophe that happened to me, but as an

Whether you perceive yourself to be the luckiest or unluckiest person alive is, largely, a choice.

experience happening for me, an opportunity to learn about resilience, presence, and what truly matters in life.

The girl with the piano had inadvertently reminded me of what my grandmother had tried to teach me long ago: in darkness, there are always stars to be found, if only we adjust our eyes to see them.

The Yellow Balloon

"The simplest objects often reveal our most complex challenges."

Gaining more motion and activating more muscles didn't make recovery easier over time. It simply became different. I discovered new challenges, new muscles to strengthen, more capabilities to relearn, and increasingly complex motor skills to master. The more progress I made, the further I realized I had to go.

At 50 to 60 percent of my arm movement, I truly believed I could accomplish anything I put my mind to. I could grab objects, hold onto rails for balance, brush my teeth, and eat properly, slowly and with minor adjustments, but I did them. I felt I was doing well. Then my occupational therapist introduced me to a sophisticated piece of equipment that challenged every last shred of this confidence: a yellow balloon.

It was just a normal-sized children's balloon, ordinary in every respect, except for the way it revealed my limitations.

Meeka had casually tossed the balloon in my direction. "Do you know the game? Don't let it touch the floor."

I rolled my eyes at what seemed like a childish activity as I reached out to hit the slow-moving, shining object upward with my right hand. To my surprise, but not Meeka's, I missed completely. Plus, the sudden movement when I reached with my left hand to save it had nearly caused me to fall on my face.

Challenge accepted.

Within a couple of attempts, I had isolated the problem. I had rough control of my arm and forearm, but I didn't have fine control over the direction and position of my hand and fingers.

After watching me struggle with the balloon for a while, Meeka changed the game. "We're going to practice throwing darts," she announced, handing me plastic darts with Velcro heads instead of sharp needles.

"I used to love playing darts and wasn't bad at it," I told her confidently. The target was about five or six feet away, close enough that I could reach out and place the darts directly on it if I wanted to.

You can imagine my shock, but again, not Meeka's, when I threw the first dart and missed completely.

I looked at her. She looked at me. Neither of us spoke. I took another dart and threw it. Missed again. With the third dart, I tried a slower, more deliberate movement, repeating the motion several times before releasing…and still missed.

Again, I could move my shoulder and elbow, but my wrist and fingers had a timing problem.

Eventually, after discussing several different techniques, I could hit the target about half the time. But I couldn't hide my disappointment and frustration. I had thought I was making excellent progress, approaching normal levels of functioning. I thought I was fine. Now I had to confront the reality that I wasn't. Not yet.

In the days that followed, I encountered even more humbling experiences. Trying to pick up a small object from a table. Attempting to write with a pen. Putting my socks on. Each revealed some aspect of fine motor control that still eluded me, some gap between intention and execution that needed to be bridged.

Meeka was an excellent guide through this process. She had a gift for finding activities that targeted precisely what I needed to work on while making the practice feel like play. We played a modified version of Cornhole, throwing ping pong balls into a bucket. She made me place cones in a straight line and then pick them up again, a task requiring precision and control. Soon, what began with a yellow balloon had expanded even beyond my physical therapy sessions. These skills were challenging my entire cognitive system.

Hitting the balloon required me to process spatial relationships, calculate trajectories, and make split-second adjustments based on visual feedback. I began to notice patterns in my mental functioning that mirrored my physical challenges with these tasks. Just as my fingers sometimes failed to follow my intentions precisely, my thoughts occasionally moved with a similar disconnect, words eluding me mid-sentence or my attention wandering unexpectedly. But the games that Meeka devised had created opportunities for complete presence. When my entire being focused on this simple interaction, I experienced flashes of clarity where all chatter ceased. Anxieties about recovery, the future, or independence all fell away, leaving only the present moment, the balloon suspended in air, and my immediate intention held to it.

While my Body Pillar had focused on visible physical rehabilitation, the Mind Pillar required equally deliberate strategies to rebuild the less apparent but just as crucial cognitive functions. Rather than becoming discouraged when these intangible challenges were made tangible, I tried to approach the tasks with curiosity: *What exactly was happening when I tried to hit the balloon or throw those darts? Which muscles were working, which weren't? What compensation strategies might help in the meantime? How could I practice specifically those finer movements that gave me trouble?* My rules for recovery served me well, too. I reminded myself to be aware of my limitations, take my time, and give myself space to heal. It was a marathon. I could celebrate my achievements, but the race wasn't over.

I knew the yellow balloon wouldn't be part of my daily therapy forever, but the awareness it had awakened could remain. This ordinary children's toy came to represent my complete framework for healing, with Body, Mind, and what I would come to realize was Spirit working as an integrated whole. As I prepared to leave the structured environment of rehabilitation to return to the messier, more complicated world of home, I held onto the truth that peace could be found anywhere, not despite the struggle, but within it.

The Grocery Store Expedition

The greatest tests of recovery can happen in the most ordinary places.

Kat wrote something new on my schedule, planned to occur just a few days before my final session in the center: "One hour Outing followed by 1.5 hours Cooking!" One of the therapists was going to take me to buy groceries, then I was to cook something for the team. I'd been looking forward to this from the moment I saw it.

Beyond offering a welcome change in routine, this activity integrated all of our training elements from start to finish, beginning with creating a grocery list. It took several attempts to write legibly with my right hand, but thanks to my fine motor skills advancements, I achieved some success. The unexpected challenge in that step was thinking about what ingredients I needed.

I'm a decent cook when it comes to simple dishes. My signature is Israeli shakshuka, essentially, spaghetti sauce with eggs cooked in it, served with good bread (preferably challah), dill pickles, and fresh Israeli salad. When I gave my list to the physical therapist who would drive me, he pointed out that I had described shakshuka as being like spaghetti, but I hadn't included tomatoes on my list.

How had I forgotten the most important ingredient? What else was missing? I walked through the cooking process aloud while he reviewed the list: "First, you fry the onion," I began. I had onions listed but not oil. He handed me the list, and I added olive oil.

I continued this way through all the ingredients, including the oil, the tomatoes, and then the lemon for the salad dressing.

I still felt I was forgetting something, so I visualized the store aisles and my usual route. It's a small store, and for the past four years, I'd shopped weekly along the same path, buying roughly the same items. At the end of the third aisle are the spices, *paprika*! I added paprika, and that seemed to complete the list.

The time had come for our trip to Trader Joe's. We walked down the familiar corridor to the entrance hall, this time making it through the two sliding doors that led to the parking lot. A dry wave of heat hit my face, carrying scents of hot asphalt and dusty vegetation. I took a moment for my eyes to adjust to the bright sun, remembering why I never used to leave home without my sunglasses.

After spending so much time within a world of brown and beige, the contrasts seemed stark. The van had two high steps with rails on both sides, which were hot to the touch. Inside the van, cool air poured from the air conditioner. And the smell of a hot summer day in suburban California mixed with the van's interior.

I gazed through the window from my seat behind the therapist, taking in the sights of cars, wide roads, scattered buildings, and dry yellow vegetation, but no pedestrians, I noticed. Then we circled out of the parking lot, suddenly activating my sense of direction. My heart rate increased as my brain processed this reconnection to the wider world.

After all those wheelchair trips we had taken trying to "get lost" in the hospital, I had given up on my instinct to always know where I was and where I was heading, realizing where I was, where I had been all of that time, was powerful. I knew that exact location, the building that I had driven by every time I went to the gym before the stroke. I'd known where we were all along, but only now did I truly recognize where my bubble, my capsule, my isolated little world actually existed.

The feeling was almost dizzying, like putting on glasses after weeks of blurred vision. Objects, colors, and letters seemed more vivid. Most powerfully, I was experiencing a collapse of the artificial boundary between "hospital world" and "real world."

Until that moment, my recovery had happened in some separate reality. Now, it hit me that I was healing within the same space where I'd lived my normal life. With a mixture of excitement and fear of returning to that life, everything became real.

After a few stop signs, we reached the traffic light at the main junction connecting the hospital with the primary road. On our left, just outside my window, was my gym. I'd gone at least four times each week for two full years, sometimes taking yoga or other classes, sometimes just working out. Over time, familiar faces and favorite trainers had created a sense of community and belonging. *Had anyone noticed my absence? Had I affected anyone's life?*

On Fridays, after yoga class, I used to drive directly from the gym to the same Trader Joe's we were going to, stopping at this same light and traveling in the same direction in which we were now headed. I usually spent those drives on the phone with Niv or my brother, or perhaps listening to a podcast. I considered myself a courteous and safe driver, but that weekly grocery trip had become so routine it was almost automatic. Now, something new was bubbling up inside me, a heightened awareness that changed my perspective. All my senses seemed to have activated simultaneously. I could almost taste the world around me.

The light turned green, and we continued through heavy traffic. I thought about all the people around us, each in their own air-conditioned world, heading somewhere or returning from somewhere as they lived their normal lives. It felt surreal, as if I were merely an observer of *living*. Like an audience member watching a show, I paid attention to everything on the other side of my window. I saw the same hotel building on the corner and the gas station across from it that I'd seen every week, but they all seemed different now.

Just before arriving at the store, we crossed over a busy highway that stretches all the way across the vast country, from San Francisco to the East Coast. It spans five lanes in each direction, all busy with traffic. So many people, each in their own bubble of existence, constantly moving, constantly changing, never standing still. So much life happening in every moment.

It was the first time in my life that I truly understood gratitude to its fullest meaning.

I didn't notice the tears until I was already crying. I cried because I was happy. Happy to be alive. Happy to be part of whatever was happening in the world. It all felt so *good*, the heat, the sweat, the smell of cars, the noise of eighteen-wheeler trucks, the sun shining overhead, the reflections from windows and windshields, the colors of signs… There was so much happening, and I felt profoundly grateful to be part of it, for however long I could be part of it.

When we reached the parking lot, Robert opened the door. *This is what I have been training for,* I thought. To get through this test, I had to apply everything I'd learned about walking, awareness of my surroundings, and cognitive functioning. I took a deep breath, held the rails, and descended the two high steps into the real world.

It was refreshing to be among "normal" people again. Not caregivers, family, friends, or other patients, just ordinary people shopping or working alongside me. I selected a cart, placed my cane in it, and began my usual Trader Joe's route, checking the destinations in each aisle against my list. I achieved 110 percent success, thanks to the ice cream I added as we passed the freezer. After all, what's a meal without dessert?

The cashier placed our items in two paper bags and returned them to the cart. Then I pushed it back to the van, removed the bags, and handed Robert my cane as I climbed the steps back into the van. He returned the cart, got into the driver's seat, and started the drive back. I stared out the window, my mind pleasantly distant as the air conditioner roared and the van made its way back to rehabilitation.

I needed help carrying the two bags and my cane down the steps of the van, but once on the asphalt, I insisted on carrying both bags myself. Back through the two sets of doors, that distinctive hospital scent and shocking drop in temperature made it clear I had returned to the bubble. The next set of wooden doors sealed off our access to natural light and confirmed our return to the brown, beige, sunless zone I'd called home.

Midway down the corridor and on the right, the gym's doors were wide open. I tried not to stare at the in-progress therapy sessions as I followed Robert to the trainers' room. Behind the doors that required a code to pass through, we entered a large area with a few dining tables, a stove, an oven, a refrigerator, and a cooking area.

Meeka arrived just in time for our penultimate session: Cooking under her supervision. She smiled when she saw my grocery bags, informing me that she hadn't brought lunch that day, "So no pressure, but it better be good."

I knew I needed to take small, incremental steps and plan them carefully in advance. But I soon discovered that skipping steps wasn't the only concern; getting stuck on a step, changing tasks, context switching, any form of multitasking, and even talking while working on something else could go extremely wrong, extremely quickly.

Carefully, I arranged everything on the counter in order of use: the vegetables split in two piles (one for the salad, one for cooking), spices, olive oil, bread, bowls, the skillet, and a large cutting knife. I admired the knife before I began. It was a good brand, similar to one I had at home, with the right handle and a blade suitable for cutting anything from meat to tomatoes. Meeka stayed close as I removed it from the drawer, washed it, and placed it on the counter. I think she was concerned. I certainly was.

I started off simply by preparing garlic, the main ingredient in any good Mediterranean meal, according to my mother. I used the large knife to give the cloves a gentle smash, then peeled them and piled them on the side of the cutting board. Once the aroma of fried garlic and onions spread beyond the trainers' room, more visitors made their way in, securing their places at the table.

Breaking eggs was an unexpected challenge. My usual technique was to clear a space with a spoon in the sauce and break the egg right into that spot. But when I grabbed the first egg with my right hand, it immediately felt wrong in my grip, too light, too fragile, like I was trying to hold a bubble without popping it. Breaking an egg perfectly requires surprising precision, hitting it at just the right speed, the perfect angle, stopping exactly after it cracks but before it smashes. It's like a tiny, everyday surgery that healthy people never think twice about. I knew I didn't have the dexterity to do it properly.

I heard my mother's voice in my head, still saving me from kitchen disasters decades after first teaching me how to cook: "Break it into a bowl first."

It's a good thing I did, because my first attempt was a disaster. After hitting the egg softly on the edge of the bowl twice without even cracking it, the third try should have been the charm. Instead, the egg exploded, with only half of it landing in the bowl. I stood there for a moment, egg dripping from my fingers, then couldn't help but laugh.

For the rest of the eggs, I developed a new post-stroke technique: crack it as good as I could, then perform an archaeological dig for shell fragments. In the weeks that followed, I became an expert shell-picker, fishing out tiny white shards from the yellow pools.

The were other lessons from this cooking experience were clear: Focus on one task at a time and never multitask, or don't try to heat bread while monitoring and stirring boiling tomatoes. (My first batch of bread burned.) Take your time and proceed in small steps, cut all vegetables before starting to fry them. (I nearly burned the onions because I hadn't finished chopping the garlic and tomatoes in time.) Be aware of your limitations, don't attempt fancy skillet-shaking with one hand or try new techniques that require you to use both hands. It only creates a mess in the best-case scenario.

In the end, while I won't detail every step of my famous shakshuka recipe, the outcome met expectations. The presentation was beautiful, if I do say so myself: a colorful Israeli salad dressed with lemon, salt, and olive oil, alongside heated sliced challah bread, and a large hot skillet of shakshuka at the table's center. It disappeared in no time, all except for the salad, typical of American dining habits.

When I first moved to the United States, I was shocked that what Americans call "salad" consists mostly of greens with thick dressing. In my culture, lots of colors with a lighter dressing indicates a better salad. I ate the rest myself, then taught Robert how to wipe the leftover sauce from the skillet with a piece of challah, an art he genuinely seemed to appreciate.

The grocery store expedition had enabled my first meaningful interaction with the outside world since the stroke, my first glimpse of ordinary life continuing beyond the medical bubble, and my first opportunity to test my recovering abilities in an everyday setting. In the midst of so many physical exercises, cognitive drills, and all the mechanics of recovery, I had almost forgotten that this was the fundamental purpose of it all, to return to life. To experience the world in all its messy, vibrant reality. To participate rather than observe from a distance.

This might be a hidden gift that sometimes comes with traumatic experiences, they can strip away the familiarity that dulls our senses to the wonder of everyday existence. When you've had everything suddenly taken away and then gradually returned, even the most commonplace experiences reveal their inherent marvel. The gratitude that overwhelmed me on the drive to the store had been visceral and immediate, triggered only by the simple fact of being alive.

My perception, my awareness, my appreciation for the seemingly ordinary had undergone a seismic shift. The tears that had come so unexpectedly were washing my eyes clear, helping me see what truly mattered on this journey.

REFLECTION SPACE

*"Sometimes, to truly understand our own journey,
we need a dramatic shift in perspective."*

"Look up. Look forward. Don't look at your feet."

My therapist kept saying this as I learned to walk again. But it became about so much more than walking technique.

When you're rebuilding your life, there's a natural tendency to stare down at the ground, at what's broken, what's missing, what you need to fix. But like driving on the 101 in my home state, you look to where you're heading, not at the car itself or your immediate surroundings.

Where are you looking right now?

Healing is as much about how you see things as it is about how you've fixed things. If you're fixated on what you've lost, I get it. The damage is real, and maybe permanent. But what happens when you lift your gaze just slightly? What possibilities exist that you can't see when you're staring at your feet? What would happen if, even for one moment, you looked up? Looked forward, beyond your feet?

I didn't start practicing gratitude because it's spiritual or trendy. It just hit me, slapped me in the face a few times and eventually shook me up. I realized I needed it like oxygen. Gratitude is where the source of resilience resides. It's the reason *why*. As Viktor Frankl wisely said, "If you give a man a 'Why' to live, he can endure almost any 'How.'" This became and still is my "Why." Those moments where I felt profound gratitude turned to how I looked up. It was how I found where my feet were going again.

Can you find something to be grateful for, even in this mess?

It doesn't matter if it's the little things or the big things. It could be anything. The color of the sky? A kind face? The smell of dinner? A song, a laugh, a small success? Could you let it in?

Here's a trick I learned: you *can* fake gratitude, and it still works! It might seem silly, but try it. You can't be grateful and resentful at the same time, even if the gratitude feels forced at first.

The day I left the hospital-bubble and saw traffic for the first time in weeks, I cried. Not from sadness, but from overwhelming gratitude for eighteen-wheelers and gas stations and people going about their ordinary lives. I was given a rare gift: the chance to see the miraculous in the mundane again. It's so easy to forget. Hold onto this knowledge, retain it, savor it for as long as you can.

You and I know firsthand that we often take things for granted until they're gone. So, look up. Look forward. The view is better from there.

PART III

THE SPIRIT

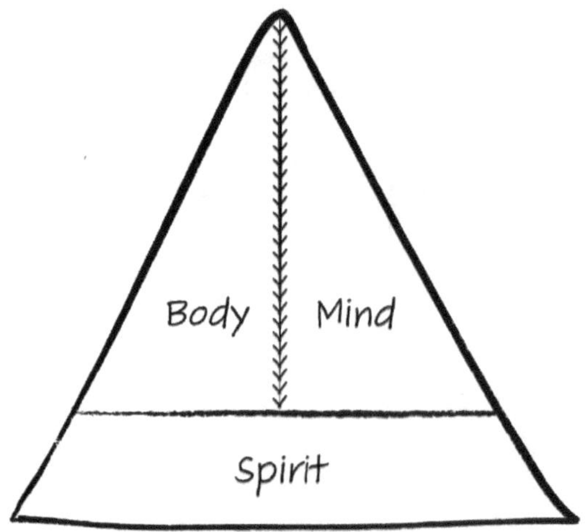

The foundation: three pillars. Body, Mind, Spirit.

12

THE THIRD PILLAR

Tears wash the eyes so they can see more clearly.

THE practice of being fully present during therapy had enhanced my body's ability to learn, and accepting my situation reduced the cognitive stress that might impede healing. The complete framework, Body, Mind, and Spirit, was taking shape.

As I gained more movement privileges, I created small rituals to ground me. I would wake up before the nursing shift change started, then meditate in my bed before getting dressed in the clothes I had chosen the night before. When the first morning nurse arrived, I would move to my chair, wash my face, brush my teeth, make a cup of espresso with my fancy new coffee machine, and wheel myself to the yard. This was a quiet, paved area with picnic tables and metal sculptures. It remained empty during the record summer heat we were having, and this early morning solitude became sacred.

With my phone on the table and coffee in hand, I would make the call that anchored my day, the one to Israel, to my mother. The time difference created a perfect window when we could connect, and I tried to make that happen at least every other day. Our conversations were short. I tried to present a cheerful face and tell her how well I was doing or what progress I was making. She would tell me about her day and about my dad. These moments gave me both emotional strength and an opportunity to exercise my speech and cognitive abilities.

Often, I saw her eyes getting red and tears forming, obviously trying hard not to cry. Later, my sister told me that my mother thought it would upset me if she cried while we spoke, but that after our calls she cried for a long time. I did the same.

As a father, I can only imagine what my mother was going through. Not knowing what was going on with her child, where he was, what was happening with him, being on the other side of the globe, it all must have felt so helpless.

There are short moments, like a shiver running up and down my neck, where I don't want to be a hero. I don't even want to be an adult man in control of my life. I just want to go back to being a little boy and have my mother hug me and make it all go away. I can close my eyes and almost feel it. In those microsecond moments, I can feel tears dropping from my eyes to her shirt and her hands squeezing me to her chest. She is much bigger and stronger than me again. She picks me up and holds me tight, kissing my head and making the whole world disappear. But then those moments are over. The whole world is between us, and it's my turn to take care of her.

This was not the first time she had to worry for my life. On one of our morning calls, she reminded me of another time she had felt this helpless, back in 2004. I hadn't thought about that experience in detail for years, but as soon as she mentioned it, I was reliving it, both from my perspective and understanding hers in a new way.

It happened just after my graduation from university, when I went backpacking in India and the Far East, traveling alone on a motorcycle I purchased. I had heard about these tiny islands that were part of India but closer to Thailand, called Andaman and Nicobar. They represented one of the less touristic, less explored places on the planet. Before leaving, I called my parents to tell them I was going away for four weeks and that they might not hear from me. I promised to make an effort to call any chance I got, but I didn't know how accessible phone or internet would be. It took four days on a ship to get there, with only a few other backpackers traveling with me and my motorcycle stashed in a guest house on the mainland.

On December 25, I slept in my hammock on one of the relatively bigger and more populated islands in Andaman. I had enjoyed the small village and beautiful beaches, and I was looking forward to going snorkeling the next morning. But something felt "off" that evening. I remember writing only one sentence in my diary before closing it and going to sleep. It was a line from a song by Mercedes Band, I had in my head in a loop: "There is a feeling that something is about to happen."

I woke up early with the same feeling. Everybody else was still sleeping, so I walked alone to the nearby village to have my cup of Chai. Before I made it to the village, the earth started to shake. I knew it was an earthquake because we had just felt one at my university not long before. But this did not end in a few seconds like the last one had. The earth kept shaking and shaking. I was on a dirt road with fields on one side, so I tried walking into the open space in the center of the field. A few other people did the same.

As I walked, I kept my balance and looked for the crack, like in the movies, when the earth cracks open and everyone falls inside. It didn't, of course. When it was over, I went back to my original plan to have my morning chai. I asked the chai person if he knew what was going on, specifically asking him about the potential for a tsunami, but he said they had a lot of earthquakes there. Maybe not as strong as this one, but that there were no tsunamis in that part of the world.

Soon after, people began running to the beach, shouting in the local language. I followed, only to see that where there once was ocean, now there was just sand and rocks. The ocean had retreated so far, I couldn't spot it anymore. I walked where there once was water and gazed to the horizon, but all I saw was foam, like waves breaking in the distance. Then I saw it. The water was coming back. And fast.

Everyone ran. We ran across the village to the only high area in the middle of the island, on the only paved road. Halfway to the high point, the older of two old women running in a pair fell to the ground. I picked her up, noticing just how light she was, like skin and bones. As I ran with her to the hill, another earthquake began. I started shouting orders for people to stay in the open, not to go under trees or power poles. By the time it was over, I had lost all of my belongings to the sea, without even a scratch on my body.

At home, my parents, my sister and brother, and my friends did everything they could to get any signs of life from me, but we had no communication with the outside world. The earthquakes continued throughout that first day, getting weaker and less frequent over time. We had food and water and sometimes electricity. When the power came on, we would gather around the television, seeing the images and videos of what happened in nearby Thailand and the coast of India. There was even a video of the village where I had parked my bike. It had all been destroyed.

Meanwhile, my sister bought a ticket to India. My family talked to extreme sport rescue companies, to the embassy, to anyone they could, asking to send someone over for me. They appeared in all the news outlets, had my picture in all the leading newspapers, and even included me on the 8 PM news.

After three days, the embassy sent a man from the sport rescue company to the island with a satellite phone, looking for all the Israelis on the island to let them call home. The second my mother heard my voice, she yelled and cried and laughed and threatened me and blessed me. For our five-minute conversation, she did most of the talking. She told me how hopeless she felt, not knowing what I was going through, not able to help me. She said that my dad knew that I was okay and that I was helping others, but that he also felt helpless. Being so far away, they were thinking the worst while hoping for the best.

I had known intellectually that my adventures worried my parents, but at the time, I dismissed their concern as overprotectiveness. Now, just imagining my daughter in similar danger made me physically ill. I finally grasped the depth of the terror my mother must have experienced during those days of not knowing.

Like any mother, she worried while I reassured her I was fine, even though I wasn't. She saw my struggle now just as she had during the tsunami. Only, back then, there had been nothing to do to alleviate her concern. I was physically isolated with no communication tools at all, no way to let her know I was safe until that satellite phone arrived three days later.

Now, I could choose how and when we spoke, what I shared, and how I framed my progress. Though I knew she would worry no matter what, I could protect her to some extent by staying in touch and focusing on positive developments when I called. I could shape our interactions in ways that balanced honesty with compassion. I could take responsibility for the emotional impact of my communication.

These calls with my mother became a fixed point in my recovery routine, just as important as any physical exercise. Each morning in that yard with my phone, I was more than a stroke patient. I was a son, still connected to my family and to my past.

In addition to reflecting on her experience during both the tsunami and the stroke, I couldn't help but notice the tremendous amount of "luck" that let me survive events. In both cases, I was meant to be somewhere else but wasn't, and it probably saved my life. There was also the notion that life can change in any given moment; when the ground isn't stable and your brain isn't reliable, anything can happen. But after speaking with my mother each morning, I'd wheel myself back through those tricky automatic doors with a renewed sense of purpose. Her strength, even when hidden behind tears, was another source of the 1 percent daily improvement I was determined to achieve.

The Question of Why

At 10 PM in the rehabilitation center, the night shift would have just completed their rounds. They would have measured my temperature and blood pressure for the last time, closing the door halfway, leaving behind the faint scent of hand sanitizer and the soft squeak of rubber-soled shoes. And I would be in bed, physically exhausted from the day's therapy session but, at least sometimes, mentally wide awake.

One night proved to be especially challenging. Two blankets covered me exactly as I preferred them, a thin one beneath, a thicker one on top, yet comfort eluded me. From somewhere down the hall, there were muffled sounds of someone crying, followed by the gentle murmurs of nurses trying to ease their suffering. The hours passed by. In the darkness, unable to sleep, a question I'd been pushing away for days finally surfaced, impossible to ignore any longer: *Why me?*

I had no family history of stroke. At forty-nine, I was in better shape than most men my age. My blood pressure typically ran low. I exercised regularly, ate reasonably well, and had just been to a medical checkup that hadn't shown anything concerning. The stroke made no logical sense. *There had to be a reason, right? Some explanation beyond a random biological accident?*

My analytical side, the problem-solver, had been trying to address this concern through medical expertise. We were in contact with both UCSF and Stanford hospitals, prestigious research institutions with world-renowned stroke units. If anyone could pinpoint a physical cause, it would be them. But something told me I wouldn't find the answer I was looking for in medical tests or expert consultations.

Earlier that day, I'd been on a group call with my oldest friends, guys I'd known for over thirty years, most of whom I'd seen just days before my stroke while on my trip to Israel and Germany. Our video conversation had been filled with dark humor. My condition provided the perfect setup for countless jokes, and we'd kept things deliberately light, promising to have deeper one-on-one conversations when the time was right. I'd laughed along, but some of those jokes had contained kernels of truth. Now, alone in the darkness, long after the forced laughter had faded, only the sting remained. I felt frustration. Anger. Sadness. And that "why me?" feeling that I could no longer suppress.

I wiped away unexpected tears with my sleeve, the question turning to a statement of self-pity looping endlessly in my mind. The stroke felt like a symptom of something else, its timing seemed too perfect to be coincidence. Then I heard my sister's voice, echoing from decades away, saying the words that had once infuriated me: "You know why. Look inside and figure out why it happened. And by the way, like everything in life, it happened for you, not to you."

The memory was so vivid I could almost smell the mint tea she'd made, a drink I never chose but she always prepared. I was twenty-three and in command of a company, at the peak of my military career. In just a matter of days, I was to lead an important operation that would likely earn me a promotion to Major. After years of training, countless dangerous missions, and building a reputation as one of the unit's most capable officers, my trajectory was clear.

Until a wasp changed everything.

During a field drill, a sting triggered an anaphylactic reaction. Even though I'd been stung before with no problems, this time they had to open my airways. I was evacuated by helicopter to the nearest hospital, where two doctors with thick accents delivered the news that ended my combat career: I could no longer serve in the field.

"That can't be," I'd protested. "Next week, I need to lead this important operation, and the week after we have graduation..." But the medical reality didn't care about my plans or even my identity. It had simply happened.

When my mother visited me in the hospital, she cried and laughed at the same time. She said, "I'm laughing because you look like a cucumber with your swollen face and head, and I'm crying because now I can sleep at night." Then she thanked the wasp for taking me off of the combat unit.

I couldn't share her relief. This was who I was, a fighter defending the country. Like my grandparents said to us numerous times, "Never again! Now we have a country, and a strong army to defend ourselves." That was how I saw myself and how others saw me. Being sidelined felt like having my identity stripped away.

After my release, my sister found me at our parents' home, feeling bitter and confused. Despite being two years younger, she possessed wisdom beyond her years. She made tea, sat across from me at the kitchen table like so many times before, and simply listened as I ranted about the unfairness of it all.

"Now listen, Nir, my big, smart, handsome brother," she finally said, her dark eyes holding mine steadily. "Shit happens *for* us, not *to* us. We might know why immediately, or we might find out later. Now take a big breath and relax. You will know why, if you don't already know. I think we both know why, don't you?!"

166

I dismissed that with a sigh and a hand gesture, but her implication was clear. The pace and pressure of my military career had consumed me. The constant adrenaline, the responsibility for others' lives, the persona I'd adopted, it took a toll that I refused to acknowledge. *Could she be right? Could the wasp be the universe's way of forcing a change I wouldn't make voluntarily?!*

Two decades later and 7,000 miles away, I wondered if history was repeating itself. *Had I been racing down another unsustainable path?* The years before my stroke had been filled with constant work pressure, family responsibilities, global travel, and the weight of solving everyone else's problems. I'd pushed through exhaustion, telling myself that I enjoyed solving problems. That the race was what fueled me. That I was being creative. That this was the pace of technology and that the speed was what made it fun.

Twenty years ago, my sister's words had infuriated me. This time, they brought clarity and comfort. Life had proven her right about the wasp. What had seemed like "disaster" at the time had redirected me toward opportunities I couldn't have imagined. The wasp had ended one chapter of my life but began another, one that ultimately led me to America, to my family, and to a career in technology. Over time, what initially felt like pure loss had revealed itself as redirection rather than rejection. Perhaps the stroke, too, was happening for me in ways I couldn't yet see.

I didn't know why I had a stroke. I still don't, and maybe I never will. But as I lay in that hospital bed, my emotional defenses were down in a way they hadn't been before. It was forcing me to let go of things that I valued: control, independence, physical capability…But was it also making space for something else? Something I couldn't yet see but might eventually recognize as valuable? It had certainly humbled me enough to receive the wisdom I had once rejected. From this perspective, the memory offered the hope that this catastrophe, like previous ones, might ultimately lead to growth rather than loss.

The answer didn't come that night, but the question itself shifted slightly, from "Why me?" to "What now?" It wasn't acceptance, exactly, I was still too angry for that, but it was the first small crack in the wall of resistance I'd built against my new, unwanted reality.

Soon, the faint light of dawn began to filter through my window. With it came another memory. This time, of something my grandmother used to say when I'd complain about life's unfairness: "Sometimes the question itself is more important than its answer." Perhaps this "why" was not a puzzle to be solved but rather a doorway leading to something I couldn't yet imagine. Could something that initially seemed like the greatest loss, the stroke itself, paradoxically become a doorway to a more authentic, aware, and meaningful life?

My body was slowly regaining function through physical therapy. My mind was rebuilding its cognitive pathways through exercises and mental challenges. Yet there was a deeper dimension of healing that neither medical treatments nor cognitive puzzles could address. That night, staring at the ceiling and listening to the distant sounds of patients and nurses sorting out their own nighttime distress, I could see a gap in the puzzle, or perhaps an opening in the doorway.

Beyond the Body and Mind pillars I had so methodically constructed, there existed a third dimension I needed to address. One I had encountered before but never fully embraced. My work on the Spirit Pillar had begun.

◆ ◆ ◆ ◆ ◆ ◆ ◆ ◆ ◆ ◆ ◆ ◆ ◆ ◆ ◆ ◆

REFLECTION SPACE

*Sometimes, the most important questions are
the ones we're most afraid to ask.*

My sister was right about the wasp, even though it took me twenty years to admit it. That sting redirected my entire life toward possibilities I couldn't see from inside my uniform. I still don't know the full purpose of the stroke. Maybe I never will. But I stopped needing to know.

That night in the rehabilitation center, asking "why me?" felt like giving up. Like I was being weak, feeling sorry for myself. But looking back, I can see that it was actually the beginning of real strength, the kind that comes from admitting you don't have all the answers.

If you're reading this in your own dark moment, maybe you're asking the same question. Why you? Why your loved one? Why now? I wish I could tell you there's a clear answer waiting to be discovered. Sometimes there is, but sometimes there isn't. And that's okay.

What I've learned, and what took me way too long to accept, is that the question itself might be more important than any answer. "Why me?" is really asking: *What does this mean? How do I make sense of this? Is there something Life (or God) is trying to tell me?*

Those are Spirit questions, not Body or Mind questions. They're about meaning, not mechanics.

Spirit work isn't about finding peace with what happened, at least not at first. It's about being honest about the rage, the unfairness, the desire to go back to how things were. Feel those feelings. They're part of the healing too.

But then, when you're ready, and only when you're ready, try shifting the question. Instead of "Why me?" try "What now?" Instead of "Why did this happen to me?" try "What if this is happening for me in ways I can't see yet?"

For now, I want to ask you:

What is your wasp story?

What unwanted event turned out to be a good thing after all?

Can you trust that one day you will find the answer to "why me?" and realize that it was "for me"?

I'm not saying everything happens for a reason. Maybe it does; I don't know. But that would make things too neat, too easy. What I'm saying is that we get to decide what happens next.

You are writing your story. This is not the end of the book, it's the twist, the cliff hanger to the next chapter...You get to choose whether this thing breaks you or becomes the thing that remakes you. Even if you don't know exactly how.

Start small, and only when you're ready. I assure you it will be the first step toward a future you didn't know you could have.

13

———

SEEDS PLANTED LONG AGO

*Life has a funny way of teaching us the same lesson
again and again until we finally learn it.*

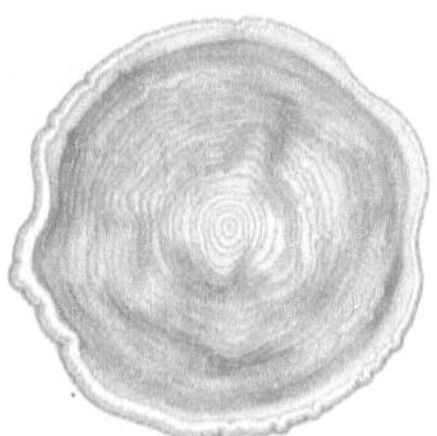

I WAS thirty-four when the motorcycle accident happened.

It was a sunny summer morning. The flat sea water of the Tel Aviv shore mirrored the few white clouds in the sky. I drove slowly down a city road, breathing in the salty ocean air and avoiding the traffic on the highway during my commute to work. There were cars parked on my right, with low bushes and a fence separating the other lane.

When one of the parked cars suddenly made a U-turn to get to the opposite side, I had nowhere to go. I pushed the brakes as hard as I could and heard myself saying, "Oh shit." The grinding sound of metal against metal was the last thing I registered before everything went black. Two days later, I woke up in the hospital to discover I had a broken femur, broken knee, broken wrist, and a crack in my skull.

The doctors told me I was lucky to be alive.

Life has a funny way of teaching us the same lesson again and again until we finally learn it. After the stroke, my approach to recovery became thorough and methodical. But back then, I was impatient, angry, and solely fixated on physical healing. I wanted my body back, exactly as it had been before, immediately.

But it took two weeks in intensive care, multiple surgeries, and months of intensive rehabilitation, and even then, my recovery plateaued. I was left with constant knee pain that conventional medicine couldn't resolve beyond the pain medication that made me drowsy and unfocused.

I hated the way the pills dulled my entire presence in the world. Every little thing would throw me off. Eventually, I stopped going to the beach, my favorite place, and avoided going out with friends. At work, they agreed to let me work at 50 percent capacity, but I could hardly manage even that. Each restriction felt like a personal failure. I grew increasingly frustrated, feeling trapped between unbearable pain and unacceptable mental fog.

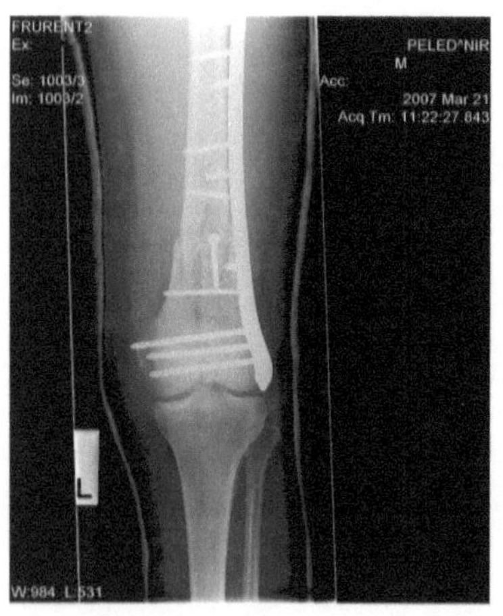

My sister, who had always been more open to alternative approaches than I was, suggested I meet her friend, an alternative therapist living in a small apartment on Shenkin Street in Tel Aviv, where all the hipsters congregated. Ever the skeptic, I imagined one of those long-haired, red-eyed tree huggers whispering words in Hindi or whatever language they all seemed to learn. But desperation has a way of opening minds that logic cannot reach.

When I arrived at the therapist's third-floor apartment, I could smell the incense from the staircase before reaching a door with a colorful Ohm sign on it. I felt awkward and more than a little bit out of place as she welcomed me into a tiny room adorned with statues and symbols from India and the Far East. But her voice was calming and non-threatening. After settling in, she instructed me to close my eyes, and we began a guided meditation.

I battled my skepticism, trying to keep an open mind like I promised my sister (and myself) that I would. I had to quiet the thoughts that came up about the incense, the statues, the experience. I had to surrender. And so, I did.

I followed her gentle voice, surprising myself as I relaxed into it. She guided me to visualize a ball of light descending from the top of my head, traveling to my knee, and healing it. A cooling sensation followed the light's path, feeling particularly soothing on my injured knee. There was no actual ice or cold water, just my brain responding to my directed awareness. Afterward, to my absolute shock, the pain had vanished. Or perhaps it simply became tolerable; either way, it was something multiple surgeries and months of physical therapy had failed to accomplish.

That meditation session should have been transformative, a turning point in how I approached healing for the rest of my life. And in some ways, it was. It taught me that I could control my experience of pain by managing the attention I gave it. Sometimes, when I shifted my focus away, I could forget about it entirely. It showed me that everything I feel and sense happens in my brain, and that I have some control over that experience.

The seed that was planted that day would remain dormant for nearly two decades. I was too analytical to let it take root, trying to rationalize what had happened rather than simply accepting its benefits. I kept asking "how" and "why" it worked instead of just embracing that it did, in fact, work. I was still looking outward more than inward, chasing external achievements rather than inner peace. So I returned to my conventional life, occasionally remembering that extraordinary session whenever pain flared up, but never committing to exploring this dimension of healing more deeply.

But the seed had been planted, waiting for the right moment to finally break through the surface.

Two Perspectives on Pain

After the motorcycle accident, I was the youngest person in rehabilitation by decades. Not quite so young as the girl with the piano, but I'm certain I stood out at least as much. For one thing, my left leg and arm were encased in plaster casts, and still, I had developed a morning routine of wheeling myself to the dining room for breakfast.

One sunny morning, I joined a couple in their forties who were already seated at a small table covered with the typical white nylon cloth. The man sat in a wheelchair with an IV pole attached, his face pale and bruised, but his expression determined. His wife sat beside him, her head partially wrapped in white bandages that contrasted sharply with her dark curly hair. They greeted me with gentle smiles, and we waited in comfortable silence for our food.

The familiar smell of eggs and toast announced breakfast before I saw it. Just as three trays appeared before us, another couple approached our table. They too appeared to be in their forties, the man in a wheelchair with one pant leg pinned up where his leg should have been, his wife trailing behind in hospital gown, pulling an IV pole with tubes connecting it to her arm.

I sat at the head of the small table, with the first couple to my left and the newcomers to my right. When two more trays arrived, we all began to eat quietly, hearing only the clink of utensils and the institutional hum of the facility around us.

The woman on my left leaned toward her husband, helping him open his yogurt container.

"This is the first time he's eating by himself," she said, her voice carrying a note of triumph, as if announcing a medal-winning Olympic performance. "Isn't that right, Avraham?"

He nodded, struggling to smile through facial muscles that hadn't fully recovered their coordination.

"He's making remarkable progress, thank God," she continued, her eyes shining. "When we came here last week after the accident, he couldn't move or speak at all. Now look at him, such a miracle."

The word "accident" hung in the air for a moment before the woman on my right responded.

"This is our first time eating outside our room," she said, her voice flat and hollow. "We're both in so much pain since the accident. Just terrible…my husband lost his leg, and we just finished sitting shiva for both our children."

Her voice broke, tears spilling down her cheeks and dropping onto her untouched breakfast. Her husband stared at his food, saying nothing.

A chill ran through me as I realized what was happening around me. The previous week, the news had been dominated by a horrific multi-car collision on the highway. A truck driver had fallen asleep at the wheel and plowed into several vehicles. The accident had claimed multiple lives, children included. Now, the devastating truth emerged: Both couples had been in the same accident. Both had lost their children. Both were grieving unimaginable loss while dealing with their own severe injuries.

Yet their responses couldn't have been more different.

The woman on my left spoke of the Rabbi who had traveled from Jerusalem to attend the shiva, how the community had rallied around them, how the doctors had performed an eight-hour surgery that saved her husband's life. "Even in our darkest hour," she said, "we can see God's hand."

The woman on my right detailed her sleepless nights, the constant pain medications, how her husband would never work again, how empty their house would feel. "Nothing will ever be the same," she whispered. "How can we possibly go on?"

The physical facts were identical: the same accident, the same devastating losses, the same broken bodies. But their experiences of that suffering diverged completely. One found fragments of light in the darkness; the other only saw the darkness deepening.

I sat frozen between them, my broken leg and arm suddenly seeming trivial by comparison. There was nothing I could say that wouldn't feel hollow. I could only witness these two fundamentally different approaches to the same unbearable tragedy.

I made a silent vow that transcended my youthful perspective: If tragedy ever struck me again, I would strive with everything in me to be like the couple on my left. Not to deny pain or pretend losses aren't real, but to consciously choose where I would focus my attention.

Now, years later, the story of those two couples became my touchstone. When frustration threatened to overwhelm me, when progress seemed impossibly slow, when the future looked uncertain, I would recall sitting at that table, witnessing two responses to an identical tragedy.

My grandmother had tried to teach me this wisdom with her saying in Hungarian, followed by the Hebrew translation, "Darkness teaches us to appreciate the light." But I had to witness it myself to truly understand. We cannot always control what happens to us, but we retain the power to choose how we experience it.

There were days after my stroke when I felt myself teetering between these two perspectives, sometimes alternating through them within the same hour. Whenever I found that my hand was shaking or when words disappeared mid-sentence, I could feel myself sliding toward that darker worldview. Willpower couldn't pull me back, it took practice. Deliberate choices, made again and again, to see what remained possible rather than only what was lost.

Rediscovery Through Necessity

My first brain scan after the stroke revealed a shape about half the size of a banana occupying nearly two-thirds of my brain's left frontal side. It was entirely black against the white brain tissue, like a terrifying stain. Even with limited knowledge of neuroanatomy, I recognized its significance as a threat to everything I knew myself to be.

The scan had been taken at the hospital, and on my last day before transferring to rehabilitation, I met with a new neurologist who would oversee my care after discharge. Having trained at Stanford, she approached my case with both scientific precision and unexpected poetry.

"Think of the brain having many connections, like paths or roads," she said. "An ischemic stroke resembles an earthquake, breaking those roads and paths permanently. We believe you might have had a hemorrhagic stroke, which is more like a blizzard covering roads with snow."

A year later, we discovered this theory was wrong. We still don't know exactly what happened, but doctors suspect I had an ischemic stroke. Nevertheless, this simple image illuminated the paths of the healing process. Rebuilding broken roads after an earthquake is challenging and often remains incomplete. But snow eventually melts. Like the rest of our body, our brain demonstrates remarkable resilience, establishing new pathways around damaged areas. This requires time. And while we don't fully understand all mechanisms, the brain can be influenced by age and general health, both of which were in my favor.

Remembering the cooling light and shift in focus that had seemed to heal my knee, I asked her about the potential benefits of meditation. She neither dismissed nor wholeheartedly endorsed it. "It helps maintain calm and lower blood pressure," she said, "and regarding healing, it won't hurt." That cautious approval was enough for me. I wanted to use every available tool for recovery, including approaches that existed beyond conventional rehabilitation.

With unlimited time in my hospital bed and a desperate desire to heal, I searched for "best iPhone apps for meditation" and reinstalled an application I had tried briefly years before. This time, I purchased the premium subscription without hesitation. This wasn't something to economize.

This quickly became the centerpiece of my morning routine, meditation first, then breakfast, then physical exercises. These began with guided meditation, usually as body scans, followed by an unguided meditation that lasted one minute longer than the previous day. When I reached thirteen minutes, I paused to maintain that duration for several days before advancing to fourteen. This gradual approach felt appropriate to my Marathon Mindset and 1 Percent Rule. Pushing too hard would derail the habit entirely, and I needed this practice to become something I anticipated. If it were merely an obligation, I would not sustain it as easily.

As the practice deepened, I discovered I could direct healing energy to injured areas, just as I had twenty years earlier on Shenkin Street. The first time I attempted to heal my brain, I imagined a healing light descending from my crown, intending to address that banana-shaped wound, the bleed in my left frontal lobe. Surprisingly, this visualization felt wrong; the area became uncomfortably warm rather than soothing. It burned. It seemed harmful in a way that frightened me.

I opened my eyes in panic, fearing I might be causing damage. In reality, I simply wasn't ready for that specific visualization. I had to learn that I couldn't force healing through willpower alone. I needed to give it time.

Building a Spiritual Practice

I continued to practice meditation daily, at least in the morning, sometimes the evening, and occasionally at night when sleep eluded me. Since then, I've maintained about twenty minutes of meditation daily, sometimes more, sometimes less. Meditation represents the highlight of many of my days, and most mornings I eagerly anticipate this quality time with myself.

But it would be dishonest to say that this practice came easily or without resistance. There have been mornings when my mind raced with worries about recovery, when sitting still felt impossible, when I questioned whether this "spiritual stuff" was just elaborate self-deception.

The analytical part of my brain, the part that had served me well throughout my career but kept me from building this practice after my knee injury, continues to demand evidence and guarantees. *What measurable difference is this making? How can I be certain I'm not wasting precious recovery time?* These doubts have never fully disappeared, but over time, they have become background noise rather than commanding voices. The experience itself has become my evidence.

As meditation became central to my recovery, I developed specific practices that supported this spiritual dimension of healing.

First, I established a consistent meditation routine. After returning home from rehabilitation, I created a small space in our backyard and another in my office for cold days. Nothing elaborate, just a comfortable chair positioned where morning light first appeared. Each day before the household awakened, I sat there, sometimes for fifteen minutes, occasionally for forty-five, rebuilding connections that might not be visible on a brain scan but are arguably more essential.

Second, I incorporated visualization techniques, drawing on my earlier experience with the alternative therapist. I visualized neural pathways reconnecting, fresh blood flowing to damaged areas, and healing energy surrounding the injured portions of my brain. I learned to approach these visualizations with respect for my body's signals, never forcing something that didn't feel right.

Third, I developed a gratitude practice for difficult days. When progress seemed elusive and frustration mounted, I discovered that you simply can't be

you simply can't
be resentful
and grateful at
the same time

resentful and grateful at the same time. On my darkest days, I would make myself look for small things to be grateful for, sunlight filtering through window blinds, a perfectly brewed cup of coffee, the soft weight of a blanket. I'd focus on the functioning aspects of my body, my supportive family, or moments of unexpected laughter. When even that felt hard, I went straight to the basics: I had survived the stroke, with access to healthcare, while still possessing the cognitive capacity to appreciate my situation. I was grateful for simply being alive.

Intentionally making space for appreciation alongside struggle shifted my perspective. Regardless of my challenges, abundant blessings remained. This also helped me learn to differentiate between pain and suffering. Physical pain, the burning sensation in overworked muscles, the occasional headaches, the fatigue, was an unavoidable aspect of recovery. Suffering, however, resulted from my relationship with that pain, my resistance to it, and the stories I told myself about what it meant. Through meditation, I discovered I could experience pain without supplementing it with suffering.

Through meditation,
I discovered I could
experience pain
without supplementing
it with suffering.

Beyond regaining function lay the deeper question of purpose. Why recover? To what end? Meditation created space for these existential questions, allowing me to envision not just a restored version of my former self, but a transformed one. Someone who might live a more authentic and purposeful life than before.

And it was only a start. I knew I was just scratching the surface of this spiritual world. I was confident that more missing pieces would reveal themselves over time and with practice. In the past, I would push away the unknown, the scary thoughts about meaning and life beyond what we can measure, by not thinking about it. Now, I was open to whatever those missing pieces might be, learning to feel and sense it even when I could not measure it.

I kept this spiritual dimension somewhat private. Some journeys travel distances that only the traveler can measure. But of the few people I shared my spiritual experiences with, only one truly understood, because she had been living this path long before I had even acknowledged it.

My sister is two years younger than me and has known me longer than almost anyone. We've always been close. Unlike me, she's spiritual, grounded, and unapologetically connected to herself. She listens to her heart, trusts her gut, and makes big decisions based on intuition. This used to confuse me, maybe even frustrate me. But deep down, I admired it.

She's not floating in the clouds. She's practical, organized, and incredibly capable. She takes care of four kids, helps our mother with bills and paperwork, keeps her house running, and somehow still finds time for everyone around her. She's the kind of person who sees a challenge and thinks, "Okay, how do I grow from this?" She's not pretending everything's okay, either. That's just how she lives. She also has a short fuse and gets angry quickly, but even her fire is rooted in love and truth.

After the stroke, our conversations deepened. She became the first person I could talk to about the spiritual layer of my recovery. She didn't need me to explain or justify anything. She would just ask, like she always has, "What does your heart say?"

That question used to stump me. I honestly didn't know. My whole life had been driven by logic and analysis. I made smart, responsible decisions, the kind a grown-up man is supposed to make. I don't regret that. My brain got me far. But something had shifted, probably that first time that I cried in the ER. That release of control evolved over time. I became more sensitive, more receptive, more open. I faced the new reality of who I was and would be. I knew who and what were important to me. I didn't want to live from the head alone anymore. I wanted to integrate something deeper. To make space for the voice underneath the noise, the voice I'd ignored for years.

This shift happened slowly, and is still happening, even now as I am writing this book.

My sister helped me feel safe in that space. When I started having early spiritual experiences like visions and unexpected moments of presence, she was the first one I told. She didn't even flinch. In fact, she lit up with curiosity, asking for every detail. Her response reassured me that I wasn't losing my mind. I could still be the logical, grounded version of me, but now with something extra.

BUILDING A SPIRITUAL PRACTICE

First, establish a consistent meditation routine. Second, incorporate visualization techniques, approaching them with respect for your body's signals. Third, develop a gratitude practice, you can't be resentful and grateful at the same time.

This spiritual dimension of recovery is rarely featured in medical literature or rehabilitation protocols. Yet for me, it became integral to, not separate from, my physical healing. Each time I visualized neural pathways reconnecting, each meditation where I focused healing energy toward my brain, each moment of profound gratitude that I felt for small improvements, it all seemed to accelerate my journey. Science might explain this through reduced stress hormones, improved sleep quality, or enhanced neuroplasticity. But the precise mechanisms mattered less to me than the results. I was rebuilding my body, my mind, and a spirit that could carry me through whatever lay ahead.

REFLECTION SPACE

*We cannot always control what happens to us, but we
retain the power to choose how we experience it.*

Life breaks your body, your plans, your heart, your sense of control. That's real! Pain is part of the deal. But suffering? Suffering is often the story we tell ourselves about the pain. The resistance. The shame. The comparison. The fear that it means something bad about us.

What changed for me, and what's still changing, is that I started noticing when I was adding suffering on top of the pain. That voice that said, "This shouldn't be happening," or, "If you were stronger...or smarter...." Once I started catching those thoughts, I remembered that it was up to me to decide which side of the table I wanted to sit on: the one with cup half empty or half full. Both sides are objectively true, but knowing I had a choice made all the difference.

What kind of pain are you in right now?

What story are you telling about it?

Can you notice, without judgment, the stories your mind creates about your pain or limitations?

Awareness itself often loosens suffering's grip.

List five things that make you lucky, that you are fortunate about in your new situation.

You don't have to solve it. You don't have to heal it all today. Just start by seeing the difference between objective pain that you're in and the subjective suffering. Recognizing when you're creating additional suffering can be the first step toward releasing it.

14

OUT OF THE BUBBLE

*The true test of recovery is what you build
when you return to your life.*

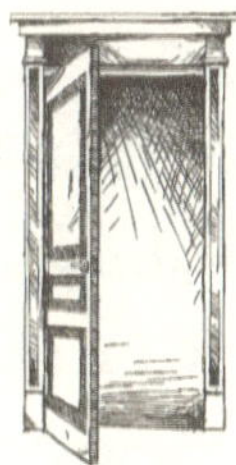

Two days away from my release date, I was overwhelmed with mixed emotions. On one hand, I couldn't wait to sleep in my own bed, be around my daughter, and even see our dog, cat, and the new kitten I'd met only once before the stroke. On the other hand, I worried about my ability to function at home, much less maintain my recovery momentum.

At home, I would be the architect of my own healing. No safety net of hospital routines. No therapists scheduling my day. No day-to-day reassurance of medical supervision. The responsibility was both liberating and terrifying. Inside, I was riddled with questions: *Would I maintain the discipline I'd developed without a printed schedule placed near my bed every night? Would I continue to prioritize all three pillars as daily life began to intrude? Could I resist the temptation to either rush the process or stop and be lazy, even when no one was watching? Who was going to guide me?*

There were more practical concerns, as well. For example, our bathroom and shower weren't equipped like those at the rehabilitation center. The staff had suggested my wife take pictures and bring measurements of our bathrooms for them to assess what modifications might be needed. That meant we could adjust our home to accommodate my limitations, but I wasn't sure I wanted to. *Did I really need grab bars and shower chairs? Would these changes be permanent reminders of my condition?* I felt paralyzed by indecision, unsure whether to plan for the worst-case or best-case scenario. Perhaps something in between? Making permanent accommodations felt like admitting I might never fully recover, and I wasn't ready for that yet.

At home I would need to stand firm in my commitment to the 1 percent approach, even when progress slowed or setbacks occurred. The greatest test of my three pillar framework would be living it, day after day, in the messy reality of home life. I knew I would face not just physical and cognitive challenges, but the emotional weight of returning changed to the place where I had been once whole.

The steady progress that I had experienced so far encouraged me, but it simultaneously confused me. As I recovered, my challenges had kept changing. Nothing stayed the same. My programs, what I was learning, the rules I was creating all had to adjust to address the next issue. I wasn't sure how to adapt to that much change on my own. And I was afraid that it might put an end to my progress.

I had heard about a curve to recovery and about the potential for stagnation, but I hadn't seen it. I wondered if I'd missed it, if I wasn't actually back to 50 percent and maybe all the progress would stop soon. Everyone was shocked by my progress, so what was really going on? I was afraid.

In one of our final occupational therapy sessions, I walked with Meeka along what I thought was the route back to my room. Instead, we continued down the corridor until we reached a locked door that looked like all the others in that beige space. Then she handed me a key attached to a long stick, like one you'd get for a gas station bathroom. As I struggled to open the door with my right hand, resisting unnecessary reliance on my left, she explained that we were going to visit their model home, a space with everything a real home would have, used for practicing daily routines.

I managed to hold the key with my fingers and insert it into the keyhole with just my right hand, but I needed help from my left hand to turn it. When I finally pushed the heavy door open, I found a queen-sized bed covered with a decorative spread and too many pillows. My first task was to change the sheets. I assessed my target, planned my approach, and set to work, joking about how my wife and I had argued about decorative pillows since moving in together. Then I recounted my father's only advice on our wedding day, when he took me aside and whispered, "Happy wife, happy life, pick your battles."

Once I had done an acceptable job with the sheets, we moved to the living room. In it, there was a sofa similar in height to mine at home. That is, *low*. She asked me to sit down and stand up several times. Since this was one of the first skills I'd mastered, it went smoothly, and we moved on to the bathroom. This had both a standing shower and a bathtub, which they had compared to the pictures my wife had sent of our shower at home. They had placed a log onto the structure to replicate our sliding door on a six-inch-high rail. My task was to step over it, simulating the way I would enter the shower at home.

Even with a rail to hold onto, this proved dangerously difficult. Instead, she brought out a sliding chair for the bathtub: a seat with two legs outside and two inside the tub, placing approximately one-third of the sitting area outside and the rest inside. The idea was to sit on the external part, turn, move my legs inside, and slide my entire body in from there. Getting out worked the same way, I could use my hands to move my leg in and out, then sit comfortably without slipping, leaving my hands free to adjust the water temperature and soap myself. Most importantly, I could do all of this independently, without supervision.

We visited the model home once more on my last day, this time with my wife and two cousins, who had planned to stay at our place for a few days after my return. My cousins seemed more nervous than I was by that point. If I followed my rules, I knew I'd be fine. Especially the most important rule: don't get injured.

My last day at rehab was the longest day ever. By breakfast, I had finished packing, made all my calls, and texted my wife to bring bags and buy thank-you gifts and cards. After breakfast, I had my final physical and occupational therapy sessions. My wife and our two cousins had arrived, with our service dog Nimmy in tow. She was accustomed to accompanying us to hospitals, since she had often comforted our daughter during her stays.

After therapy, we made our farewell rounds. We took pictures with key staff members and exchanged contact information. Then we sat in the dining room, waiting patiently for my release forms and other last-day paperwork. I stared at the clock, counting minutes until the case manager appeared and declared, "You're all set!"

Then I walked through the familiar corridor, through the wooden doors to the entrance hall with its bright windows and the long staircase that had tried but failed to defeat me. The first set of glass doors slid open, then the second, and we stepped into the blazing heat. I paused to put on my sunglasses, then carefully walked to our car.

I didn't look back. But as I stepped outside, an unexpected wave of mixed emotions hit me. Relief, fear, and excitement all rushed forward in one confusing moment. I wanted the freedom to work out and practice at any time of the day, to eat when I wanted to and what I wanted to. But I was equally worried about cooking, buying groceries, and where I would work out. I was afraid of not having a call button or nurses around me day and night or facilities that were safe for someone like me.

I was excited about being in my own home, with my daughter and wife and even guests, but that also meant I would need to consider their needs. Here, I only had to care about myself. And how would my wife and daughter handle me? It was going to be a big change for everyone.

Like finishing a good book or movie, I felt a sense of nostalgia about leaving the safety of the rehab center, knowing that I'd never return. Even though I was going home, I was also walking to the unknown. It was the beginning of a new chapter in my recovery journey and, really, in my life.

I scanned the parking lot as we walked, noticing the van that had taken me grocery shopping parked in its usual spot, imagining how hot it must be inside. Then I got into the passenger seat of our car, *my* car, buckled up, figured out something to do with my cane, and we left.

There were conversations happening around me in the car on the way home, but I wasn't paying attention. My mind was quiet, peaceful, as if in a dream I'd had many times before. I had driven this route to our home several times weekly, roughly four miles with eight lights and four stop signs. I knew each one well, even where to change lanes to avoid being sprayed by sprinklers in the morning. The closer we got to home, the more real everything became. The dream was ending; this was actually happening.

My heart beat faster as I realized I was home and it was time to enter back into my real life. The familiar mess of our garage with its familiar garage-like smell welcomed me as I prepared to climb out of the car. Everything looked exactly the same, but it felt different now. Somehow smaller and a bit unfamiliar.

My focus returned, instincts kicking in as it was time to focus on a new skill. This was my first time getting out of this car, and my "don't get injured" rule took over. My wife and cousins seemed more nervous than I was. While I knew what

I could and couldn't do, they didn't, and they undoubtedly feared the worst. I wanted to appear smooth and confident, preferably executing this movement without assistance and definitely without mistakes. I wanted to assure them that it was going to be okay. That I was fine. That we are all okay.

I surveyed my surroundings. The door opened wide enough that I could turn 90 degrees and rest both my legs outside. Then I would need to push myself slightly so my feet would be properly positioned on the ground. I hesitated about using the cane, but remembered the two rails that had helped me in the van. I felt around the door frame for a place to hold with my left hand, then moved the cane to my right. Bending forward slightly, I incrementally shifted more weight to my feet, and stood up.

"Great success!" I announced, mimicking the voice of Borat, from one of our favorite comedies.

Therapy at Home

During the first few weeks at home, physical, occupational, and speech therapists came to us. I created a schedule around these visits, turning our living room (and the rest of the house) into my new gym. The first session with each therapist began with an evaluation, almost identical to those at rehabilitation before my release.

In both physical assessments, I failed at standing on one leg. My new physical therapist, Joy, suggested I work on activating my core muscles, which she thought I might remember from yoga classes. These muscles surround the abdomen and lower back, providing stabilization, and "activating" them means tensing them proactively rather than allowing them to passively engage. Surprisingly, this suggestion worked! I broke my previous three-second record (which barely qualifies as standing) and set a new twelve-second record, extending it to seventeen seconds by day's end. It was a promising start to my recovery at home.

Initially, I needed complete focus for this exercise. I couldn't multitask, listen to music, talk, or listen to others speaking. So, in our next session, Joy challenged me to count backward from 100 in steps of seven while balancing. She explained that I needed to train my brain to stand on one leg without consciously thinking about it. I needed to multitask. Later challenges would include catching and throwing a ball made out of towels while balancing on one leg, which required both coordination and maintaining balance.

I seized every opportunity to practice. From this point forward, everything became my responsibility, my recovery, schedule, work and insurance matters, doctor appointments, eating, sleeping…Everything. I had never been particularly organized, but I always maintained discipline and focus when motivated. Thankfully, I was more motivated than ever.

My principles still applied, from the Marathon Mindset to the Variety Rule and everything in between. To hold to these rules, I needed a routine that allowed me to train while also meditating, resting, spending time with family, handling necessary chores and appointments, and even having a social life. It needed to include fixed times but with enough flexibility to accommodate changes. I decided to leverage the early-sleep-early-wake pattern I'd attained in the rehab facility to finally become a morning person as I'd always wanted to be.

The quiet morning hours, when I was the only one awake and it wasn't too hot outside, worked well for meditation. After my daughter woke up, we'd have breakfast together and prepare for school. It would still be early in the morning when she left, so having had my coffee and with my energy at its peak, I would exercise. Around one or two in the afternoon, I would have accomplished quite a lot and would typically be very tired. Instead of fighting it with another cup of coffee as I used to, I decided to listen to my body and take a nap.

Before my stroke, I used to say that any day when you can take a midday nap is a great day, and I meant it. Naps felt like luxuries that I didn't always deserve.

If I napped, it was only on a day when I had no plans and no chores, and even then I had to make sure I had nothing better to do. This is not how I was raised. Growing up in a small town in northern Israel, everyone in my community took a midday break. Signs requested silence between 2 to 4 PM, and my parents closed their small photography shop during that time to come home for lunch and a nap. But I was living at a different pace. From the army to the world of high tech, sleeping is seen as a waste of time.

If I were giving anyone else advice in my situation, however, I would tell them to give themselves a break. So that is what I told myself as well. Just looking at the calendar was enough to show compassion for myself, only a few weeks ago, I was not okay, and that was okay. I remembered what the experts said about sleep, and I used all the reasoning I could find to convince myself that napping wasn't lazy or reserved for the very old or very young. It was a strategic recovery approach, helping cells and neurons rebuild themselves in the middle of a long day. Naps were another way to heal.

I adopted the routine that my parents had modeled and began to nap after lunch. Soon, those naps started to feel like a necessity and the schedule became second nature. And once my whole body knew what to expect and was ready for it, persistence became easy. Each nap was proof that I was finally learning to listen to my body rather than pushing beyond its limits.

My world had changed dramatically, but I was establishing a new normal. We arranged delivery services for groceries, used Amazon for most other needs, and I used Uber for transportation. My wife drove our daughter to her activities, and I tried to minimize how often I needed her to drive me around for mine. I had a structured routine, a supportive environment, and a clear framework for continuing my recovery.

Moving from an environment that was completely focused on rehabilitation to one where recovery had to coexist with the ordinary demands of family life had been my greatest challenge yet. But in this challenge there was also an opportunity to test and refine my three pillar approach in the real world. I had reached an important waypoint on this journey: I was home. And I was ready to continue rebuilding strength, neural pathways, and resilience within this new chapter of life.

REFLECTION SPACE

*Recovery in the real world means becoming your
own therapist, coach, and cheerleader.*

The hardest part about returning to "normal" life wasn't the physical work, it was knowing that, from here on out, the next step was mine alone to take. In the hospital or rehab, there's structure, support, and someone always checking in. At home, that safety net is gone. Every decision, every action depends on you. That freedom can feel heavier than the injury or illness itself.

If you're in that place, coming home, returning to work, or reentering a life that kept moving while you were healing, know this: the fear you feel isn't weakness. It's awareness. It means you understand what's at stake, and that you're awake for what comes next

So here's what I want to ask you:

Where do you still need someone to tell you what to do?

Could you choose one or two things and make them part of your daily routine? What's something like my morning routine that would give you the feeling of movement, of "doing"?

What's your motivation now that no one's watching?

I created my rules for the days when I couldn't answer that question. What do you need to remind yourself of so you can keep showing up, even when it's hard?

The truth is, most of us do better with someone else telling us what to do. But real growth begins when we start choosing for ourselves. That's when the healing deepens and becomes our own.

You don't need to do it all. But you can do the next right thing. And that's enough.

Be gentle with yourself along the way. Healing yourself, by yourself, might be the hardest and loneliest job in the world. Have compassion. Give yourself credit for every step you take, even the invisible ones.

15

MY NEXT MOVEMENT

The mind must lead the body.

AT home, I became obsessed with overcoming a critical limitation in my movement. I could move my knee forward in a kicking motion, but I couldn't fold it, and I had zero control over my heel and foot. I tried all the exercises they had taught me in rehab and practiced new ones with my at-home PT, but nothing was working.

Eventually, I remembered how my first finger movements had begun: with dreams and visualization before physical movement. To follow the blueprint I'd set out for myself, then I needed to act as thought the breakthrough would happen in my head first, likely while sleeping or in that twilight state between sleep and wakefulness.

Drawing on my emerging third pillar, I incorporated this challenge into my daily meditation practice. I directed my awareness to my knee area and visualized the motion as if I were actually performing it. In my mind's eye, I saw little sparks of neural activity, tiny green sprouts growing in the damaged area of my brain. I imagined my leg folding while lying down, sitting, and standing. I visualized healing light flowing through my entire body, from the crown of my head down to my toes, repairing everything in its path.

Four days into this meditative practice, I woke up in the middle of the night, still half-dreaming, and felt the weight and texture of my blanket on my knee as I was folding my leg. The sensation was vivid, I could clearly feel my knee bending, pushing against the blanket. But when I tried to deliberately control the movement after I was fully awake, it all vanished. I couldn't move my knee at all.

I couldn't be certain if it had been real or a dream, but it felt just as real as it had with the other joints. My first movements were in dreams that seemed to bridge the gap between imagination and physical reality. Regardless of whether or not my leg had actually moved, I knew I was getting close. The neural pathways were forming; they just needed more encouragement.

Over coffee the next morning, I shared the experience with my wife.

"I think I moved my knee last night," I said, trying to contain my excitement.

"In your sleep?" she asked, looking up from her phone.

"Sort of. I was half-awake. I could feel it bending."

"And now?"

I attempted to demonstrate, concentrating intensely. Nothing happened.

"Maybe your leg is like one of those shy performers," she suggested with a smile. "Only works when no one's watching."

I laughed. "Great. I've got the neurological equivalent of stage fright."

Revisiting the Blueprint

Feeling inspired by this visualized progress and ready to move into the next step of the blueprint, just a sign of life to confirm the connection was there, I devised a new exercise. In my makeshift home "gym," I lay face-down on a thick yoga mat and used my left leg to fold both knees more than 90 degrees. Then I tried to hold that position with my right leg when I released the left.

Since I already had the "kick" motion, I could already move my leg from about 100 degrees to close to 90 degrees. The challenge was keeping it there without support. It required minimal force to bring it there, just enough to counteract gravity, but I couldn't maintain it. The moment my leg crossed the balancing angle, it would drop down, and if I didn't block the fall with my left leg in time, my toes would hit the floor with a painful "thud."

This was the hardest single joint movement I had attempted. There's something uniquely draining about trying to activate dormant neural pathways. I don't know precisely why it's so tiring, but the mental exertion is as real as any physical workout. My breath created condensation on the yoga mat I was lying on. Sweat pooled under me and rolled down my back. It felt ridiculous to be so exhausted by *not* moving. Yet despite intense concentration and complete exhaustion, I had zero success. After ten failed attempts, I flopped around onto my back, panting as if I'd run a mile.

The mind-body connection had never been so obvious or so frustrating. Every attempt required intense concentration, visualizing the movement, sending the command, monitoring feedback, adjusting, trying again. It was a full cognitive workout alongside the physical one. Recognizing this as a marathon, I decided to pace myself according to my 1 Percent Rule: after ten attempts, I would take a break. After three or four sets, I would switch to a different exercise for a different part of my body.

By my second session that morning, I could already feel a change. As my leg started to drop, I noticed it was falling slower. Not fully in my control, but for those first critical sections, I was able to brake its descent.

"Yes!" I shouted to the empty room. "That's it, we have contact!"

The signs of life were there: I knew I had at least one functioning neural connection for that movement. Now it was just a matter of practice, practice, practice.

Before I paused for lunch and a nap, I could slow the drop for roughly five times out of ten attempts. I was proud of making such enormous progress and couldn't wait to show my wife when she returned home.

"Watch this," I said, positioning myself on the mat.

I demonstrated the knee bend exercise and the slight control I'd gained in slowing its descent.

"Is that what I think it is?" she asked, her eyes widening.

"Yep. I think NASA has less excitement when they make contact with Mars than I had when I made contact with my own knee."

These tiny movements, barely noticeable to anyone else, meant everything to me. They were proof that all my hard work, patience, and frustration were finally paying off. Now I just needed to keep practicing that single movement, gradually increasing resistance as I improved.

After slowing the drop, I progressed to stopping it completely, first for just a second, then two, then several seconds at different points and angles. Eventually, I could pull it back up as well, initiating the bend from increasingly smaller angles. After a few days of diligent practice, I could lie flat on my stomach with my toes touching the mat and bend my right knee all the way up past 90 degrees without any assistance.

Then I added more challenges: first wearing shoes while performing the movement, then adding small ankle weights. I was elated with my progress, celebrating each milestone and letting the progress fuel my determination to keep pushing forward.

When my physical therapist, Joy, arrived for our next session, she was also impressed with my progress.

"Someone's been doing their homework," she said, watching me demonstrate my new knee control.

"Just following orders," I replied. "Though I'm starting to think my leg works for you better than it works for me."

"That's because I don't accept excuses," she said with a wink. "Ready to try something new today?"

"New is good," I said, remembering my Variety Rule.

I had noticed a tendency in myself to keep doing the exercises I had mastered, going deeper wherever I already felt successful or competent. To avoid the trap of convenience and routine, I had to deliberately force myself to try new things. This was a cognitive exercise as much as a physical one, requiring me to push through my natural resistance to change and learn new patterns.

Each new movement sequence demanded that I build new mental models, anticipate different sensations, and establish new feedback loops between intention and execution. The mental work often exhausted me before my muscles felt any strain.

"Rest the front of your knee against the wall," she instructed. "Now, try to bend it."

Once I achieved full range of motion while using a surface for support, we gradually added weights. The final progression was to perform the movement without support, maintaining my leg in position while flexing only at the knee, a much more precise and challenging task.

To practice, I took a daily walk in the backyard alongside the house wall, where I could grab the wall for support if necessary instead of walking with a cane. I even attempted walking backward, which I had failed to accomplish in rehab. This challenge was primarily cognitive. When moving forward, you can see exactly where you're going, so it's easy to know where to place your foot. Moving backward demanded different awareness, better balance, and constant vigilance against tripping.

"I feel like I'm piloting a spacecraft in reverse," I told my wife as she watched me cautiously step backward along the length of our patio. "Houston, we have a problem: I have no idea where I'm going."

"You're doing fine," she assured me. "Just don't back into the pool."

Revisiting the Stairs

We live in a single-story house with a spacious backyard and just one step at the front and back entrances. While I was grateful to not have to think about stairs often, these single steps became my next challenge. I tackled the lower one at the garage entrance first, planning to graduate to the taller one in the backyard afterward.

Until then, I had cheated on the stairs I faced, always leading with the strength of my left leg. I also had to stand far away from the stair and lift my straight leg forward to place it on the step. But thanks to my newly developed knee-bending abilities, I was determined to climb properly. I learned to stand with my toes touching the stair's edge, lift my leg with a bent knee, and position my foot anywhere on the step without dragging my toes.

I still wore the brace on my leg, which served two crucial functions: preventing my ankle and foot from dropping when I walked, and protecting against turns that might cause injury. My next frontier would be gaining control of my ankle and foot. Mastering this would allow me to walk without the brace like a "normal" person, maybe even run, ride a bike, or drive again.

Joy and I worked intensively on activating my ankle. One key technique was practicing conscious, mindful walking, taking each step in slow motion, placing my foot down heel-first, gradually rolling through the bottom of my foot to my toes, maintaining proper alignment without turning inward or outward, then lifting my heel and pushing off with my toes.

This movement required participation from my entire body, without any single muscle or nerve acting alone. Once again, I was in awe of how truly magnificent our bodies are in their complexity. Climbing even a single stair is a full-body, whole-brain operation that involves numerous muscles, precise coordination, exact timing, and considerable strength.

"Think of walking as meditation in motion," Joy suggested. "Each step requires complete presence."

"So, I'm basically doing a walking meditation whether I want to or not," I replied.

"Exactly! Most people have to work for years to achieve this level of mindful walking," she said with a laugh.

"Lucky me. I get enlightenment and physical therapy all in one package."

I meant it.

In rehab, I had seen the stairs as symbols of my limitations or purely physical obstacles to overcome. But in the familiar context of home, and as time passed, that step became something more profound. Each time I approached that step, I had to slow down completely. There was no rushing through on autopilot. I needed total concentration to feel my weight shift, keep balance, engage precise muscles in sequence, and time each movement exactly. This enforced a level of mindfulness that gradually evolved from frustration into presence.

Just like my meditation practice, the stairs allowed me to be present and aware both in and of the moment. It facilitated the integration between body, mind, and now spirit. What began as necessity had become a sacred practice, converging my spiritual and physical journeys on this one, humble threshold.

Progress remained incremental. The brace had some flexibility, allowing limited ankle movement, but it took months before I could execute even half of this walking sequence properly. Even now, a year later, I'm not at 100 percent. Still, I combined isolated ankle exercises with regular walking practice, taking a "small steps" approach (pun intended). We started by standing in a forward stride position near a counter for support, right leg in front of the left, shifting weight forward and back through my heel. After several repetitions, we progressed to standing with both feet together as I attempted to rise onto my toes. We also incorporated extensive stretching, particularly for my calf muscles. I quickly discovered that stretching had a calming effect on me that often left me feeling energized, yet another intersection of the Body and Spirit pillars.

Revisiting First Steps

During the final week of our at-home sessions, Joy surprised me by suggesting we walk outside. When I opened the door, she stood there for a moment as I hesitated, making sure I wanted to venture beyond our controlled indoor environment. It was a summer morning and not yet hot, but I was afraid of walking on uneven, unforgiving asphalt without a wall or counter within reach to prevent a fall.

Instead of giving in to this fear, I feigned enthusiasm: "I was waiting for you to ask! Hope you'll be able to keep up."

"Oh, it's like that, is it?" she responded, raising an eyebrow. "Should I grab my stopwatch?"

"Maybe an hourglass would be more appropriate," I joked. "I'm going for the slow and steady approach."

There were two routes to our front door: either four wide steps or a sloping path that also led to the garage. I chose the stairs, which proved to be a wise decision, though I didn't know it at the time.

We didn't walk far that day, just back and forth a few times in our quiet suburban neighborhood. There were no cars or people around, so the session was uninterrupted. I practiced turning and picking up small rocks from the ground. I tested my shoe grip on different surfaces, sidewalk, paved road, small side slopes, gentle inclines and declines. Then, on our return journey, I decided to try the slope instead of the stairs. It wasn't particularly steep and only about 15 feet long, but after taking just one step, I felt myself losing balance. Instinctively, I sat down immediately to avoid falling.

Joy's face went white and she rushed toward me, never far behind, asking if I was okay.

"Just taking a quick break," I said, trying to play it cool while sitting awkwardly on the ramp. "Thought I'd admire the view from down here."

She had tried to warn me about ramps, but I hadn't given her the chance, dismissing their potential difficulty. The stairs had seemed much more challenging than a flat, wide, shallow ramp. I had assumed that since I managed the stairs going down, the slope would pose no problem. I was wrong.

"So," I said, still sitting on the ramp, "I'm guessing this wasn't part of the plan?"

"I tried to tell you about ramps," she said, helping me up. "They're actually trickier with the brace than stairs."

"I think I got that memo now," I replied. "Delivered express to my backside."

Joy explained that the brace excelled at keeping my foot and ankle straight for walking on flat surfaces, but that same rigidity became a liability on the slope. When I took my second step, the inability to flex my ankle while my foot was flat on the inclined ground forced my body into an awkward, unstable position. She advised either avoiding ramps entirely or approaching them straight-on or sideways, always with my cane positioned on the downhill side for stability.

Feeling a wave of humility wash over me, I took this advice seriously, once again admitting to myself that some things weren't just about effort or determination. I didn't attempt that ramp again for many months, and I still exercise extreme caution on inclined surfaces.

Recovery required me to respect my new limits, at least until I was strong enough to challenge them safely, and progress required strategic adaptation.

Some challenges couldn't be overcome with sheer willpower; they required technique, tools, and a willingness to find alternative paths when needed.

REFLECTION SPACE

"The breakthrough starts in my mind first."

That day on the ramp, sitting on my backside after one overly confident step, I learned something crucial: recovery is about knowing the difference between a challenge and a limitation. About recognizing where your growth edge ends and where you need to humbly respect your limits.

It's a thin, shifting, curvy line that we have to find and rebalance every single day.

How do you know when you're at your growth edge versus when you're pushing too far into territory you're not yet ready for?

Can you be honest with yourself and read the signs when you're getting close to that line?

Can you identify your "ramp" and, just for now, avoid it? Maybe make it tomorrow's edge instead of today's?

Is there anyone who can help you see that line clearly?

Maybe there's an expert who can help you know what's an edge and what's a limitation, especially when your vision gets clouded by frustration or false confidence. Listen to them. This isn't about giving up. It's about being smart. There is strength in effort, but there's also strength in restraint. Sometimes, the bravest thing is to pause, reassess, and come back wiser.

Keep showing up. Keep listening. You're not failing when you fall, as long as you learn from it and get up again.

16

FINDING PATTERNS IN PROVIDENCE

Healing is an inside job.

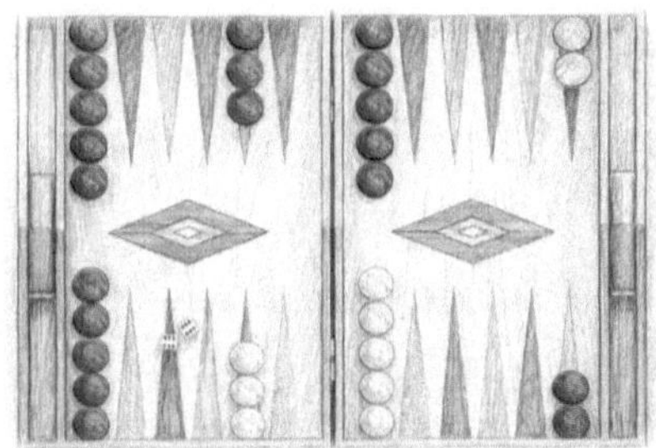

WHEN people heard I'd had a stroke, their eyes immediately went to my leg and my cane, the physical manifestations of my condition. They could see me limping, notice my awkward grip on objects, observe my slower movements. The subtle but significant changes in how my brain processed information, recalled memories, and managed complex tasks remained invisible. There was no formal assessment or direct way to see my progress in cognitive rehabilitation, so I had to test my capabilities in real-time and remain conscious of my limitations on my own.

Speaking presented the initial challenge. Then came short-term and long-term memory issues, problem-solving, multitasking, and other executive functions. I continued to seek out cognitive training apps and used them every opportunity I had (not just in the bathroom). And in my weekly speech therapy sessions, we practiced multitasking, memory, or both.

The therapist recommended Sudoku if crosswords weren't suitable due to my dyslexia. They demanded intense thinking, memory skills, logical reasoning, counting, and conditional logic, all valuable cognitive exercises, and I became obsessed. I even participated in online Sudoku tournaments and achieved high rankings. But my bubble burst when I told her about my amazing achievement. With little to no emotion, she replied, "So you figured out how to solve Sudoku. It's like figuring out how to solve a Rubik's Cube; you learned how to."

I thought my Sudoku success had demonstrated broad cognitive recovery. After all, each puzzle was a unique challenge requiring fresh problem-solving skills. But I'd simply mastered a specific algorithm, a series of patterns and techniques that, once learned, I could repeat to solve a puzzle. I was no longer using my brain as I had in the first few times before I "mastered" it. I was just mechanically executing a memorized sequence.

This distinction was crucial. True cognitive rehabilitation required variety. I needed to force my brain into uncomfortable and challenging tasks so it could create new connections rather than reinforcing existing ones. Mastering Sudoku had placed me in a comfort zone that felt like progress but was actually a plateau. Embarrassingly enough, that was exactly why I'd created the Variety Rule in my recovery. It prevented me from getting obsessed with one type of exercise and losing focus on what was important.

Watching for Signs

My progress in speech recovery had been measured both by the lack of reaction from people who didn't know me before the stroke and by honest feedback from those who did. Once basic communication was restored, I was ready to challenge myself further.

Before my stroke, I had regularly mentored young entrepreneurs, founders of technology startups seeking guidance on their ventures. These mentoring relationships had been intellectually demanding but deeply rewarding. I decided this would make a perfect cognitive workout. *What better way to test your swimming abilities than by jumping into the deep end?* So I reached out to one of those founders I'd been advising before my stroke and cautiously resumed our sessions.

The experience proved to be a partial success, and a humbling reality check. My deliberate, measured speaking style could pass for thoughtful confidence to those who hadn't known me before. But I was acutely aware that I wasn't operating at my previous level.

Multitasking had once been my superpower in these dynamic discussions. I could jump from topic to topic, and my calendar was always full with back-to-back meetings on all different topics. While on calls, I could also send emails and instant message. Throughout the day, I could manage chores, handle all the financials, navigate investments, and take care of everyone plus myself. I never "just" folded the laundry, or "just" cooked diner or "just" walked on the treadmill. I was always doing something else. Now, even the smallest overlap of tasks completely overwhelmed me.

The most concerning change was my lack of confidence in my own reasoning and decision-making. Previously, I could quickly analyze a business model, identify critical issues, and propose creative solutions all in one session. Now, I was second-guessing every insight, wondering if my cognitive "glitches" were affecting my judgment. This experience provided a sobering measurement of the work still ahead, and a great deal of motivation to do it. The deep end hadn't drowned me, but I also wasn't swimming with the grace I once had.

Reading was its own challenge. I hadn't attempted to read a book yet, but even reading phone messages or signs and billboards took longer. I would stare at words, no matter how familiar they seemed, then process them letter by letter.

Everything that had once been automatic now required conscious effort.

Typing presented another significant obstacle. My entire career depended on computer use, and I had been a quick typist before the stroke. Just before I was discharged to go home, I asked my wife to bring my work laptop so I could deal with work and insurance matters. Unfortunately, simply opening it, literally grabbing the lid and pulling it up and away, proved difficult.

When typing, I had to try hard not to rely solely on my left hand's fingers and to use more than one finger on my right hand. Over time, I was able to type with multiple right-hand fingers, but with much less accuracy than I preferred, often pressing two keys simultaneously or missing the letter completely. Additionally, after several failed attempts to use a mouse, I abandoned it altogether and only used the touchpad with my left hand.

At home, I had a more ergonomic setup with a split keyboard featuring wrist rests and a vertical mouse. Surprisingly, these were even more challenging to use. Instead, I placed my laptop on the desk and practiced growing my abilities with a standard keyboard and mouse. To practice, I used the desktop interface for WhatsApp to send messages to my wife, mother, siblings, and friends. I began with short messages and gradually progressed to emails, all of which took more time and effort than I hoped, with many errors and double keystrokes. I did learn to use the backspace key, constantly.

Like any new skill, typing exhausted both my mind and body. My hand, palm, and wrist muscles needed frequent breaks. Ironically, I couldn't even shake my hand to release tension. I could move it side to side deliberately, but I couldn't control it precisely enough to shake it. Instead, I used my left hand to grasp and shake my right hand, which didn't quite create the level of relief I expected.

I tried not to let this progress affect me emotionally, but my entire career depended on computer use, with typing as the primary interface. I frequently reminded myself to be patient and not get frustrated. But sometimes, especially after multiple failures, I broke down. I even flipped the keyboard away in frustration a few times, growling at my hands and walking away from my desk in anger. It was a painful reminder of just how much I had lost and what that might mean for my future.

During these breakdowns, no logical explanation or self-talk could immediately dispel the rage. Only deep breathing and time could change my focus and reduce the frustration to manageable levels. I would go exercise, choosing something satisfying like resistance-band workouts, and hope that breaking a sweat would distract me from the frustration and anxiety. Then I would remind myself of my recovery framework: that this was a marathon, that I had anticipated difficult days, that tomorrow would be different, that my best improvements came from mistakes, that change was happening even when I couldn't see it…

I had to pay attention to subtle signs of improvement. The growth was there, but it primarily revealed itself in the absence of mistakes rather than in positive achievements. Fewer instances of difficulty finding words, less mental fatigue after conversations, improved ability to follow complex discussions, these were not as easy to spot as how far I could lift my arm or bend my knee.

To compensate for these deficits, I leveraged my professional knowledge as much as I could. Since all of my work interactions were virtual, I gradually created a comprehensive system of tools and techniques to support my struggling brain. For example, I recorded every conversation, then used AI tools to transcribe and summarize them. These systems identified action items, tracked their completion, and even sent me reminders when tasks were due. Creating, integrating, and working with these tools required its own focus, memory, and executive function, precisely the areas where I struggled, but in a controlled environment, where initial mistakes wouldn't have serious consequences.

Surprisingly, what began as compensation for deficits evolved into something more valuable: I discovered that this structured approach actually improved my efficiency. It forced me to become more organized than I'd ever been before, as I traded my previous speed and agility for methodical order and precision. What started as a crutch became an enhancement.

One evening, about two months after returning home, I closed my workday by meditating in my home office as sunset painted the walls with golden light. A profound realization surfaced: Maybe my grandmother and my sister were right. Maybe this stroke hadn't happened to me, maybe it happened *for* me. Maybe it was an inflection point, where life offered a change in direction that I was invited to accept.

The stroke had taken so much, but what it had ultimately given me was much greater: a more authentic relationship with myself, a deeper appreciation for each moment, and a clearer sense of purpose. I understood then that the most important healing occurred in dimensions no MRI could capture. Therapists had helped rebuild my body. Cognitive exercises strengthened my mind. But only I could reconstruct my inner landscape.

Beyond Luck

It was a bright, sunny Sunday morning, almost five months into my recovery journey. The morning sun warmed my skin. Birds chirped from our neighbor's tree. I had done my morning meditation practice and had breakfast with my daughter. Then she went straight to her new Switch game, the one she kept reminding me had been purchased with her own money, and I went outside to our backyard.

My mood was odd. Not happy, not sad, but "just okay." It was a feeling I had started to get used to but didn't like.

I sat on the gray outdoor sofa, running my hand over the stained fabric, marked by last summer's barbecues and the winter's rain. I needed to clean it. *Deep clean it.* I was sure those would be the first words my wife would say if she came out just then.

As if I had called to her, the glass door slid open and my beautiful wife poked her head out right then. She was still in her PJs, and both that and her hair indicated she had just woken up.

"Good morning, love. Remember you have a blood test today, and after that I'm going to have my nails done. We'll have to leave at 9:30 the latest."

"I'm ready," I responded. "Just let me know when we are leaving." I lifted my hand off of the sofa and blew out a kiss.

"This is dirty, how can you sit on it? You need to clean it. Like, deep clean it. Bleach it or something?" Then she blew a kiss back and slid the door closed behind her.

Chores were now part of my recovery plan, gentle challenges for my mind and body that have easily measurable success and create a sense of accomplishment afterward. But I still didn't feel like it. I felt like talking to my mother. Conversations with her were always about what was going well, what was improving, and plans for the future. She will not give me things to do, I thought. The stroke had stripped away many of my defenses, making it easier to admit such things.

She picked up the video call before it even rang.

I could tell she was outside as well. The bright sunlight cast a shadow on her face and illuminated the tall green bushes in her backyard that I used to trim when my grandmother lived there. I imagined her sitting on the old swing chair my dad built when my brother was born. It wasn't swinging anymore, but it was sturdy.

"Nir-oosh! So good to see you! How are you feeling today?" Her face lit up the screen, lines wrinkling around her eyes as she smiled.

I was in no rush, and neither was she. I listened to her recount the day, all about who she met with and where she went. She had visited my father at the care facility, bringing him fresh clothes and new shoes, though he barely recognized her now. She'd had coffee with her friend Hannah, who asked about me, and she'd started watching a new show on Netflix but didn't remember what it was called.

I told her about my progress and that I was walking every morning by myself, without the brace but still with a cane, just in case.

"That's wonderful," she said, her eyes misting slightly. "I'm so proud of you."

I don't know what triggered her next question. Possibly because we already exceeded our usual conversation length, or because this was a question she'd tried hard not to ask and couldn't hold it in anymore. After having me recount the story of the stroke again, she asked: "Do they know what caused it? Was it the flight? Was it stress?"

"No, Mother, they don't. Not for sure. I am seeing two of the best stroke research institutes probably in the world. They have a list of hypotheses, theories of what could have caused the stroke, and we are working on eliminating each one of them. But it will take time. They also said that we might never know for sure."

She nodded slowly, digesting this information. Her hand moved to touch a small pendant around her neck, something she always did when she was thinking deeply.

"I'm glad that it happened when you were home," she said, then continued, "I'm not 'glad' that it happened. But imagine if it happened on your flight?!"

"Yes, Mom. I was supposed to be on a flight or in a hotel in Portland that morning, but I didn't catch the flight," I responded. "I guess I was lucky."

Then I tried to joke by continuing, "Come to think of it, it was the perfect time and place to have a stroke. The only better time and place to have a stroke would be in the hospital while the doctor that treated me was starting her shift." It was way too soon and not the right crowd. She took it literally, and simply nodded her head in acknowledgement.

Then she leaned closer to the camera, her eyes suddenly intense. "I told you; someone is watching over you. Do you remember the first time I told you that?"

I paused to think. She had said it on a few occasions, but when was the first time? Before I could answer, or even remember, she continued.

"Do you remember your trip to Sinai just after your graduation?"

That night came back to me with surprising clarity, the breeze off the Red Sea, the stars impossibly bright overhead, the laughter around the fire…just before the explosion.

"Ah ha," I confirmed. "I was very lucky. Very."

Sinai Desert was "only" four hours from my university, and it had everything I loved: sun, an endless virgin beach, the bluest and clearest water in the world, and a desert mountain on the other side. It was also isolated. No electricity or phone or stores or restaurants. Just scattered straw huts and a central, single-floor building that served as a "restaurant" using a generator that worked only sporadically. It was peaceful there. Everything slowed down.

The central building was attached to a large tent with carpets and palm logs, creating a gathering place where you could light a fire at night. There were tens of those places along the Red Sea shore in Sinai desert, but I went to the same one every time I had a few days to escape.

To get there, I crossed the border in Eilat with my traveling partner, and we took an Egyptian taxi the rest of the way. A two-hour drive to nowhere sets you in the right mood. I recognized the turn to my favorite beach by the broken sign, tilted onto its side. The taxi turned there, and after a short drive on a dirt road, we had arrived.

The owner approached us as soon as we arrived, telling me in perfect Hebrew that he was sorry but he didn't have any huts for me. He pointed at the place nearby.

"They have a place, I'm sure of that. It's only 100 meters." Then he teased me, "You are welcome here later if you want to lose again in backgammon," and laughed.

Later that night, we sat on a palm log covered with a rug, waiting endlessly for our food in the place that he had suggested to us. There was no moon, so it had been too dark to walk to my friend's to beat him in backgammon. The sky was beautiful. I remember saying out loud, "I have never seen so many stars. Not even in Sinai."

It was quiet, as expected. Just the night sounds of crickets, a few conversations around us, dice hitting the wooden backgammon board, and someone playing a guitar. I didn't hear the explosion until after I saw the flash of light. A split second after, it felt like something had hit me, pushing me off balance and off the log I was sitting on. I looked up to see a red mushroom ball of fire coming from the other gathering tent. The one that was full. The one that it had been too dark to walk to.

In the morning, we learned that it had been a suicide car bomb that drove straight to the people in the gathering tent. Two people were killed and a dozen more injured, most of them students at my university. There had been another explosion at the hotel near the border, as well, taking the lives of over twenty people. We saw the hotel on our way back across the border, half of it was broken, like it had been cut by a surgical scalpel.

"You are my gift child," my mother interrupted my thoughts, correcting me for saying I was just lucky. "You were given to me as a gift fifty years ago, and many times again since. I thank God every day for that." Her voice grew soft. "You always come back to me. You are my gift."

As she spoke those words, something shifted inside me, deep in my chest, like a knot loosening. For the first time, I truly connected the dots between that night in Sinai and what happened five months ago when my stroke hit.

If the huts at my favorite place hadn't been full...if my partner and I had chosen a spot closer to that gathering tent...if we had decided to join the group rather than play backgammon...

If my daughter had been wearing her headphones like she usually did...if my wife hadn't been home...if I had caught that flight to Portland, if I hadn't forgotten my ID at home that morning...if I had been alone in a hotel room rather than at home where my family could call for help immediately...

All these tiny coincidences, these little shifts in routine, these seemingly random circumstances weren't just luck. They were part of a pattern I'd been too stubborn to see. And the pattern extended beyond those two incidents. There was also the tsunami, the robbery, the wasp, the motorcycle accident, and cancer.

Yes, they all contained a mix of pure luck, guardian angels, karma, or being at the right or wrong place at the right or wrong time. But more importantly, each experience had given me the opportunity to notice a mismatch between my heart and what I was doing or where I was going. Sometimes, I had been blinded by ego, as with the cancer or army experience. Other times it was love that clouded my judgment, as during the bombing incident, the robbery, or the motorcycle accident. The tsunami simply came when I was still finding my way in life.

The stroke contained elements of all these experiences, but it also gave me the opportunity to see death as a realistic outcome. And not for just a second like it had during the robbery. This had been a slow drift toward the end of my life, a "curtain closing" that provided both the time and environment to reflect on life and death alike. Like the others, it had called attention to how far I had wandered from myself. But it had also issued the challenge to find my way back.

Once again, my grandmother's words came back to me: "Darkness teaches us to appreciate the light." Now, I had to apply the lessons from all of my brushes with darkness. I had to recognize what was being revealed to me and evolve from it.

After we hung up, I sat there on the dirty sofa for a long time, thinking about all things I had taken for granted. I realized that my third pillar had been missing a crucial element, something beyond meditation routines and visualization techniques. I was missing a deeper level of gratitude, specifically for the "coincidences" that had placed me exactly where I needed to be, even when it didn't feel that way at the time.

I found myself saying out loud, "I am always where I need to be."

Perhaps the biggest "stroke" of luck wasn't surviving the bombing or even surviving the hemorrhage in my brain. Maybe it was finally waking up to the truth my mother and grandmother had been showing me all along, that sometimes our worst moments contain within them the seeds of our greatest transformation.

REFLECTION SPACE

Even in the darkest night, your eyes eventually adjust.

My journey has had two tracks: the visible and the invisible. This chapter focused on the second one, the hidden path. The one no one sees but you. For me, that path ran through my mind and my spirit. My cognitive jitters, emotions changing, and the quiet meanings I started to be open to. This path turned out to be the glue, the thread that held it all together, connecting the work of healing my body and my brain with myself and the world.

What are the hidden parts of your recovery? The things that only you know you're struggling with?

When do you notice them? New emotions you're not used to having? Cognitive challenges? Fears? Thoughts? Things you're saying to yourself?

Those things are harder to measure and easier to fake. So this one is up to you, which makes it harder. But you've got this!

Can you notice moments where something bigger seemed to nudge you?

It could be in a religious way, if that speaks to you. It could be a pattern, a message, a sense that you were exactly where you needed to be. Something beyond coincidence.

What would happen if you let yourself believe, even a little, even just for a moment, that there is meaning in some of what you've been through? Not answers, not "for a reason." Just a little meaning.

Doesn't it feel better just knowing that, maybe, this is true?

Healing often looks like patience, surrender, and trusting yourself again. They might look like nothing from an outside perspective, but they're still a big deal. Maybe more than anything else.

17

———

EXPANDING HORIZONS

*The body can achieve more when the mind
and spirit are fully engaged.*

"So, this is it?" I asked Joy as she prepared to leave for the last time. Our final at-home session marked a significant transition. We focused on practical matters, showering safely, taking out the trash, getting in and out of the car. Basic tasks that would determine my independence at home. Then the therapists packed their equipment and handed me their final recommendations.

She smiled encouragingly. "This is just the beginning of the next phase. You've got all the tools now. Time to put them to work."

An important stage of my recovery journey was coming to a close.

> "This is just the beginning of the next phase. You've got all the tools now. Time to put them to work."

FIRST STAGE OF RECOVERY

The first stage had been about survival and basic functioning. It started when the paramedics lifted me from my office floor and continued through the ER and ICU. I had minimal control and was completely at the mercy of medical systems and protocols. All I could do was hold on while doctors and nurses worked to stabilize me and assess the damage.

THE SECOND STAGE OF RECOVERY

The second stage had been about rebuilding fundamental capabilities. Through intensive therapy, first at the rehabilitation facility and then at home, I had relearned basic functions: talking coherently, using the toilet independently, feeding myself, standing up, turning around, and eventually walking with assistance. By its conclusion, I was functioning at about 60 percent of my pre-stroke self, a tremendous achievement considering where I'd started.

THE THIRD STAGE OF RECOVERY

Now I was entering the third stage, what I called the "refinement phase." My goal was to reach 85 percent of my previous capabilities. This meant strengthening my right side and entire body, making newly relearned skills instinctive rather than deliberate, and functioning smoothly enough that strangers wouldn't notice anything unusual. For those who knew me before, I wanted any differences to be subtle enough that they'd only notice "something" different after spending time with me.

Ultimately, I wanted to walk normally, ride my bike again, practice yoga, participate actively in work meetings both virtual and in-person, and all with the same mental sharpness I'd had before. Unlike the dramatic improvements of the earlier stages, I anticipated this refinement stage would bring slower, sometimes imperceptible progress toward these benchmarks. There might even be periods of regression. I prepared myself for this reality, knowing that if I expected it, I wouldn't be surprised or discouraged when it happened.

The rules I'd developed in the previous stages remained my guide. I was still running a marathon, and I'd need to push consistently but not excessively. Variety would prevent boredom. I needed to work on all aspects of recovery simultaneously and seek expert guidance when needed. And above all, I needed to keep my spirit motivated. This last part, maintaining psychological resilience through slow progress, would likely prove more challenging than before.

One morning, I was standing by myself in my living room, looking at the stack of printouts my therapist had left me. They were the same exercises I'd been doing for a while, but looking at them now created a quiet sense of dread. It was the weight of knowing this was what progress looked like now. Not dramatic. Not exciting. Not new.

The substantial early gains, like standing on one leg or walking to the mailbox, were behind me. Now came the subtler, less visible work.

When I shared these thoughts with my sister, she told me, "You need to leave room for sadness. You can't be positive and determined every minute of every day."

Reflecting on previous difficult periods in my life, I realized that in times when I'd fallen into dark places or experienced depression, there had always been legitimate reasons for sadness, even if I had not allowed myself to feel it. The situations were objectively challenging. Allowing space for sadness would have meant occasionally feeling sorry for myself, taking breaks from constantly pushing forward, and simply feeling my feelings. These emotions deserved acknowledgment and expression, including tears when necessary.

I also resolved to treat myself as I would a best friend, with compassion, wisdom, and perspective. I would remind myself of truths that are easy to know intellectually but difficult to embrace emotionally: that the future holds hope and mystery; that when one door closes, many others open; that these doors had always been there, but now I could see them; that what seems painful or limiting in the moment often leads to growth and renewal.

This was hard-earned wisdom set into motion.

Years before, when I had cancer and went through aggressive chemotherapy treatment, I had reached a point where I barely had the strength to breathe, where my whole body ached down to the bones. During one particularly dark moment, where I wished it would all simply end, a song played in the background with a line that I clung to: "Tomorrow, tomorrow, there will always be a tomorrow…"

That simple truth had sustained me then, and it could support me now. No matter what happened, tomorrow would eventually come. This difficult phase would end. Each day brought me closer to recovery, even when I couldn't perceive the progress.

KISS, Keep It Simple, Stupid

> ### KISS, KEEP IT SIMPLE, STUPID
>
> To maintain momentum through the slowness and inevitable setbacks, I adopted another principle: ease over perfection. Or, as we say at work, KISS, *Keep It Simple, Stupid*. In a journey where overthinking and perfectionism could easily become barriers to progress or might lead me to push too hard, simplicity became my most reliable ally. No need to optimize. Start with what's doable. Refine later.

For example, while the professional gym that I used to attend offered superior equipment, getting there involved significant "administrative time," packing a bag, waiting for an Uber, traveling, changing clothes, then reversing the entire process to return home. If going to the gym cost too much energy just to get there, what was the point? Instead, I relied on a personal gym I had converted the living room into. At home, I could exercise whenever I wanted, wearing whatever was comfortable, without wasting precious energy on logistics. My equipment was more limited, but it was entirely adequate for my current needs. Not fancy, but functional. And most importantly, sustainable.

I refined my schedule into a reliable daily routine that accommodated the rhythms of my household:

6:00 AM: Wake up, meditate for thirty to forty-five minutes

6:45 AM: Breakfast with my daughter while she prepares for school

7:30 AM: After she leaves, make breakfast for my wife, then call family in Israel

8:30 AM: Computer time for cognitive exercises

12:00 PM: Lunch, followed by a short nap if needed (which was often)

1:30 PM: Afternoon physical exercises until my daughter returns at 3:00

6:00 PM: Family dinner

8:00–9:00 PM: Family time

9:00 PM: Sleep, usually the first to retire, exhausted from the day's efforts

This structure strategically integrated all three pillars of my framework. Physical exercises rebuilt my body, cognitive tasks strengthened my mind, and meditation and family connections nourished my spirit. The routine provided psychological security, a foundation from which I could gradually build my capabilities.

Still, even a solid structure couldn't prevent the slow fade of motivation. As I expected, the repetition quickly became monotonous. Doing the same exercises each day felt robotic, and without the energy and encouragement of a therapist, it was easy to lose focus. My body showed up, but my mind wandered. I needed something to shake me up.

That's when I turned to YouTube.

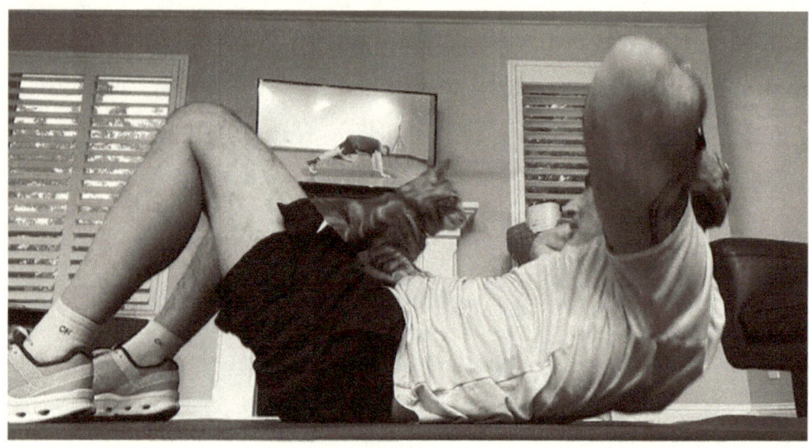

I started searching for beginner workouts I could do at home: "strength, no equipment, recovery, rehab." To my surprise, I found hundreds of videos. Some were terrible, but others had exactly what I needed. They were full of energy, variety, and a sense of momentum. Instructors talked directly to the camera like they believed in me. I didn't care if it was pre-recorded, I needed to have someone cheering me on.

Then I added small tools to make the experience feel more real: a full-length standing mirror like the one I'd used in rehabilitation, resistance bands in varying strengths, and ankle weights. These simple additions made the exercises more engaging and effective. I also attempted beginner yoga but quickly realized I wasn't ready. Most poses required a level of balance, strength, and range of motion that I still lacked. So I added "being able to do beginner yoga" to my list of milestones that would signal advancement through this recovery stage.

To combat my tendency to fall into comfortable routines, I put my Variety Rule into action again, deliberately seeking out new instructors, new methods, and new exercises to keep both body and mind engaged. Variety was brain training. It kept me present and forced new neural connections rather than allowing autopilot to take over.

This balance, between simplicity and variety, between structure and flexibility, became central to my long-term recovery strategy. Boredom led to adaptation which refined structure. Recovery at this stage wasn't about breakthroughs. It was about consistency. It was about showing up, even when I didn't feel like it. *Especially* then.

"Just remember," I reminded myself, "eighty-five percent will be more than enough."

I believed it. I had to. It was the only way to keep going.

Single-Minded Focus

Not long after my formal at-home therapy concluded, my father-in-law and his wife arrived for a visit. He's an eighty-year-old water scientist with the curiosity, and sometimes behavior, of a ten-year-old boy. A brilliant mind, constantly fascinated by new technologies, and eager to learn about anything unfamiliar.

Despite his age, he also maintains impressive fitness through daily walks and morning crunches. "Haven't had back problems since I started," he often declares, and it's a claim I've come to believe.

The evening after they settled in, he asked about potential walking routes near our house.

"There's a nice half-mile loop around the neighborhood," I suggested, then impulsively added, "I could join you if you'd like."

"Splendid idea," he replied with characteristic enthusiasm. "Tomorrow morning? First light?"

Now that we were both early risers, thanks to my new routine, we agreed to meet around 6 AM. I suggested we each prepare for the walk separately, then meet by the front door, knowing that any pre-walk conversations could easily consume the entire morning before we even stepped outside.

It was still dark out when I entered the kitchen the following morning. The sun hadn't yet appeared, but gray light had begun to illuminate the streets. He stood by the door, fully equipped for his constitutional, walking shoes, oversized sun hat, and long-sleeved UV-protective shirt.

"Shall we confirm our walk together?" he asked formally, as though verifying an appointment.

"Confirmed," I replied, matching his tone. "Just need to put on my brace and shoes."

Our wives hovered nearby, poorly concealing their concern. They checked the location-sharing apps on their phones, requested we review the route one more time, and repeatedly asked if I was certain I didn't want more company.

"We'll be fine," I assured them, strapping my cane to my arm. "It's just a short walk."

As soon as we stepped outside, my father-in-law launched into a detailed monologue about the intersection of big data and agricultural technology, with a particular focus on water conservation innovations in California and their parallels to Israeli developments. He asked if I knew certain professors working in the field, seeming surprised when I didn't, as though all Israelis must certainly know each other.

He possessed that rare quality I've always appreciated in colleagues and friends, genuine passion for his expertise, knowledge unavailable from public sources, and pure joy in sharing it. Though I only retained perhaps half of what he explained, his tendency toward elaborate technical tangents being what it was, the information itself wasn't the point. The connection, the sharing of enthusiasm, was what mattered.

Before either of us had realized what we'd done, we completed not one but *two* complete circuits of the neighborhood. When we passed our house the second time, we decided to go inside for water and continue our conversation at the dining table.

Only then did it hit me: that was the longest continuous walk I'd completed since my stroke! Engaging my mind had allowed my body to surpass its previous limitations.

The following morning, we embarked on an even longer route, where I believe we both approached our physical limits. During the final three-minute uphill climb to our house, conversation ceased entirely as we concentrated on simply finishing.

The body can endure much more than we think it can. Without his company, I would have given up much earlier, and it would have been justifiable. But I wouldn't have grown as much. When we reach the edge of our abilities and our mind and body tell us that it's hard, that we can't do this, that it is time to stop, that is where our spirit comes in. It tells us that we can. That we have the resilience. That we are not our thoughts or our aching body, but we are so much more.

> When we reach the edge of our abilities and our mind and body tell us that it's hard, that we can't do this, that it is time to stop, that is where our spirit comes in.

SINGLE-MINDED FOCUS BODY

Because I was engrossed in our conversation, I was not thinking about how long we had or how far we went. I was just focused on the step in front of me, placing my foot the right way, moving the weight from one leg to the other. When my mind and spirit were fully engaged, my body could achieve more. This is made possible by focusing only on the present moment.

This is made possible by focusing only on the present moment. Because I was engrossed in our conversation, I was not thinking about how long we had or how far we went. I was just focused on the step in front of me, placing my foot the right way, moving the weight from one leg to the other. When my mind and spirit were fully engaged, my body could achieve more.

We maintained this routine throughout their visit. By the week's end, I realized with a mixture of pride and amusement that I was now walking better than an eighty-year-old man, a modest achievement, perhaps, but a clear sign of progress.

I maintained this morning walking routine even after they left. I would wake early, meditate, have breakfast with my daughter, then prepare for my walk. My brace, cane, fanny pack (which kept my hands free for the cane), and earbuds became standard equipment. Then after she left for school at 7:30, I would wait a few additional minutes before heading out, at her explicit, teenaged request not to be seen with her by any classmates.

Without my father-in-law to converse with, I listened to audiobooks to keep my mind engaged. A therapist recommended *Autobiography of a Yogi*, mentioning that Steve Jobs had kept it on his iPod. While the content itself was only moderately engaging, the narrator's deep, soothing voice became the perfect soundtrack for my morning journeys. Even after I finished the book, I would often replay random sections just to maintain that comforting vocal accompaniment.

Because I had maintained good cardiovascular fitness before the stroke, the physical exertion of walking wasn't particularly challenging. The real work lay in refining the quality of my gait. I had to walk with conscious awareness in order to place my right foot with intention, precision, and care. Maintaining this focus proved surprisingly difficult. My mind constantly wanted to wander, requiring frequent reminders to return attention to my steps.

I also needed to maintain awareness of multiple factors around me: the surface beneath me (was it wet, slippery, dry, uneven?), my broader surroundings (where was I heading, where were potential hazards?), traffic when crossing streets, and any curbs and slopes beneath me. It was a complex cognitive task requiring continuous attention.

Yet amidst this intense level of concentration, I also enjoyed unexpected moments of beauty. The morning light that illuminated the dewdrops hanging from grass blades. A butterfly that seemed to follow me for several minutes. One morning, I photographed an enormous spiderweb adorned with water droplets that sparkled in the sunlight like Christmas lights. The architect sat proudly at the center of her web, both majestic and fearsome with her striped body and impressive legs extended. When I passed the same spot days later, both spider and web had vanished, a reminder of life's impermanence that resonated with my spiritual pillar.

I maintained consistent routes each week, gradually increasing either my pace or my distance, but never both simultaneously. Though my smartwatch tracked the metrics of these walks, I didn't need technology to tell me when it became easier. My body knew. Whenever the challenge became comfortable, I would extend the route.

What began as a ten-minute walk with my father-in-law expanded to two half-mile rounds before he went home, and then to thirty minutes on my own within weeks. After a month, I could maintain a good pace for forty-five minutes. The following month, I completed 2.5 miles without any unusual fatigue.

I also incorporated at least one weekly rest day for my body to recover. After skipping a day or two of intense walking, I noticed that my next outing would feature improved strength, precision, and overall quality. This observation reinforced my Rest Rule and confirmed that progress wasn't solely about continuous pushing; strategic recovery was equally important. In response, I featured this principle in my routine. In between challenging sessions, I would pause for a day of low-intensity activity (perhaps just stretching) or complete rest.

Three months into this practice, I felt ready to attempt a significant challenge: a five-mile walk. That morning, I prepared meticulously, extra water in my fanny pack, hat, sunscreen, and notably, no cane. I had abandoned it the previous week after realizing it had become unnecessary and potentially problematic. It required one hand to hold, complicating tasks like checking my phone or adjusting earbuds, a complexity that could actually cause accidents rather than prevent them.

Before I set out, I stood at my starting point, activated my tracking app, and repeated a mental mantra: *the most important goal today is to not injure myself.* I knew my personality. Once I began and my heart rate increased, adrenaline and excitement would build alongside the sweat and heavy breathing, and maintaining this safety awareness would become challenging. I needed to implant this priority into my mind so that it would remain accessible even when my cognitive resources were primarily devoted to physical exertion.

Midway through the walk, my prediction proved accurate. Breathing hard, sweating profusely, walking faster than usual, I checked my heart rate to see that it was over 140 beats per minute. I had entered that mental zone where oxygen prioritization limited me to perhaps one conscious thought. That thought became my mantra: *don't fall, don't fall, don't fall.*

I repeated it with each step, maintaining caution in foot placement, ensuring I lifted my right leg with intention rather than dragging it. At my current speed, a single dragging step could send me face-first onto the pavement. I even scanned for patches of grass along my route, preferred landing zones should I stumble in spite of my precautions.

On normal days, I would make eye contact, smile, and offer a "good morning" to the people passing by. But while I was in "the zone," I had to focus all of my attention toward the physical process of walking. Being in that moment required me to control my thoughts, not to drift to other places, not to think about anything but my walk. Making eye contact would have been a distraction that could prove disastrous. Just one imperfect step when my focus shifted to say hello and I would be on the ground.

There was just one exception: an elderly couple I encountered daily, perhaps in their late seventies or early eighties. They always appeared impeccably prepared for the weather, hats, long-sleeved UV shirts, walking shoes, and always held hands while they walked. We never spoke beyond greeting each other, yet I felt a special connection with them and the perpetual smiles illuminating their faces. Whenever we made eye contact, the man's face would light up with a genuine smile that encompassed his mouth, his eyes, and his entire countenance. I believe I smiled back the same way. In my mind, we exchanged more than pleasantries. We shared silent acknowledgment and encouragement: *I know what you're going through. Good job. Well done. I recognize your struggle and respect your effort.*

As I approached them from behind during my five-mile challenge, I deliberately slowed my pace. They walked unhurriedly, so I knew I would still pass them even at reduced speed. I wanted to be able to exchange our usual greeting. As I drew alongside them, I turned slightly, and engaged the steps I had anticipated: I said, "Good morning," waited for their warm response, then returned my gaze forward and resumed my focus on breathing, conscious walking, achievement, and the neurochemical rewards of setting and meeting a challenging goal.

I returned home triumphant and drenched in sweat. My wife was there with the location-tracking app open on her phone, waiting anxiously by the door.

"Five miles?" she asked, eyebrows raised. "That seems a bit ambitious for your first big challenge."

"Had to be done," I replied between deep breaths. "The hardest part wasn't the walking."

"What was it then?"

"Remembering not to fall when all I really wanted was to go faster."

She shook her head with a mixture of exasperation and pride. "You realize eighty-five percent doesn't mean you have to do everything at eighty-five percent *intensity?*"

"Of course," I said, grinning as I wiped sweat from my face. "Some things deserve a hundred."

This accomplishment had required the interaction of all three recovery pillars. The physical achievement was obvious, but equally important was the cognitive discipline of maintaining safety awareness under exertion, as well as the spiritual dimension of pushing boundaries while accepting current limitations.

As I showered away the sweat of achievement, I reflected on how far I'd come since those first tentative steps in rehabilitation. The cane was gone. Five miles were possible. My world was expanding. Though I remained far from complete recovery, each step literally *and* figuratively carried me closer to the life I was rebuilding, not identical to what came before, but richer for having been so consciously constructed.

REFLECTION SPACE

"Simplicity is the ultimate sophistication."
–Leonardo da Vinci

This phase of recovery is where things get quieter. If you're in this phase, you know exactly what I mean. The exercises that once felt like victories now feel like chores. The routine that saved you can start to suffocate you. Everyone thinks you're "better" because you look fine, but you're still fighting for percentages they can't see.

There's less cheering. Fewer therapists. Fewer dramatic improvements. No more first steps, first words, first anything. All that remains is the daily grind and its tiny, invisible gains. It's easy to wonder if you're even moving forward at all and hard to keep showing up every day.

So, I want to ask you:

What's keeping you from slipping, or from pushing too hard just to feel something again? What do you say to yourself? For me, it was the rules, repeated like a mantra in my head.

Are you giving yourself credit for showing up, day after day?

When things get boring or too easy, can you bring back both simplicity and variety to your process? Are there small shifts, routines, or tools that could spark new energy?

The mind is a powerful tool. It can push you or it can hold you back. Can you tell when you need to engage it, like walking with someone to keep you distracted, and when you need to stay laser-focused, like repeating a mantra with every step?

This part of recovery is about staying grounded and showing up even when it's quiet. Even when no one sees. True strength is built here, one steady, invisible step at a time.

PART IV

BEYOND 100 PERCENT

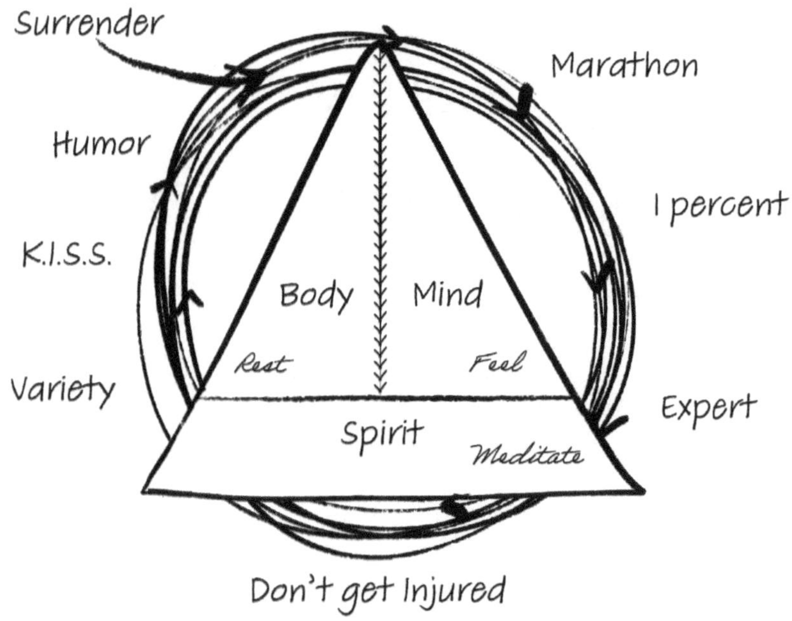

The Recovery Framework: A foundation to build from, and a journey with a clear beginning and no endpoint.

18

———

HEALING THROUGH CONNECTION

The privilege of a lifetime is being who you are.

My fiftieth birthday was coming up. Originally, I had wanted to celebrate with my wife and daughter locally and then party with "the boys" somewhere in the world. We had considered going to Berlin again, or maybe Ibiza, or even Burning Man, but none of those were real options for me now. Still, I was at about 65 percent of my pre-stroke abilities, and I wanted to see my friends.

This need for connection was an essential part of my third pillar of recovery. I desperately needed the company, laughter, silliness, and male companionship of my friends. While physical therapy rebuilt my body and cognitive exercises restored my mind, only genuine human connection could heal certain aspects of my spirit.

"Since you can't fly, what about Vegas? You can drive there, can't you?" Ofir

239

suggested one option during our video call. "Low-key, you know."

We all laughed. "Vegas and low-key is like saying 'stroke' and 'convenient timing,'" I replied.

That idea was dismissed quickly. I couldn't drink, needed more sleep than before, wasn't that stable on my feet, and couldn't afford to fall.

"Why don't we rent an RV and go somewhere?" I suggested. This idea sparked immediate interest. It would be a contained environment where I could rest when needed. No flights were required. And we'd have the freedom to set our own pace. The decision was made.

As the local guy in California, I took responsibility for all the administrative details. They just needed to get to LAX on the date we had picked; everything else would be taken care of. I found an RV to rent for the week, mapped a route with minimal driving, and made reservations at various parks. I also ordered an absurd amount of gear online and had it delivered to my home.

Two days before the guys were set to land at LAX, my brother Roy flew to Sacramento to help me get ready. Together, we packed my car up, and he drove us to Los Angeles to pick up the RV. Throughout that night and the next morning, we collected the rest of our friends as they arrived on different flights. I gave each one a welcome package containing a blanket, pillow, sheet, flashlight, and, most importantly, a strong hug.

A Much-Needed Break

Motti took the lead when we stopped at the grocery store. It turned out, he had become a healthy eater with many dietary restrictions, which immediately became the subject of many jokes. Motti could usually keep a straight face like nothing bothered him, but those of us who had known him since high school could detect exactly when his shield was cracking. When it did, we doubled down until it broke completely.

At one point, he suggested we separate so that he could do his own shopping while we did ours. Obviously, we refused. Partly because we wanted to tease him some more, but also because, though none of us wanted to admit it, we had all started eating healthier in our middle age. Each had his own dietary preferences, and Motti's shopping list gradually became our list too.

More of these roles emerged within our temporary flock of men, naturally falling into patterns established over thirty years of friendship.

Motti became the salad man. He constantly talked about new ingredients that "we" (meaning he) could add and new dressings "we" could make from what we bought. First thing in the morning, and again each time we started thinking about food, he was already up chopping vegetables and encouraging us to try his latest recipe. I have to admit, everything was delicious. Without him, we would have survived on meat, coffee, and beer alone.

Ofir became the meat guy. From the minute we took out the grill, he was hovering around it. The first time we cooked, I had assumed control of the grill, but then quickly handed him the spatula when he started commenting on my technique.

"Close it and let it warm," he instructed. "Where's the fork? Get the onion and some oil." Clearly, he knew what he was talking about. Thinking back, he had always assumed this role in our gatherings, from the beaches of Tel Aviv to our backyard barbecues.

Uri's contribution was to keep everyone's cup full. He ensured our glasses always contained cold beer, soft drinks (non-sugary for Motti), or whiskey. Uri also slept enough for all of us combined. He would fall asleep as soon as we hit the road and not wake up until hours after our arrival. I still don't understand how he managed to sleep through our morning routine of picking on Motti, the smell of coffee filling the RV, our loud voices, and our stamping feet. But we all envied this ability of his.

Roy, my brother from the *same* mother, was everywhere all the time. His role was to be the fixer, joker, and promoter of "let's try it" adventures. He definitely has ADHD, but that comes with a great sense of humor and boundless energy that is a welcome boost when everyone else is drained. If we needed more wood for the fire late at night, he would suddenly appear out of nowhere with a pile in his arms and a "you won't believe what just happened" story.

Roy was also the only one I trusted to drive that beast of an RV. As soon as we parked, he would immediately start setting up what we called the "Zoola," a shade structure with folding chairs around a fire pit and a table loaded with snacks and drinks.

Our first destination, Joshua Tree, provided the perfect backdrop for our time together. We did nothing but exist in each other's company in that beautiful, magical place. It felt like no time had passed since we had been young men together in Israel. I often found myself laughing so hard that tears streamed down my face as I begged for air, usually for no objectively good reason. The jokes weren't that great, and nothing particularly funny happened, but there was this overwhelming feeling of release, freedom, and life itself in our time together.

What struck me most was how they treated me. Not as a recovering stroke patient who needed special attention, but as the same friend they'd always known. They didn't avoid the topic of my stroke, we joked about it frequently, but they didn't define me by it either. When I needed help with something, they provided it matter-of-factly, without making it a big deal.

I can only speak for myself, though I'm certain it was true for all of us: we were simply present. We had all taken a break from our lives, driving or flying across the world for a few precious days together, and we were all truly there. In this temporary universe, it was just us. No judgment, no chores, no kids, no work. Just five days in a remote desert in Southern California, named for the U2 album we had all owned as teenagers.

One night, the conversation around the campfire turned unexpectedly deep. Ofir, who is normally sarcastic and cynical, suddenly asked, "Does anyone else feel like we've created our own little world out here?"

"That's exactly it," Uri said. "We've stepped outside of regular life. I haven't even looked at my emails since we got here."

"Regular life," Motti echoed with a small smile. "I didn't realize how much I needed a break from that until now."

A Walk on the Beach

After several days in Joshua Tree, we moved on to the coast. I wanted them to experience the Pacific Ocean's power, so different from the gentle Mediterranean Sea we had all grown up with.

"This isn't the sea you're used to," I warned as we neared the shore. "You don't just run into these waters, I learned that lesson the hard way. This ocean is huge, cold, and powerful. Home to white sharks and blue whales."

We walked along the beach, moving slowly enough that I could keep up. We stopped as we walked, feeling the wet sand between our toes, breathing in the salty air, and listening to seagulls crying out. We spotted dolphins and possibly distant whales. Motti took out his expensive camera and started taking pictures. As the sun set in spectacular oranges and pinks, we climbed the long staircase from the beach to our campground on top of the cliff.

That last evening together felt different. We were quieter, more thoughtful. We all knew it was ending soon, though we didn't talk about it directly. We had each called home, checked flight details, and mentally prepared to return to "real life." We went to bed earlier than on other nights and, unusually, all woke up at sunrise, even Uri. Then we shared a final breakfast, complete with the inevitable salad from Motti, talking little, each trying to make these final moments last longer.

The drive to LAX was mostly silent, with only Ofir's playlist and the sounds of the highway in the background. We hugged at the terminal, promised to meet again soon, then Roy and I returned the RV and drove home.

As we drove north on I-5, I thought about what the trip had given me beyond simple fun. For five days, I had lived without being defined by the stroke. My friends saw and treated me as the person I've always been, not as a patient or a rehab success story. This feeling, that the core of who I am remained intact despite my physical and cognitive changes, gave me a kind of healing no formal therapy could provide.

> For five days, I had lived without being defined by the stroke. My friends saw and treated me as the person I've always been.

I also realized how far I'd come. Just six months earlier, I had been in the hospital, barely able to move. Not long after that, this trip still would have been impossible, not just physically, but mentally and emotionally. I wouldn't have had the energy for long days, the ability to handle group dynamics, or the emotional strength to fully engage without the protective structure of therapy.

The RV trip didn't heal my brain pathways, improve my right-side coordination, or enhance my memory. Not directly. But it had supported my third pillar, enhancing the recovery of joy, social connection, complete immersion in the present, and my identity beyond my medical diagnosis. My friends had given me the precious gift of being seen not for what had changed but for what stayed the same. Beneath the stroke's visible and hidden effects, my essential self had remained intact.

> Beneath the stroke's visible and hidden effects, my essential self had remained intact.

During one of my morning meditations on the trip, I realized that the first two pillars of my recovery, body and mind, required professional guidance. This third pillar flourished in ordinary moments of genuine connection.

Back home, I was profoundly grateful to find sand in my shoes, solid proof that what already felt like a dream had actually happened. That gritty reminder symbolized my progression beyond regaining function and into making new memories. The laughter around a campfire, the shared silence watching a sunset, the familiar rhythm of old friendships…

These were essential components of my path to wholeness.

◆ ◆ ◆ ◆ ◆ ◆ ◆ ◆ ◆ ◆ ◆ ◆ ◆ ◆ ◆

REFLECTION SPACE

"A friend is someone who knows all about you and still loves you."

It is so powerful to be around people who knew you before it all happened, who see past the limp, the memory gaps, the emotional edge. Who don't treat you like a project or a patient, but just as their friend. Who laugh with you, not despite what you've been through, but including it.

That trip taught me something no therapist could: I was still me. Not "me, considering the circumstances" or "me, doing pretty well for someone who recently had a stroke." Just *me*.

Who are the people that remind you who you are?

Who can you be fully yourself with, no explanations, no apologies, no pity?

Who can you reach out to now, not just to catch up, but to help you reconnect with the parts of yourself that haven't changed?

Think about the kind of friend where you don't even think twice about putting your feet on their table or lying down on their couch. You just feel at home.

If no names come up right away, that's okay.

What kind of connection would feel good to make right now? Maybe there's someone who's walked through something similar. Where might you find them?

It's easy to let recovery become the thing that defines you. But it's just one part of you and your story. For example, I'm short, bald, and hairy, but that's not who I am. Same with my stroke. Same with whatever you're healing from. It's part of you, but it's not the whole you.

You don't need an RV or a desert to discover this truth. The container doesn't matter. What matters is the space, one where you're not performing recovery or proving progress. Just being. Just *you*.

19

———

COLLECTIVE RECOVERY

Behind every person who has overcome adversity,
there is someone else whose life has been equally
upended yet rarely receives equal attention.

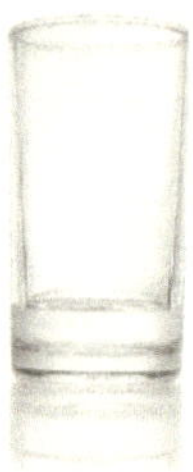

THE brain bleed had changed more lives than just mine on that fateful June morning. My daughter had found me lying on my back, not able to move or talk. She called my wife, who came running from the shower with only a towel wrapped around her. My wife immediately called 911, which became the action that saved my life. Without her presence, I wouldn't have survived that day. But this traumatic beginning was only the first of many challenges she would face in the months to come.

I later learned that she chased behind the ambulance, frantically explaining to hospital security that her husband was behind those doors and she needed to be given access. Even as she processed the shock of what was happening to me, she still had to manage our daughter, who had remained with neighbors and needed to get to her activities and eventually return home.

We didn't utter the "D" word, death, for many months, though it was constantly present for both of us. During those first critical days especially, the unspoken question of "What if he won't make it?" hovered over her head. What she had endured was emotionally as difficult as my own experience, and probably even more so.

On my last day at the rehabilitation unit, just before being discharged to go home, my occupational therapist had shared an important insight with me and my wife: "We often mistakenly think medicine is only about the patient, but in reality, it's about healing the entire system surrounding the patient."

This truth continued to be validated in the months that followed. Recovery doesn't happen in isolation. It occurs within a web of relationships, with caregivers forming the most critical connections in that web.

My progress depended not just on my determination and the skills of my medical team, but on my wife's daily, unheralded efforts to create an environment where healing could happen.

> Recovery doesn't happen in isolation. It occurs within a web of relationships, with caregivers forming the most critical connections in that web.

Life had slapped her hard across the face that morning, just as it had me. Before she could comprehend what was happening, her entire world had turned upside down, and there was nothing she could do to change it. While I was told to take it easy and avoid stress, she was expected to function, to do whatever needed to be done. When I needed to surrender, she was expected to dominate. When I was weak, she was expected to be fearless.

She went "all in" on this role and, to quote my aunt, "fought for you like a lioness!"

That first night, she had "slept" on two chairs pushed together beside my bed. She made only the most essential phone calls herself, creating WhatsApp groups to communicate with everyone else. Then she leveraged every contact and influence possible to connect with the best stroke research units in California, securing top specialists for second and third opinions.

"Your psycho bitch of a wife made this happen," the nurse told me during my weekend discharge to the rehab unit. "She just doesn't take no for an answer."

I was surprised. "What was supposed to happen?" I asked.

"There are advocates, social workers that are supposed to support patients," the nurse explained. "But there's nothing like family. Everybody here knows your wife and is a little bit afraid of her."

I smiled, feeling a surge of pride. This was my wife, relentless, determined, unwavering in her commitment to my care.

It All Matters

Even the smallest light can dispel great darkness.

While our closest loved ones have the greatest impact on us, there are other circles of influence that can be just as important. Like Andrew bringing me black coffee or the Rabbi coming to visit each Friday, these small gestures of kindness extended far beyond what any of them could have realized.

One day, while I was still in the ICU, busy with yet another attempt at recording a message for my mother, the nurse popped in with an announcement: "You have a visitor. He says his name is Nay. Should I let him in?"

To get through the ICU doors, you either needed a hospital badge or a nurse to open them for you. They limited visitors strictly to family and staff, allowing just a few of even those privileged guests in at a time. I looked at my wife for an answer, and she immediately understood my confusion. "Nay, the drum teacher," she clarified.

Nay owns the music school where my daughter learns drums, and he's the only instructor she genuinely likes. He's gentle, patient, a good listener, and, on top of all that, he's cool. Though, honestly, if I didn't know him from the music school and saw him approaching me in a dark alley, I'd probably cross to the other side. Hardcore clothing, long hair, and tattoos covering his neck and arms make him appear tough and, if you're not accustomed to that look, intimidating. I was not accustomed to that look.

I leaned forward slightly, glancing toward the ICU entrance, and there he was, walking awkwardly, eyes fixed on the floor, clearly uncomfortable in the clinical atmosphere. Then I noticed he was holding the hand of a small child beside him. The nurse noticed too and quickly escorted both of them back outside, children weren't allowed in the ICU. My wife followed the nurse out the door to go speak with him. When she returned, she told me that Nay had been worried about me, deeply shaken by what had happened, and had desperately wanted to see me. "He didn't know he couldn't bring his kid, but he really wanted to see you." Then she added quietly, "He even cried."

I didn't know what to say. I barely knew him, and the thought of visitors still felt overwhelming. As gently as I could, while still searching for words, I told my wife, "Please, no. I don't want to be rude, but I don't have the energy for small talk right now." She understood.

Months later, I finally saw Nay again while dropping my daughter off for her drum lesson. I hugged him and told him how much his visit had meant to me. Then I put on ear protection and smiled as the two of them began to play a song by the Pixies, one of my favorite bands.

It's strange how deeply we can be shaken by something bad happening to someone we know personally, even if they're not close. One day, you casually see someone and maybe share a quick conversation, and the next thing you know, they're seriously injured, ill, or even gone. It's shocking, unsettling, and forces us to face something we normally avoid thinking about: our own mortality. We realize how fragile life is, how quickly it can shift or end. This awareness makes us feel vulnerable, reminding us, even if only for a short, worrying moment, of the delicate line we all walk between being here today and gone tomorrow.

On the drive home from that drum lesson, I thought about Nay and the others like him, people outside of my closest circles who still made efforts to support me. My wife had often shared with me how many people wanted to visit, how many were calling, praying, and asking about me. My hospital room was decorated with drawings from my nieces and the kids in our community, as a simple, beautiful reminder that people cared. Friends, coworkers, even acquaintances, people I never imagined would care so deeply. Initially, I didn't know what to say or think. *Should I thank them? Could their thoughts or prayers even help me?*

Looking back, I realize now how crucial these gestures were. It didn't matter if the visitor was a close friend, a distant coworker, or a community member, every gesture mattered. Everything made a difference: meals brought to the hospital, flowers sent to my room, gift cards for groceries or Uber, handwritten notes, or even text messages sent to me or passed through my wife. Each small action helped me feel less isolated, less alone, and gave me a deep sense of belonging. To someone facing life's toughest challenges, these acts of care are profound.

Never underestimate the power of kindness. These actions quietly reassure that person: "You matter. You're not alone." They create a sense of connection and, I'll admit it, love, a word I rarely use but have learned to appreciate deeply throughout this experience.

This connection, this love, is essential for healing. It gives us purpose, strength, and hope when we need it most. Sometimes, simply knowing someone cares can become our main purpose, the reason we keep going. The reason we can keep fighting through even the hardest moments.

Seeing the Cost of Care

What I didn't fully grasp at the time was the toll that this care was taking on my wife. As I started my slow recovery journey, measuring progress at 1 percent a day, she had hit the ground running at full speed. For her, there was no learning curve, no gradual adaptation, only an abrupt transition into a role she never asked for but chose to embrace completely.

The cost was steep. She was alone, physically and mentally fried, beyond exhaustion. Fortunately, her brother Adam had come over immediately from New York to take care of our daughter, who later flew back to NY with him for a few weeks. Niv was there too, but mostly for me. And then there was Nici, her best friend since childhood. Beyond helping with the endless chores that kept piling up, Nici did something even more vital: she supported my wife emotionally. She listened, hugged her, wiped her tears, and hugged her more.

"Sometimes I just needed to put the boulder down and cry," my wife later told me. With Nici, she could simply be, not anything for anyone, including for me. She could make space for her sadness in all the surrounding chaos. Not solving problems, not fighting battles, not pushing boulders uphill. Just being.

As the weeks progressed, my wife's role evolved from advocate to full-time caregiver, a position she had taken on in addition to her regular job. The physical demands were relentless. She bent and lift and carried when I couldn't. She drove everywhere because I couldn't. She prepared meals, managed medications, and handled thousands of daily tasks that had suddenly become her responsibility alone.

Research confirms how stressful the caregiver role can be, emotionally and physically draining, unrewarding, and profoundly isolating. While the person recovering receives encouragement and acknowledgment, caregivers work in the shadows. Their achievements aren't marked by first steps or lost abilities regained. They are measured in problems solved, schedules maintained, and emotional stability provided in the countless small moments of endless days.

To be honest, I didn't feel grateful all of the time. There were days when I was resentful and angry, and at times she was the only one there for me to take it out on. She absorbed my frustration, anger, and despair throughout my recovery, becoming an emotional lightning rod without the benefit of therapeutic attention of her own. I deeply regret the things I said in those moments, but I can't take them back. And despite all of that, she stayed. She took all the punches I threw at her and still stayed by my side.

One warm evening, well into my recovery, we were sitting outside together after dinner. She laid her head on my shoulder, her hair carrying a familiar scent that I loved, as we gazed at the full moon peeking between the pine trees. We had been talking about the future, but my mind drifted. A strong feeling of gratitude washed over me. I realized that, beyond a casual "thank you," I had never really told her what her presence meant to me.

I sat up, interrupted our conversation, and looked into her eyes. "I want to tell you that I saw everything," I said. "I saw the tears and the sleepless nights evident in your eyes. Your struggle to manage everything while feeling you were failing at all of it. I saw your loneliness. The guilt. The constant worry and fear. It is too much for one person to carry alone. And I want to tell you two things: *Thank you.* And you are not alone. I love you and I see you." I paused. "Okay, that wasn't two things."

We smiled, and then we cried together. I tasted the saltiness of her tears on her lips, and she tasted mine.

"We are in this together, don't you forget it," she said to me. Then she added,

"Thank you for saying that. I needed to hear it."

The Caregiver's Journey

The caregiving experience encompasses all three pillars of recovery, body, mind, and spirit, but from a different perspective than the patient's.

Physically, caregivers endure their own marathon. By day's end, my wife was often as exhausted as I was, but without the socially sanctioned right to rest that patients are granted. I remember finding her asleep with her clothes and shoes on our bed one evening, grasping her phone close to her chest while tucked into a fetal position, her mouth slightly open. She was physically and mentally exhausted. I gently took the phone away and removed her shoes, then covered her up and turned the light off behind me.

Mentally, the burden may be even heavier for the caregiver than it is for the patient. One afternoon, I walked into our bedroom to find her sitting on the edge of the bed. The afternoon light came through the white curtains that she loved so much. She wasn't crying, just staring at the floor a few feet in front of her with an emptiness in her eyes that scared me more than tears would have.

I could hear the wheels in her head spinning fast, like a runaway train racing downhill. Each thought added speed, the physical demands of my care accelerating it forward. The flashbacks to finding me on the floor pushing it faster. The "what-if" questions adding momentum. Her work responsibilities that she couldn't neglect adding weight. Our daughter's needs piling on top of the insurance paperwork, the medical decisions, the household management, the uncertain future looming ahead. All of it gaining more speed, propelling this runaway train toward an imminent crash.

When she noticed me, she simply whispered, "What if I'm not enough?"

She had carried the mental load for both of us for so long. I sat next to her and hugged her close. I told her that she is more than enough, that most people would have jumped off that runaway train long ago. I told her that I love her, that I see her, and that all I needed was to know she loves me.

Spiritually, caregivers face an even more profound sense of isolation. Her social world had contracted precisely when she needed it most. We both realized how lonely we were, but especially how lonely she was at that time. Even when talking to friends and family over the phone, most of the conversation revolved around me, my "remarkable recovery," how I was doing great, how it had been a miracle, and how grateful we both were.

I decided to develop strategies that would support her as a caregiver just as I'd made my own framework for myself. Each day, she should have "me time," where she must do something for herself. Not me, not the house, not our daughter, and not work. She resisted, but I put my foot down, I can be persuasive when I need to be! Her me time was non-negotiable unless there was an actual emergency in the way.

One day, in my fourth month of recovery, I peeked into her office when she wasn't on a call.

"Why don't you go somewhere?" I suggested.

"What do you mean? Go where? Are you already tired of me?!" she responded with a smile. I could see the weariness behind her humor.

"I want you to go somewhere for a few days where you don't have to take care of anyone, just yourself." I saw the questions in her face and answered them before she could speak. "I will be fine. And just in case, Niv can come over. Please, go to Nici, go to Napa, go to Esalen, go anywhere you want. You need it."

She stared at me for a long moment, and I saw something shift in her eyes. It was permission to consider her own needs without guilt.

"You know what, I will!" And she did.

That weekend, she took off to spent time with Nici at a famous hotel with a spa. When she called to check on me, I could hear a lightness in her voice that

I hadn't heard in months. And everything at home was just fine. This became another lesson in our recovery: sometimes, separation creates the space for both people to heal in their own ways.

Most importantly, we acknowledged the reality of caregiver burnout. My grandmother's wisdom came back to me: "You cannot pour from an empty cup." The marathon metaphor I applied to my recovery applied equally to her caregiving journey, perhaps even more so, since my marathon had clear milestones and an expected finish line, while hers had neither.

As I grew stronger, new challenges emerged. She had to learn when to step back and let me struggle with tasks I needed to master independently. I remember the first time I took back my duty to empty all the trash cans in the house, take them out, and take the big trash cans to the front of the house before the next morning's trash day.

"I'll take out the trash," I called out loud. I started emptying the bathroom cans to a trash bag, tying it with effort, then taking the trash bag from under our sink and tying it up too. With both bags in my hand, slowly making my way to the garage, I noticed her standing there with hands clenched at her sides to keep from rushing to help. Then she walked behind me keeping safe distance, as I rolled it to the side of the road.

"Are you following me in the dark?! Creepy," I joked. "That wasn't that hard," I added once I had finished.

"Okay, you get your old job back," she said. "But watching you struggle when I could make it easier was harder for me than for you."

What struck me most throughout this whole process had been how little attention the medical system paid to her, or to caregivers in general. While my rehabilitation team provided excellent care for me, my wife received minimal guidance about her critical role. She was expected to absorb complex medical information, implement therapy recommendations at home, monitor medications, and manage psychological support, all with virtually no training.

When I mentioned this observation to my neurologist during a follow-up appointment, she nodded knowingly. "Caregivers are the backbone of recovery," she said, "but we don't have systems in place to support them properly." She explained that studies show caregivers have higher rates of depression, anxiety, and even physical illness than the general population, yet receive little systematic support.

If you are reading this while supporting someone through recovery, please know that your work is seen and valued, even when it seems invisible. Your journey matters just as much as the person you're caring for. Your body needs rest and care, your mind needs space and support, your spirit needs nourishment and recognition.

And if you're the one in recovery, take a moment to truly see those who wait with you, who walk alongside you, who sometimes carry you when you cannot walk at all. Their recovery journey is just as real, just as challenging, and just as worthy of acknowledgment as your own.

The wisdom I gained through this aspect of recovery was perhaps the most humbling of all: healing is always a collective achievement. My three pillars of recovery existed not just within me but within the ecosystem of care that surrounded me. And in that collective effort, those who wait and watch and work behind the scenes are not supporting characters but co-protagonists in the story of recovery.

> healing is always a collective achievement

About six months into my recovery, I found my wife sitting on our patio sofa staring at the stars. I joined her, and we sat in comfortable silence for a while.

"You know," she said finally, "I think we're both recovering."

"Yes," I agreed. "Different injuries, but both healing."

"I'm not the same person I was before that morning," she said. "I don't think

I'll ever be that person again."

"Is that good or bad?" I asked.

She considered the question. "Both, I think. I'm stronger in ways I never wanted to be tested. I understand fear and hope differently now. I know what I can endure." She took my hand. "I wouldn't choose this path for either of us."

"No," I agreed. "But since we're on it, I'm glad we're walking it together."

REFLECTION SPACE

*A caregiver's journey matters just as much
as the person they're caring for.*

Your trauma creates ripples. Some people get swept into the tsunami while others feel the waves from shore. The closer they are to you, the harder they get hit. You didn't choose it, but they did. They had a choice, and they have stayed with you anyway. They're recovering from a life-changing event that happened to a person they *love*. That is a life-changing event on its own.

Who is helping you even though they don't have to? A little or a lot, recognize that they don't have to.

Whose recovery are you not seeing? Can you pause and really see those people? Not as supporting characters, but as partners in this story.

What have they lost? What have they carried?

What have they sacrificed? What do they need now?

When was the last time you said thank you? Are you doing it often enough?

Tell them not just "thank you," but "I see you." I see your sacrifice. I see your exhaustion. I see that you're recovering too.

For the caregivers reading this: Your recovery is real. Your exhaustion is valid.

Your need for space isn't selfish. You're not "just" supporting someone, you're healing from your own invisible wounds while helping someone else heal theirs.

The rules for recovery apply to you just as much as they do to them.

Recovery is never a solo journey. From the person who fights like a lioness for you to the drum teacher who just wants to check on you, they're all part of your healing, and you're part of theirs.

20

THE FOURTH STAGE

The journey back to independence follows many roads,
some entirely unexpected.

WE typically take our family vacation during the month of December. School is on break for the holidays, my work slows down, and the additional days off make planning simpler. The year after my stroke was different. That year, we desperately needed a vacation. We craved a change of scenery and realized we both longed to be around people again. So, my wife and I set our sights on the Big Apple.

We love New York City, and our daughter adores visiting my brother-in-law Adam in upstate New York. It's quiet and remote, and since both he and his spouse are artists, their home is a haven for my artistic daughter. During those first weeks when my wife was extremely stressed, worried for my life, and stretched impossibly thin, Adam had flown in immediately. While he was there to help his sister, his primary concern was clearly his niece who had experienced the trauma of finding her father collapsed on the floor.

Then Adam, a teacher, therapist, and artist who shares a special bond with my daughter, proposed something that turned out to be exactly what she needed: a few weeks at what soon became known as "Camp Uncles." There, she painted in Adam's studio, hiked through the surrounding woods, stayed up late watching movies, and cooked alongside Joe in their cozy country kitchen. Most importantly, she was given the space to simply be a teenage girl again, in a safe, loving, and stress-free environment.

When she returned, the change was visible. She couldn't stop talking about "the uncles" and their home, a place where, through art, conversation, safety and love, they had given her tools to process what was happening while reminding her that joy remained possible amid uncertainty. It was the healing for my daughter and for our family that I couldn't provide myself.

Vacationing there would be a perfect arrangement for everyone.

However, my doctors still advised against flying. This posed a challenge, until I had what seemed like a brilliant idea. Why not take a train? Throughout my journeys, I've ridden the bullet train in Japan, the high-speed trains in China, and countless trains across Europe. But aside from subways, I'd never taken one in the U.S. As it happens, there's a four-day train route from Sacramento all the way to New York City. We'd have a private compartment, and there was a dining car with full service onboard. I knew my wife wouldn't be interested in such a lengthy rail journey, but I suggested that perhaps our daughter and I could take the train while she flew and met us there.

My daughter loved the idea, both the train ride and that the trip would reunite her with "the uncles." So on December 22 at 9 AM, she and I boarded the Amtrak train from Sacramento to New York City, with four suitcases in tow. The views were breathtaking.

We crossed the continent in winter, witnessing a spectacular display of American landscapes. We talked, created art, read books, played games, pointed out wild animals, or simply sat quietly together watching the frozen and untamed landscape unfold through the large window. We never discussed the stroke, but we bonded in the way only two people sharing a small compartment on a four-day train journey could. I have an amazing daughter who is rapidly becoming an extraordinary woman, and I felt fortunate to have this opportunity for such closeness with her.

Upon our arrival, New York offered a sharp contrast to the serene train ride and our quiet suburban life at home. It is loud, busy, and almost like visiting another planet. Each evening, my wife and I attended performances, primarily stand-up comedy and other shows, and we laughed and enjoyed non-alcoholic beers. During the day, we visited museums and art exhibitions, and mostly walked the streets, absorbing the big city energy. Food played a central role in our visit. We attempted to visit every restaurant on our ever-growing list of recommendations from friends and Adam.

On mornings that were too cold for walking, I used the gym in our Airbnb apartment's semi-luxurious complex. It was a respectable facility with standard equipment and free weights. It lacked fresh air, but so did the city outside. Large windows offered views of the awakening city as I maintained my exercise routine. Unlike our quiet California suburb, there were always people on the streets and cars on the roads.

I was getting cardiovascular exercise from our long walks, but I needed additional activities to strengthen and improve my flexibility. Whenever I was alone in the gym, I used my phone to follow trainers on YouTube. When others were present, I put my phone away and followed my own regimen, attempting to work all muscle groups, even the less favored ones like my legs.

Fortunately, I was usually alone in the facility. This gave me the space to be fully present, observant of my body, and conscious of my thoughts. I assessed my condition, comparing my right side to my left, measuring my progress with each movement. The differences between them were shrinking, no longer visible to casual observers, but still unmistakable to me. I couldn't shake my right arm or leg naturally, and their range of motion and precision remained limited. I couldn't hop on my feet or stand on my toes. My foot had lagged the most in recovery; I still couldn't fully control my right foot and toes. It was my final frontier. As I progressed slowly into the third stage of recovery, my toes remained stuck in the second, barely moving, their range of motion frustratingly small.

I estimated my overall recovery to be at 85 percent, with my foot at 60 percent and toes at 20 percent. But that 85 percent! That had been my goal. Not bad for seven months of rehabilitation.

There were some days of our vacation when my wife had to work. I ventured out for walks alone then, acutely aware of how precarious my recovery remained. My greatest fear wasn't getting lost in the unfamiliar city. It was ending up back in a hospital. One millisecond of inattention, one foot not lifted high enough, one step placed carelessly, could undo months of progress. The stroke had taught me how quickly life can change course, and I had no intention of giving it another opportunity for a detour.

I took careful precautions, this awareness guiding every step. My first solo excursion was limited to an hour-long walk in any direction, my smartphone serving as both navigator and lifeline. On my second outing, I brought a portable charger, knowing my safety depended on my ability to maintain communication.

I meticulously planned routes that avoided the most crowded areas, navigated uneven sidewalks with deliberate attention, and approached curbs and intersections with strategic caution.

Amidst this hypervigilance, as I moved through the crisp winter air under brilliant blue skies, a shift occurred. In spite of my intense focus on the way I walked, the way I moved through the crowd, my marathon-mindset calculations, and don't-get-injured priority, I found myself simply enjoying the moment. My face relaxed into a smile that I couldn't suppress, and remarkably, New Yorkers smiled back. For those brief, beautiful moments, I was just another person experiencing the city, my recovery finally moving out of the foreground of my existence.

To everyone around me, I was just another person weaving in and out of the crowds on Fifth Avenue. No one stared at my gait or offered unsolicited assistance. I wasn't "the stroke patient" or "the man in recovery." I was simply a man walking down a New York sidewalk, indistinguishable from thousands of others. While waiting for a light to change at a crosswalk, I caught my reflection in a store window, a confident man, standing tall among the gathering crowd. For a moment, I didn't recognize myself. I had reclaimed a version of myself that I had feared I'd lost forever.

I walked tens of miles during that trip. I climbed countless stairs, navigated crowded spaces, rode the subway and taxis, all without requiring, being offered, or requesting assistance. I functioned completely independently. Though I wasn't as quick-witted or verbally agile as before and couldn't always translate the jokes in my head into words, I maintained conversations, including those with multiple participants. At a dinner with friends, someone expressed shock when I mentioned having had a stroke seven months earlier, and how I'd been unable to speak or move after it happened. "I would never have known," she said, studying me with newfound curiosity.

This should have filled me with pride and satisfaction. I had met my goal. This is where I wanted to be. *Eighty-five percent.* I had made unprecedented achievements that would have seemed miraculous had someone predicted it during my hospital stay. Yet I felt a strange mix of emotions, gratitude for how far I'd come, paired with worry and fear. *Was this my ceiling? Had I reached my maximum recovery? What did this mean for my career, my freedom, my capabilities? Was regression or recurrence possible?* The realization that this might be "it," that this could be the future best version of me, was scary. Everyone had told me I would reach a plateau where recovery would slow down from there and then stop. The thought of reaching it, especially now, was scary. The thought of staying at 85 percent was depressing and defeating.

I tried to dispel these thoughts through logic, repeating my marathon mantra to myself and offering self-compassion, but the feelings persisted. And I had no one to talk to about it, no one who could understand what I was really feeling. I could already hear the responses from the people I wanted to confide in, brushing it off with things like, "Look how far you've come," or "You're such an overachiever," or "Don't worry, just give it time." I had to be the one to give myself the advice I needed, the strength to stay patient, and the courage to keep going.

The next morning, as I sat in my favorite breakfast spot, sipping coffee and watching New Yorkers rush past the window, I realized that these percentages weren't fully accurate. My journey wasn't just about returning to who I was before. The 1 percent improvements, the Marathon Mindset, the three pillars of recovery, they had all carried me remarkably far. But they had also changed me in ways I was only beginning to understand. My physical recovery had outpaced my comprehension of what it all truly meant. While progress had begun to slow as I neared that mark, my new 100 percent was going to look different than my old self. I needed to aim higher. I needed a more ambitious goal, something beyond 100 percent, to keep propelling me forward.

I ordered another cup of coffee and sat with this idea, trying to visualize my new goal. But I couldn't quite see it, not yet. I did know exactly how it would feel. It reminded me of a question I was often asked as a child: *What do you want to be when you grow up?* At thirteen, I had no answer. Even at twenty-four, I still didn't know. But I followed my interests, trusted my instincts, and carved my own path.

I focused on each next step, and eventually, I arrived at where I was meant to be.

Now, I would do the same. I would visualize my goals while staying focused on my next step, watching for signs of life without rigid specifics about what that might mean, concentrating on milestones, and trusting my intuition to guide me.

I was entering the fourth stage of my recovery. My vision for myself had evolved over the past months, and it would continue to be refined. Now, it was up to me to define what my next step might be.

REFLECTION SPACE

What if your recovery isn't about getting back to 100 percent of who you were? What if it's about discovering what your new 100 percent looks like?

For months, I'd been chasing a number. Then I got there, and instead of celebration, I felt...empty. I was close to my ceiling, and I realized this might be the new me.

Have you hit your own plateau? How did it feel?

I panicked, like everyone expected me to be grateful, but inside I was grieving.

Are you caught between who you were and who you're becoming? Not whole yet, but no longer the same?

What if your recovery isn't about getting back to 100 percent of who you were? What if it's about discovering what your new 100 percent looks like?

Can you sit with the discomfort of not knowing what comes next?

Someone once said, "Suffering lives in the gap between expectation and reality." I don't know if that's always true, but I do know I had to change to meet my new reality.

Before smartphones took over, we used to play card games all the time. In Israel, the most popular one was Taki, a version of Uno with number and action cards in different colors. Then came the second generation of the game, and with it, new action cards. The +3 card was especially brutal. But the one we all *really* hated? The Crazy Card.

If someone placed the Crazy Card, everyone had to switch their cards with the person next to them. Total chaos. You'd spent the whole game building your hand, getting used to the cards you had, maybe even thinking, *just a little more luck and I've got this*. And then, boom, everything changes. You're holding new cards. You don't know if they're better or worse. Just that they're not yours.

We used to vote against using the Crazy Card before we even started the game. Most of the time, we just took it out of the deck.

Recovery feels like adapting to being dealt new cards in the middle of a game. The drastic, unexpected, unwanted change in the "cards you're holding" might not be all bad, but it's not what you expected or planned for. And it can feel crazy.

Maybe your new 100 percent includes a wheelchair, but also wisdom.

Maybe it includes speech challenges, but deeper connections.

Maybe it comes with limits, but also freedom from who you thought you had to be.

I couldn't visualize my new goal that morning. But I knew I had to stop measuring myself against my former self. That person was gone. The question wasn't how close I could get to being him again. The question was, who did I want to become?

My advice to you is what I needed at that time: stop looking backward and start looking forward. Even if, or *because*, forward looks nothing like you planned.

The fourth stage of recovery is terrifying because there's no map, no clear improvement percentage to chase. But it's also where you discover that maybe, just maybe, you are becoming a better version of who you were.

What do you want to be when you grow up?

STAGE 4: BEYOND 100 PRECENT

I was entering the fourth stage of my recovery. My vision for myself had evolved over the past months, and it would continue to be refined. Now, it was up to me to define what my next step might be…

The fourth stage of recovery is terrifying because there's no map, no clear improvement percentage to chase. But it's also where you discover that maybe, just maybe, you are becoming a better version of who you were.

21

____

FREEDOM REGAINED

It's not about going back. It's about going forward,
in your own way.

I RETURNED to California on the same train, alone, while my wife and daughter flew back in time for work and school to resume. I used this time to contemplate the new stage of recovery that I'd started and what my next move might need to be. I also started writing this book. Besides typing practice, I felt like I needed to document what I had gone through, like a recovery journal that I could later use to help others if I ever decided to share it. By the time I reached California, I had clarity about my path forward.

The day after arriving home, I renewed my gym membership that had been on hold since I had my stroke. Though I generally dislike large gyms and tend to judge their clientele, I had joined specifically for the classes, which run throughout the day. My favorite was called Warrior Sculpt, a full-body workout combining

HIIT (High-Intensity Interval Training), yoga, cardio, and strength training, conducted in a heated, darkened room with loud music. It provided a consistent challenge, where I could always push harder and find room for growth. Once the music started and my breathing intensified, the outside world disappeared. Those sixty minutes became my sanctuary, a place where thought ceased. Only breathing and physical effort existed.

When I attended my first class since the stroke, I saw many familiar faces, and several people including the instructor mentioned not seeing me for a while. I shared little about what happened, mentioning only that I had "medical issues" I had to take care of. Then the class began, and proved disastrous.

Nothing worked for me. During cardio segments, I couldn't perform jumping jacks, mountain climbers, or jump rope. During strength portions, lifting even three-pound dumbbells overhead caused shoulder pain. The heat made my blood pressure rise to an uncomfortable level. Before class, I had promised myself to listen to my body rather than pushing too hard. I told myself, "This is only your first time back, take it easy," and I remained until the class ended, mostly lying on my mat stretching and following the instructor when I felt that I could.

Despite it all, I did appreciate sweating and the room's energy, reinforcing my sense that this environment represented my next challenge, my next step. I made a silent promise to myself that I would return one day. When I was actually ready.

In the meantime, I needed something with extensive movement and no jumping. Since the next class in that room was a yoga flow, I decided to stay.

Learning to Flow

I had been introduced to yoga in college and had practiced it sporadically throughout my life. In my twenties and thirties, I am not ashamed to say I had attended mostly for the girls, and in my forties it was whenever I needed a less intense workout and some stretches. I had also attempted yoga trough YouTube videos shortly after returning home from rehab, but I couldn't perform the poses with my right side still significantly impaired. Still, something drew me to stay for this class. I thought it might be curiosity to see how I'd do at this stage in my recovery, but there was something else that I could not put my finger on. In any case, my instinct told me to stay, and I had nowhere else to be.

The class began with us lying on our backs. The teacher's voice guided me inward, focusing on my breath, my body's contact with the mat, my heartbeat, how my body felt. She gently led us through various poses while emphasizing breathing, repeatedly reminding us to "follow your breath." Nothing else was on my mind but following my breath and moving slowly between poses.

My right leg and arm struggled but did their best. Maybe it was her voice, maybe the music, maybe the energy in me or in the room or all of those made me approach the practice without judgment or frustration. I embraced it with excitement, compassion, and love. I was in my zone.

There was a dissolution of duality that felt absolutely transformative. I felt like no one was watching even as the instructor watched over us. I was completely alone and at the same time I was part of the energy in the room. In those moments on the mat, all divisions disappeared. My mind was following the instruction, my body was moving to get to the poses, my strategic thinking gave way to music and sensation, my analytic thinking and planning gave way to flowing in the moment. I felt no judgment and was not trying to improve. I was not observing or being observed, just being my whole self exactly as I was, body, mind, and spirit. It was a spiritual experience, and a unification of all of the pillars of my recovery.

During the final component, we lay down in savasana, slowing our heart rates and breathing. I attempted to understand where I had been during the past hour and what had transpired, the instructor whispered the exact words I needed to hear.

She told me that the way I showed up today was the way I moved through life, with power and grace. That I wasn't just surviving. I was choosing to fight. For joy. For compassion. For life.

Her final words still echo in my mind, words I'd only recently come to understand as deeply true: *I am exactly where I'm meant to be, right here, in this moment, in this place.*

These were messages I had told myself, but coming from someone else, in that precise moment when they *felt* true, touched me on a profound level.

Before the class ended, we moved to sitting, with our legs crossed and the palms of our hands touching near the heart center. I was still caught up in my world, in that rare state of being fully present in my body rather than analyzing it from a distance. And I felt tears dropping from my eyes. They kept coming, until I covered my face with both hands and cried into them. It was a profound release that transcended all my careful measurements and recovery calculations. I simply sat there on my mat, simultaneously crying and laughing, not attempting to conceal my emotions. I felt profound happiness, the best feeling I'd experienced since the stroke.

I knew exactly what I needed next: more of this.

This was integration, body, mind, and spirit working in harmony rather than as separate projects to be managed. For the first time since the stroke, I didn't feel like I was repairing a broken machine. I felt whole, exactly as I was, even with my limitations. As we raised our hands to our foreheads and joined in the collective chant of "Namaste," expressing gratitude for the experience of oneness, I found myself reciting the Shema once again, an instinct I appear to have when there are no other words. In English, the Shema means, "Listen Israel, God is our Lord, God is one." While I recited it before when I had nowhere to turn, this time it was a declaration of oneness, much like Namaste, right where I was. This time, it was a "thank you."

After everyone departed, I stayed behind, my legs still shaking from the effort and my heart still full from the emotional release. I wasn't sure whether to hug the teacher, though I desperately wanted to. I cleared the tears off my face, though I was still emotional when I shared my stroke story, explaining that this was my first day returning to the gym after seven months of methodical rehabilitation.

Her eyes softened with recognition and offered the hug I'd been craving. A few more tears slipped out before I released the hug. Then she mentioned something that seemed almost too perfectly timed: A new yoga teacher training course that she herself had completed would be starting soon, with the same instructor.

"It completely transformed my life," she confided. "Not just how I move on the mat, but how I move through the world."

Registration was closing the following day. She pointed to a table at the entrance with a prominent sign and brochures that I had completely overlooked when entering, as I had been focused on just surviving the class.

By this point in my recovery journey, I no longer believed in coincidences, only opportunities. My pillars approach had prepared me to recognize when all three dimensions were aligning toward something meaningful, so I took a brochure and discussed it with my wife that evening. I needed her support for this time-consuming commitment, another reminder that recovery never happens in isolation.

With her encouragement, I registered that same night, and the training would begin the following week.

My vision was beginning to crystallize. This knowledge, this extraordinary experience I was undergoing, had taught me lessons too valuable to keep to myself. I wanted to share them, using them to help others, not just stroke survivors but anyone facing difficult circumstances.

The first three stages of recovery had gradually built on the pillars: physical rehabilitation of the body, then cognitive restoration of the mind, and finally the spiritual awakening that meditation had initiated. Now the fourth stage would engage all three pillars simultaneously.

While I had initially aimed for 100 percent restoration, returning to who I was before, I now looked for 110 percent. The stroke had taken things from me, yes, but it had also created space for new growth I might never have discovered otherwise. My new self would surpass the old, physically, mentally, and spiritually. The oak tree my grandmother had shown me years ago was growing stronger, and it was beginning to provide shade for others.

Relearning to Drive

Months after the stroke, removing the cover from my car felt like an unveiling ceremony. I stepped back to appreciate the moment before opening the driver's door, getting in, starting the engine, and taking it for a drive.

The experience wasn't as glamorous as anticipated. Instead, I felt nervous. I was worried about forgetting something, becoming distracted, or experiencing one of my "glitches." It was like staying focused on my walks, only this time the stakes were higher. I reminded myself to not multitask, even if it was to set the radio or make a phone call. Each time I moved my foot from the brake pedal or the gas, I had to remind myself to think about my next steps so I didn't hit the gas when wanting to stop or vice versa.

I had to talk to myself constantly: "Watch the road," "Stop sign ahead," "Careful merging left," "Not too slow," "Not too fast." By the time I returned home, I was exhausted. My wife had been right, again. I disliked saying those words ("Yes, you were right"), and she loved hearing them. I'd like to say it didn't happen often, but lately, I'd found myself conceding that point more frequently than before.

After a week of solo driving, I did feel comfortable and confident transporting others, including my daughter. Our first journey together was purely recreational.

We have a tradition of drives without destinations, sometimes picking up food from Panda Express and eating in the car, just talking along the way. She manages the music on these drives and carries the conversation, while I primarily listen and drive, impressed by her music collection and taste. Then we park somewhere to eat, usually by the lake, discussing music, animals, playing "Would you rather?" or going over my routine of dad jokes before heading home.

During one of these drives, I found a quiet moment to ask if she wanted to talk about finding me on the floor during my stroke. She simply said "no." I didn't want to push her to talk before she was ready, so I just told her I was here to listen whenever she wanted to, and left it at that.

It's hard for me, knowing how traumatic it must have been for her, to let time do its healing work instead of trying to fix it. There have been signs that she's processing it in her own way. Recently, when I was being my deliberately annoying dad-self and she got frustrated, she suddenly blurted out, "Are you having a stroke?!" You should have seen her mom's face, shock transforming into uncertain laughter as our daughter said, "Too soon? *Too soon?*" We all ended up laughing together, which felt like its own kind of healing.

This moment of shared laughter over something once unthinkable demonstrated the freedom we have to reclaim difficult experiences through humor. To transform fear into something we can face together. Freedom is understanding that we are not our body or our minds or our emotions. They do not define us; they are vessels through which we experience our reality. Just as I was finding new ways to navigate physical spaces, my family was discovering new ways to navigate emotional ones. My entire family is finding their way back to a new normal, right alongside me.

These moments of reclaimed freedom symbolized a deeper level of recovery, that of self-determination and agency. More than physical capability alone, independence is the freedom to make meaningful choices about one's own life.

Even when adaptations remain necessary or perfect restoration isn't possible, finding new pathways to self-determination honors who we were before the traumatic incident and who we are becoming after.

The road to freedom after any life-altering event rarely follows the route we might have predicted. My path included trains instead of planes and yoga instead of high-intensity workouts. All led to the same destination: a renewed sense of agency in my own life.

As I continue this journey, I carry with me the understanding that freedom isn't the absence of limitations but rather the creative adaptation to them. And sometimes, these adaptations lead to discoveries and destinations that are more meaningful than those we might have reached on our original path.

REFLECTION SPACE

Sometimes, adaptations lead to discoveries and destinations that are more meaningful than those we might have reached on our original path.

What does freedom look like for you right now?

Not someday. Not when you "get back to normal." But now, inside the life you're already living.

Before my stroke, I thought freedom meant having no limitations. Now I know it starts with perspective. I can find freedom in my mobility. In the way I create and communicate. In the way I feel and connect. In new ways that still feel fully mine.

Freedom isn't about what you can do, it's the feeling underneath it. Take driving, for example. Maybe what we really crave is solitude, motion, a sense of direction, or a favorite song with the windows down. If the old version of that freedom isn't possible right now, how else can you get that same feeling? A walk in nature? A quiet moment in the park? A shared playlist on a road trip with someone you trust?

What does real freedom feel like to you? Not the action, but the feeling it gives you.

Is there something you miss doing, and could it be that you're actually missing how it made you feel?

What are some new ways you might find that same feeling today, as the person you are now?

What's one thing you thought you lost but are beginning to reclaim in a new form?

Sometimes freedom looks like letting go of the idea that you need to break free at all. Like the rest of our recovery journey, it's the forward movement that matters, in your own way, in your own time, and on your own terms.

22

———

BEYOND 100 PERCENT

True healing is discovering something more
valuable than what was lost.

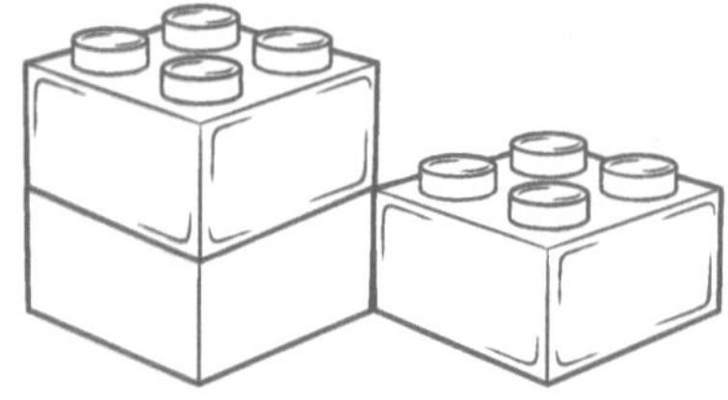

I JOINED the yoga teacher training program in the early weeks of the new year. The twelve-week, 200-hour intensive course required practice, reading, and preparation between our weekly meetings. In my pre-stroke life, I would have considered this schedule impossible alongside my other responsibilities. Now, it had become my central focus.

Our instructor created a space that welcomed practitioners at all levels, including those with physical limitations. The training group was diverse: fourteen participants, mostly women, including a twenty-something student, a new grandmother, a single mom of two kids, a winemaker around my age, a tech salesperson, several businesswomen, and even a professional golfer recovering from his own serious motorcycle accident.

Our physical abilities varied, but we were united by our shared curiosity about the deeper dimensions of yoga. The poses, yes, but also the philosophy, the breathwork, and the way it could change how we moved through life.

During one of our first sessions, we formed a circle to share why we'd joined the program. When my turn came, I hesitated, then decided on complete honesty.

"Seven months ago, I had a stroke," I began, noting the surprised expressions around the circle. The words came out without thinking, like something inside me wanted to share with this group of near-strangers.

"I couldn't move the right side of my body or speak. In the hospital, I set a goal of 100 percent recovery. I've worked hard on physical rehabilitation and cognitive exercises, and I've made remarkable progress, I'm at about 85 percent today."

I paused, not sure if I should continue. Then I dismissed that thought and kept going.

"But somewhere along the way, I discovered there's another aspect to recovery that I can't put a name to. I call it 'spirituality.' It ties all my physical, emotional, and cognitive energies together, fuels them, directs them toward something beyond just walking or talking, something holistic. It gives me the 'why,' the reason for it all."

I wasn't sure why I used hand gestures for quotation marks, but I did.

"This wasn't my first brush with death, not even the second or third, but this time was different in ways I'm still figuring out."

I finally stopped there, not ready to go deeper. Not yet. Sharing even this much felt like enough vulnerability for one evening.

The room fell silent before our instructor nodded. "Thank you for sharing. I can see it wasn't easy. Yoga is precisely there, in the intersection of our physical body, our mind, and 6,000 years of spirituality."

At home that night, I reflected on the evening. At first, I regretted sharing so much, exposing myself to the group, being open and vulnerable in front of a group of mostly women. But in all honesty, it felt good. *Really* good. I was breathing easier, felt lighter. I remembered my commitment to feel everything, so I made a promise to myself for the next twelve weeks: I was going to give it everything I had. I'd be all in and as open as possible. I'd treat it as an experiment, and in the worst-case scenario, the damage would be contained to fourteen people.

Physically, the training was exactly what I expected. It challenged my balance, flexibility, range of motion, stability, endurance, and strength, all areas where my right side still lagged behind. Mentally, it required me to read several books and employ memorization, sequencing, instructing, and multitasking skills that I was still trying to rebuild.

But I hadn't expected to traverse the uncomfortable territories of vulnerability, authenticity, and empathy that my pre-stroke self would have avoided.

The yoga philosophy reinforced my own spiritual beliefs, not in a religious way, but in how it sees the world. That this life is a journey, that everything is connected, that we are not our bodies or our thoughts or our emotions. It aligned perfectly with my spiritual pillar and my curiosity. We also learned about what they called "doorways," or stages of a class. This takes you from exactly where you are when you enter the room, gradually ascends toward a climax where you're in the "zone," vulnerable, open, receptive, and present, then gently descends back for you to observe the experience.

In one of our final classes, the instructor walked in after break and wrote the stages on the whiteboard with our names beside each one. Then she turned to us and said, "It's our tradition that during graduation weekend, you'll all teach a class to your friends and family. Each of you will teach one stage, alone or with a partner, one doorway, as assigned on the board. We'll rehearse next time. Please prepare."

I saw my name next to the main doorway, the peak of the climax.

After class, I approached the instructor with my concerns. Before I could say a word, she smiled and said, "You're perfect for it! Just be yourself and you'll be fine."

In our final rehearsal, I felt anxiety creeping in as I stood in front of the class. But when my turn came to teach, I knew exactly what to do. I closed my eyes, took a deep breath, centered myself in the moment, then opened my eyes again. My new friends were there, standing on their yoga mats, breathing hard from the training, staring at me with anticipation.

I nodded at the teacher to play the soundtrack I'd chosen for my section. Although I'd written down what I planned to say and practiced many times, I didn't have to think about what came next. As the music came up, the words just flowed.

The first sounds of piano keys filled the room, and I instructed them into a pose I knew was physically very hard to hold. I asked them to lean into it.

"Yoga teaches us that we are not our body, we are not our emotions, we are not the thoughts in our head," I started with a soft but confident voice. "I'm asking you now, for just this moment, to feel your body, be aware of what emotions are surfacing, notice the thoughts that come up. But don't let them define you. You are much more than that!"

Soon, mine and my daughter's favorite Linkin Park song broke the silence in the room, and I followed the lyric "It starts with one" with a louder voice: "Everyone in this room personally knows that life can sometimes be tough, hard, unfair, frustrating, scary. The way you show up here on the mat is the way you show up for yourself when you leave this room. Notice your thoughts. Notice what emotions are coming up when it gets hard and your body aches and muscle starts to shake. What are they telling you at this moment?"

When the song reached "I tried so hard," I continued: "What would you tell your best friend, your daughter, your son, when you see them struggling? Say those words to yourself now!"

I saw a few of them falling or getting out of the pose, then said, "It's okay to fall. Falling is not failing. It's learning. It's getting stronger. Get back in and try again, even for a short moment. Give it all you've got, because this is what life is all about: being ourselves, doing our best."

The words coming out of my mouth were the exact words I'd desperately needed someone to tell me during my own dark times. When my thoughts spiraled and fear took control. When I fell. When depression convinced me there was no way out, that I was stuck in the darkness forever. Now, I knew these words were true. Not because someone had told me, but because I'd lived them.

All those brushes with death, the climb back after the stroke, it had all taught me lessons I couldn't have learned any other way. And now they were flowing out of me, naturally, without effort or planning. I wasn't thinking about percentages of improvement or timelines or where I should be by now. I wasn't measuring my progress against who I used to be. I wasn't thinking about recovery at all. I was simply present, completely alive, speaking from a place that had been forged in the fire.

I continued to have them hold that single challenging pose, walking between them, making eye contact, raising my voice, encouraging them to find strength within themselves. Telling them that they were capable of anything. That they were worth it. That I saw them.

I urged them to lean in deeper and reach higher, to observe their own thoughts and emotions. To feel their bodies shaking, but to not let those things define them.

When the final piano chord ended the song, I offered one final instruction: "Get to the top of your mat, close your eyes, and feel. *FEEL EVERYTHING.*"

There was a moment of silence in the room after the music stopped completely. Then everyone clapped and cheered. I even saw tears on a few faces.

"I knew you'd be perfect for this part," the teacher said.

Looking Forward

A few days later, I wrote about the experience in my digital diary. This was an activity that had started as physical rehabilitation for my fingers and cognitive training, so it also measured my typing speed. I noticed that I'd improved by 2 percent since my last measurement. And that's when it hit me.

I pushed away from my desk as the realization fully landed: I had been measuring myself against who I was on June 26. That was my 100 percent. But I was moving forward, not backward. I'd never be that same person again, not physically, not mentally, and definitely not spiritually.

The person I was on June 26 was smart enough, articulate enough, and would have certainly been through his share of struggles to be able to teach the class as I just did. But he probably never would have. And more importantly, if he had tried, it wouldn't have been authentic. He would have had to think about what to say, to plan and organize his thoughts, delivering his wisdom from his head, not his heart.

I sat back in my chair, reflecting on that 2 percent typing improvement. I considered what I'd been calling my limitations, and I realized that they had actually forced me to develop what became my superpowers.

I'll probably never type as fast as I did before, but that has only improved the content I write. I'll never speak as fast, but because I need a moment to find my words, I choose them carefully and take my time before I speak. Besides improving my communication, these improvements also present a more reliable persona, more solid, stable, and even professional.

My lack of ability to multitask has made me more present in everything I do, at work, with my wife and daughter, even when I'm cooking or at the gym or doing yoga.

Yes, I need more sleep, so I have to better organize my day and plan my week, which leads to better efficiency and focus.

My memory isn't as good, so I use technology for summarizing meetings and tracking tasks and more. I don't need to remember everything, and I also don't forget anything.

There are also things I can do now that I never would or could before, like the class I'd just taught. The three pillar strategy I came to live by. My relationships with the people around me, my job, and mostly myself. Or living every day as if I might not wake up tomorrow.

I'd seen my stroke as a catastrophic interruption to my life, but it was revealing itself as a gift. One I would never have chosen, but whose value I could now begin to appreciate.

Looking Inward

Graduation weekend was a celebration full of laughter, tears, sweat, hugs, and even dancing. The hardest part was saying goodbye to my new friends. We promised to keep in touch, but we all have our lives outside of yoga. We knew that our jobs, families, and responsibilities would gradually pull us back into our separate worlds.

Two weeks later, I met up with Carmen, an energetic and charismatic woman I'd felt a strong connection with during training. We'd talked about doing something together, for ourselves and for the community, and now we wanted to bring that to life.

She texted me coordinates of a place she wanted me to see. When I arrived, it was just a dirt road on a hill with nothing else around. I parked behind her on the gravel shoulder, wondering what she had in mind.

"Trust me," she said with an infectious smile. "You'll see."

She led me up what turned out to be a five-minute, easy climb. On the way up, we spotted hares, deer, and even a turkey that seemed completely unbothered by our presence. She pointed out plants that were all native to the area. Then she explained that she and her husband had bought this land a few years before. "I think it's the perfect place for that community gathering we talked about," she said.

When we reached the top, I understood exactly why. We were at the highest point in the area, looking west. The air was crystal clear, with Folsom Lake shining bright in the distance, the high-rises of downtown Sacramento on the horizon, and the setting sun painting the sky in brilliant oranges and reds.

We looked at the landscape, then each other, and said simultaneously, "Perfect!"

"It's not hot, and there aren't even any bugs like I thought there would be at this time," I added, swatting at the air just to make sure.

Carmen laughed and agreed, and we started brainstorming everything we'd need: sound system, yoga mats, water, snacks, maybe even a portable toilet. The list kept growing as we got more excited about the possibilities.

"You know what," I said, interrupting our planning session, "let's first set a date and work backward from there."

And so we did. We divided the chores between us. I took charge of anything involving technology, like invitations, spreadsheets, to-do lists, etc., as well as my part in the event.

Soon, the planned evening arrived, and everything was meticulously in place. There were soft lights and tiki torches lighting a gentle path, rugs for the yoga mats, tables with drinks and snacks, and fire pits ready to be lit. More than twenty close friends and family came, filling the space with warmth and familiarity. Then we started our practice an hour before sunset, flowing through poses as daylight softly faded.

We reached the climax of the practice exactly as the sun dipped behind the horizon, creating a magical twilight moment. When it was over, we slowed down the practice. I softly guided everyone to put on warmer layers and settle into a comfortable seated position, then led them through the meditation that had helped me regain movement after my stroke and had continued to deeply ground and connect me with life.

I wanted them to experience the profound feeling that I had. The subtle sensation of new neural connections forming in my brain. The body healing and spirit reconnecting with life itself.

When we opened our eyes, a beautiful night sky glittered above us, with countless stars above and the light of the city in the distance. We moved to sit around the fire, where we shared stories, laughter, and quiet moments of friendship. It was truly magical.

Josh, a friend from the yoga teacher training, the guy that had been in a serious motorcycle accident and was still recovering, was sitting next to me. He leaned over and quietly said, "I felt it. I felt my body healing. Just a little bit, but it did."

In that peaceful glow, I knew that the wisdom I'd gathered throughout my life's recoveries, particularly my journey through the stroke recovery, hadn't been for me alone. It was meant to be shared, to help others navigate their own challenging paths.

My intuition told me, clearly and completely naturally, that this was my path forward. Whether that would mean leading meditation, teaching yoga, giving advice, sharing the strategies and tools I had developed, or simply offering compassion and empathy, I knew what I was meant to do. And I knew that it would not come from a place of knowing better, but from genuine empathy. I'd been there myself. I'd lived by my principles far beyond my yoga practice, and they were guiding me toward a more authentic relationship with my body, mind, and spirit.

This transformation had rippled throughout all my relationships. My partnership with my wife has deepened as we integrated the experiences of patient and caregiver into a more balanced interdependence. Communication with my daughter has opened into new territories of vulnerability and authenticity. My approach to work holds greater clarity about what truly matters, and I have become more selective about projects that align with genuine value rather than mere status.

The three pillar approach that I'd developed for recovery has evolved into a framework for living. Each day has included intentional attention to my body through movement and rest, my mind through curiosity and learning, and my spirit through meditation and connection.

As I approached the one-year anniversary of my stroke, I realized I'd achieved something I never anticipated when lying in that hospital bed, struggling to move my fingers. This was not 100 percent or even 110 percent recovery, but something far beyond.

It reminded me of a phone call I had with someone in the beginning of my third stage of recovery. Just before we ended the call, she asked me, "Should I expect to hear that you moved to Tibet and began living as a monk? You already have the right haircut?"

I just laughed, understanding where she was coming from. When "life-changing events" like having a stroke at forty-nine happen, we often hear that people change their entire lives, from one end to the other. But, no, I didn't sell my car and move to live on a mountain. I didn't get on a flight one day, never to return.

My life did change. It just took many days, with the change occurring 1% at a time.

In fact, I'm still making those changes, and hopefully I always will be. Because life is a journey, and the journey truly is the destination. I am right where I want to be, exactly here, moving, learning, growing, developing, changing.

I am not afraid of dying, I just want to make sure I live.

❖ ❖ ❖ ❖ ❖ ❖ ❖ ❖ ❖ ❖ ❖ ❖ ❖ ❖ ❖ ❖

Epilogue

From my wounds came my strength.

–Rumi

My daughter and I often play the "What if" game. One evening, around the one-year anniversary for my stroke, my daughter surprised me when she asked, "What if you could only remember one thing from the stroke? What would that be?"

I didn't even have to think. "If I could remember only one thing from my stroke experience, and, you know what, from all of my experiences in life, it would be that there is always a path forward!"

I saw her rolling her eyes at me, but I continued. "It may look nothing like what you imagined or wished for, but when you get there, it is exactly where you would want to be."

"Yap," she said, a teenager-shaped acknowledgement that she actually heard me, thought about it, and agreed with what I said.

One year before, I had only hoped to return to exactly who I was before the stroke. A full recovery meant 100 percent restoration of my previous self, same abilities, same identity, same limitations. My rational mind saw the challenge as essentially mechanical. I had to rebuild what was damaged, restore what was lost, and return to baseline functionality.

I grew to understand how profoundly limited that conception was.

To grow beyond 100 percent is not to reach an achievement but to discover a new dimension. It is to release attachment to who you were and become

> To grow beyond 100 percent is not to reach an achievement but to discover a new dimension. It is to release attachment to who you were and become curious about who you might be now, after everything changed.

curious about who you might be now, after everything changed. It is to understand that everything is *constantly* changing, your body, your mind, your environment, you. Accepting those changes is accepting the new you that you wake up as, every morning slightly (or significantly!) different than you were in the past. This is how transformation occurs. Not by forcing change through sheer willpower, but by showing up consistently, responding to each moment's invitation, and remaining open to possibilities beyond your current imagination.

When I was five or six years old, my father and I had a weekend tradition. We'd dump out all our Lego pieces on the living room floor and build something together. No instructions, no plan, just whatever came to our minds with the parts that we had. A castle, a spaceship, a weird hybrid of both. We'd work on it for hours, sometimes across multiple weekends, playing with our creation, making up stories about it.

Then came the part I dreaded: my father would announce it was time to break it down.

"Why?" I'd ask. My mother would echo from over his shoulder, "Why can't we just keep it on the shelf?"

I don't remember his exact answer, or if he even gave one. But somehow, every time, he would make the breaking the best part of the whole experience.

Sometimes he took a picture of me holding what we built, and then we'd count down together, "Here comes the wrecking ball!" and crash our hands down, demolishing our creation back to its smallest pieces.

What started as heartbreak became a celebration. After all, the destruction meant we could start fresh. We could build something new.

Beyond 100 percent is the new structure you build after life knocks down the old one.

Today, I am not rebuilding the same person I was before. I am working with the old parts that survived and new parts I discovered I needed. I have pieces I can use differently and pieces I didn't even know existed until everything fell apart.

> Beyond 100 percent is the new structure you build after life knocks down the old one.

Not everyone gets this opportunity to build again. But when you do get the rare chance to rebuild from the ground up, remember that the breaking can be the best part. We might not have wished for the wrecking ball of life to deliver a major blow, a stroke, an accident, a loss, but here it is. Take it. Recognize it as an opportunity and seize it with both hands.

I hadn't wanted to break what I worked so hard to build, not when it was a Lego design, and not when it was my whole life. But once all of the parts were back on the floor, I could see an opportunity to build something better, something new, something that I couldn't have built unless the old structure had been demolished.

My beyond 100 percent self is still in construction. It resembles the old one, before the stroke knocked it down, but it's different in so many ways. Some pieces are all still there, scattered on the floor of my life.

Whatever comes next, I want to meet it with the wisdom gained through the breaking and rebuilding. The question isn't whether I *can* build something more from here. It's whether I will continue to see the breaking as a beginning, not the end.

One breath at a time, one step at a time, one percent at a time, the journey continues.

Acknowledgments

To my wife: You fought for me like a lioness when I couldn't fight for myself. You became my advocate, caregiver, and anchor while processing your own trauma. You absorbed my worst moments and still chose to stay. The nurses were right, you're a little scary when someone you love is threatened, and I'm grateful for that fierce protection every day.

To my daughter: You found me on the floor and made the call that saved my life. Your strength at that moment, at your age, amazes me. Thank you for letting me be your slightly broken but still annoying dad, and for teaching me that "Too soon?" can actually be perfect timing.

To my mother: Your voice across the ocean became my daily anchor. This wasn't your first time watching your son from thousands of miles away, fearing the worst. I can't imagine what it's been like. I'm sorry. Thank you for seeing angels and patterns where I saw only chaos, and for never giving up on your gift child, no matter how many times I've scared you.

To my siblings: Vered, for knowing this was happening *for* me long before I could see it. Roy, for making me laugh until I cried from a hospital bed in another hemisphere. You've both been through this drill too many times. I can't promise this is the last one, but I can say I'll try my best. Our connection transcends any distance. You both carried me when I couldn't carry myself.

To Niv: My brother from another mother. You dropped everything and flew across the country to sit with me when I couldn't even say your name right. You reminded me how to laugh when I'd forgotten it was possible. True friendship is showing up in a hospital room and still treating someone like themselves.

To Adam: You flew in immediately when we needed you most and became exactly what our daughter needed, a safe haven at Camp Uncle, where she had time, space, and love to simply be a kid and heal in ways I couldn't provide myself. Thank you for giving her that precious gift while everything was falling apart.

To Nici: You were my wife's lifeline when she was drowning. Thank you for letting her put down the boulder and cry, and for being the friend who shows up not to fix but simply to be present. Your friendship carried both of us.

To Lillian and Eliane (our Oakland cousins): You arrived ready to help the moment I came home, before I even knew what kind of help I'd need. Your presence made the transition possible.

To my lifelong friends: To thirty years of friendship that could survive anything, including my brain breaking and all the other times you've had to worry about me. You've gotten too many of these calls over the years, too many dark jokes at my expense. To video calls that kept me connected when connection felt impossible. To the RV road trip family, Motti, Ofir, Uri, and Roy, you gave me five days of being just Nir again, not "stroke patient Nir." Desert sunsets, terrible jokes, and the reminder that some friendships are forever, no matter what happens to our bodies or brains.

To Andrew and Andrea: You brought me perfect black coffee or warm food almost every day, offering quiet support to both me and my wife. No fanfare, just showing up. Those small, consistent acts of love meant more than you could possibly imagine.

To my community: To Viktoria, our neighbors who quietly cared for my family. To Rabbi Yossi, who showed up every Friday. To Nay, who cried for someone he barely knew. To everyone who sent prayers, drawings, meals, and messages, you might think these were small gestures, but when you're wondering if you matter, every act of care becomes proof that you're not forgotten and that love shows up in countless unexpected ways.

To the readers: Thank you for trusting me with your story by letting me share mine. Recovery is lonely work, but it doesn't have to be done alone.

And finally, to anyone still fighting their way back: Keep going. There's always a path forward, even when you can't see it yet.

About the Author

Nir Peled is the grandson of a Holocaust survivor, born and raised in northern Israel. After serving six years in the Israeli Defense Forces and traveling the world for two years, he eventually settled in California as a technology executive with his wife and daughter.

Throughout his life, Nir has survived more than his share of life-changing events: a bombing in the Sinai Desert, wasp-induced anaphylaxis that ended his military career, a tsunami in the Andaman Islands, an armed robbery in the Amazon, cancer, a serious motorcycle accident, and most recently, a stroke at age forty-nine. Each experience taught him something different about resilience and rebuilding, but the stroke became his greatest teacher, showing him how all those lessons could come together and revealing his calling to help others navigate their own difficult transitions.

As a technology executive, Nir initially approached his stroke recovery the way he approached business problems, with data, systems, and measurable goals. But somewhere between relearning to walk and rediscovering his voice, he realized that true healing required more than physical rehabilitation. It demanded an integration of body, mind, and spirit that his analytical background had never prepared him for.

A certified yoga instructor and meditation and resilience teacher, Nir now helps others discover their own paths forward. He brings both the systematic thinking of his technology career and the hard-won wisdom of someone who has rebuilt his life multiple times, understanding that each breaking can become a new beginning.

What started as a personal recovery journal became his first book when Nir realized he had developed strategies and tools that could help others navigate their own life-changing events. It's written for anyone who needs proof that there's always a path forward, even when you can't see it yet.

Nir continues to recover, grow, and discover what lies beyond 100 percent. He lives in Northern California, where he can be found walking the neighborhood each morning, practicing yoga, and writing about the ongoing adventure of becoming who he's meant to be.